EVERYTHING
YOU'D
BETTER
KNOW ABOUT THE
RECORD
INDUSTRY

~

By Kashif

With Contributions By Gary Greenberg

~

Visit our web site at:
http://www.pacificnet.net/~kashif

or

E-mail Kashif at:
kashif@pacificnet.net

"It didn't surprise me when I heard that Kashif had written the book that everybody is talking about. It's a complete piece, filled with practical information about the do's and don'ts of the often treacherous recording industry. It's filled with warmth, humor and boundless insight."

~ Gordon Chambers ~

Essence Magazine Entertainment Editor & Grammy nominated songwriter

• •

"The information contained in Kashif's book is realistic, important, useful, interesting and presented very well. But what I like best about it is that rather than being patronizing, Kashif assumes you're a credible musician who must manage a long term career."

~ Nicholas Batzdorf ~

Editor, Recording Magazine

• •

"For years when musicians and singers, promoters, and managers asked me if there was a book they could read that would give them a complete overview of the record business, I've had to say no there isn't. That book has finally been written, and Kashif is the perfect person to have written it."

~ Quincy McCoy ~

Urban Editor, Gavin Report

• •

"Dear Kashif, I just finished reading "Everything You'd Better Know About The Record Industry". An excellent book. Congratulations. The personal approach in the writing style puts the reader into various scenarios you utilize in the book. The practical information is easily presented and immediately useful."

~ Jim A. Progris ~

Director, Music Business and Entertainment Industries
University of Miami School of Music

"This book should be required reading in every high school, university and college that has a music program."
~ Kenny Gamble ~
Legendary songwriter, producer and CEO of Philly International Records

....

"A book like this has been needed for a long time. I am not only fascinated by the contents but also Kashif's writing style, which makes the reader feel like he's talking directly to them."
~ Jennifer Thomas ~
Producer NBC Nightside Television

....

"It's about time someone took the time to school newcomers about the realities of the music industry.
My hats off to you Kashif."
~ Steve Halsey ~
The Michigan Chronicle

....

"Yo, where was Kashif and this book when I was first starting my career? I'm down with the way he sets the record straight.
Word life to you Kashif."
~ G. Rap ~
Epic Street recording artist

....

"Everything You'd Better know about the Record Industry is a great book. It is concise, pragmatic and filled with instructions for anyone interested in pursuing a career in the music industry.
I recommend this book!"
~ Dr. Lyn Schenbeck ~
Coordinator, Music Industry Program
Georgia State University School of Music

"Everything You'd Better Know About The Record Industry"

BB
—
B

Brooklyn Boy Books c/o RIIS
P.O. Box 3029
Venice, California 90294-3029

ISBN 1-885726-03-1

Available in audio cassette & audio CD.

Cover Design by MC DESIGN 818.788.3835

Edited By Elsa Boyd

Additional Editing by Alison Faith
Additional Research by T. Scott Bolden

This book is dedicated to the memory of
Eddie and Vandella Simpson, my mom and dad
and
Robert Wedlaw, my father in music.
I miss you all tremendously.

~

Robert Wedlaw & Clive Davis

There are two persons to whom I must pay special homage, as they have been both role models and sponsors of my career at different times in my life.

Robert Wedlaw was my junior high school music teacher. My first serious musical experiences came in the form of his teaching me trumpet, piano and drums.

Clive Davis granted me my first record contract and heads the label with which I have had my biggest successes. For that I am eternally thankful.

To all of my friends. Life would not have been the same had I not crossed paths with all of you. You have made life full and have helped me tremendously. I wish my memory were more proficient. If that were so, I could remember every name that deserves to be on this list. Those of you whom I did not include, please know that it is not because you have not touched me, but only that I am imperfect, and I ask your forgiveness. The space at the end is where you should insert your name and do so with the greatest of confidence that I would approve.

ACKNOWLEDGMENTS:

Lisa Butler
Tanya McConnor Jones
Kathleen Figueira
Kama Cook
Alana Cook
Raymond Jackson
The Maui Tradewinds
Steve & Debra Atchison
T. Scott Bolden
E.E. Pressley
Gary Cohen
Joel Weinstein
Bobby Summerfield
Travis Smith
Los Angeles Public Library
Gary Greenberg
Greg Phillangaines
Jay King
Mike Fisher
Karen Kimmons
Erica Nuri
Monty & Kamya Seward
Cynthia McConnor
J.R. Reynolds
Evelyn "Champagne" King
Robbi Mitchell
Eric Nuri
King Davis

Kenny G.
Stephanie Mills
B.T. Express
Howard Hewett
Melba Moore
Kevin Harewood
Robert Wright
Jermaine Jackson
Freddy Fox
Howard Johnson
Whitney Houston
Clive Davis
Colleen McCrary
Kim & Jennifer Watson
Jonny Kemp
Melisa Morgan
George Benson
Doug E. Fresh
Al Jarreau
Coming Of Age
Delain Roberts
Michelle Thomas
Barry Mayo
Maisha
Stacy Lattisaw
Debbie Allen
The Uh Huh Girls
The entire UCLA Extension Staff

Jerry & Ruth Golod
Rodney Frazier
Ana Rodriguez
D.C. Wilson
Mike Smith
Land Richards
Roy Lott
Glenn Jones
La Forest Cope
Dionne Warwick
Gene Page
Tony Aikens
The Future 2000 Band
Dennis Payne
Ken Reynolds
David Nathan
Vasily Shumov
Jan, Joyce & Kenny Blythe
Dianne Quander
Nathan East
Bashiri Johnson
Monifa & Jelani Jah
Shiba Freeman
Shiela Eldridge
Milton Allen
Latifa Slaughter
Kwaku, Afi, Sekou &
Nadira Saunders
Charles Bananty
Brad Naples
Thea Inoue
Adrian Salley
Uncle Sonny, Sharon &
Carol Salley
Russel Sedelsky
Raymond Katz
Donny Simpson
Warren Wilkerson
Victoria Rowell

Charles Alexander
Paul Jackson
Steve & Debbie Atchison
Thurmon Bailey
Lee Bailey &
Bailey Communications
Alan Bergman
Bo Blinski
Barbara Ann Bueno
Don Patterson
Harvey Mason, Jr.
Wayne Beyers
Cleaster Cotton
Russel Chan
Roy Comier
Mike Fisher
Steve Cunningham
Dave & Sherry Dean
Kathy Doy'en
Aeisha Grice
Darrel Gustamachio
Charles Huggins
Donny Ienner
Alphonse Ketner
Sandy Stein
Bernard King
Hussein Khashoggi
Ricky Lawson
Lynn Fiddmont
Wayne Lindsay
Linda Minor
Rob Jenkins
Arsenio Hall
Marcus Miller
Phile Wilde
Mike, Gail & Jaleel White
Marques, Kimberlee, Beverely &
Bob Elliott
Rick Oriole

Leeds Levy
Rachel Fields
Norby Walters
Sandy Davis
The Rices
Billboard Magazine
Vicki Sum
Fred Zarr
Jeff Smith
Larry Smith
Tyrone Demmonds
Darnell Spencer
Bryce Johnson
Brad Johnson
Kendall Reid
Kendall Minter
Denise Smith
Darnell Gray
Morrie Brown
Paul Lawrence
Marty Lane
Melba Moore
Carmi Cohen
Charles Alexander
Galit Erdman
Richard Imamura
Music Connection Magazine
Musician Magazine
Jamie Brown
Sister To Sister Magazine
Steve Feldman
Nancy Catapano
Michael Chu
Alexine Frank
Jim Scott
Marie Brown
Elsa & Herb Boyd
The Society For Seamans- Kids
The Entire Arista Records Staff

Cathy Windom
Charrise Browner
Rick Cummings
Iona Morris
Ian, Henry, Stewart,
at Manny's Music
Steve Rice
Susan Pardon
Alison Faith
Rick Shoemaker
Denise Weathersby
Sherri Saba
Joyce Taylor
B. Stroll
Thomas Blaylock
Patrick Parker
Deanna Williams
IAAAM
Copy Page
Dominique Deprima
Eileen Woodbury
Raycito Griffith
The Beat 92.3
KMEL
Davie D.
Chuy Gomez
Russell Gatewood
Gary "GSpot" Baca

SPECIAL THANKS TO:

Marina Pointe Apartments
and Recording Studios,
Marina Del Rey, CA for
providing the space for
research and development of
this project, its audio series
and interactive CD Rom.

Partial Discography of Productions, Executive Productions and Writing Credits

EVELYN CHAMPAGNE KING
"I'm In Love"
"Love Come Down"
"Back To Love"
"Becha She Don't Love You"

WHITNEY HOUSTON
"You Give Good Love"
"Thinking Bout You"
"Where You Are"

HOWARD JOHNSON
"So Fine"
"Keepin' Love New"

JONNY KEMP
"Just Another Lover"
"Just Got Paid"

MELBA MOORE
"Take My Love"
"Love The One I'm With"
"Living For Your Love"

DEBBIE ALLEN
Entire Album

KENNY G
"Hi, How Ya Doin?"
"I've Been Missin' You"
"Tribeca"
"Love On The Rise"

DIONNE WARWICK
"Reservations for Two"
(Duet with Kashif)

ME'LISA MORGAN
"Love Changes"
(Duet with Kashif)

TRAVARES
"The Loveline"

GEORGE BENSON
"Inside Love (So Personal)"

AL JARREAU
"Edgartown Groove"

STACY LATTISAW
"One Night For Love"

JERMAINE JACKSON
"I'd Like To Get To Know You"

B.T. EXPRESS
"Time Tunnel"

KASHIF RECORDINGS
(5 albums including these songs)

"Lover Turn Me On" "Say Something Love"
"Personality" "Kathryn"
"The Movie Song" "The Mood"
"Send Me Your Love" "Are You The Woman"
"Dancin' In The Dark" "Help Yourself To My Love"
"Baby Don't Break Your Baby's Heart"

Copyright Information

Sending your songs to the copyright office of the Library of Congress does not actually copyright your material. Your material is actually copyrighted when you finish writing it and record it in some physical form, such as sheet music or a demo tape. By sending in your material to the copyright office, you are insuring yourself the maximum recourse available in case your songs are plagiarized.

Use the information below to copyright your material before sending it out to anyone.

Address:
Copyright Office
Library of Congress
Washington, D.C. 20559

Copyright Public Information Office
(202) 707-3000
Office hours: 8:30am-5:00pm Eastern Standard Time.
Any general questions you have concerning copyrighting can be answered by this office.

To order copyright forms call:
The Copyright Forms Hotline at:
(202) 707-9100
This line is accessible 24 hours daily.

Listed below are the various forms to request.
Also note the description of their uses. This should help you determine which forms to request.

Forms:

Form PA (published and unpublished works for the performing arts)
Form SR (for published and unpublished sound recordings)

Circular #1 (copyright basics)
Circular #50 (copyright registration for musical compositions)
Circular #56 & #56A (for sound recordings & musical compositions)

There should also be circulars available to better help you understand copyrighting in general.

TABLE OF CONTENTS

~Making Your Dream Come True~

~Keeping Your Dream Alive~

INTRODUCTION

Scenario #1
SOULMAN & THE FUNKY BEAT

One night after performing a concert in Washington, D.C. at the famed Constitution Hall, I was persuaded by a few members of my band to take in the night life. My band members were particularly hyped because the concert had gone well and the crowd had given us the usual warm welcome that D.C. audiences are known for. As a result, they were primed to go. I, on the other hand, was not accustomed to going out after performances and instead had my heart set on spending the remainder of my evening watching reruns of the Honeymooners in the cozy warmth of my hotel room. It was winter and it was cold. But after a little goading from my guitarist who accused me of being a hermit, a book worm, and a recluse, I finally conceded.

Our destination was the Club Starlight, where we would hear the popular local band SoulMan & the Funky Beat. As we drove up we could hear the music and see the excitement on the faces of the crowd as they waited to get in. The band was playing with the kind of intensity and volume that made the walls of the small club vibrate and pulsate. We could feel the fever they were working the crowd into before we even entered the doorway. The band lived up to its reputation and more. I was impressed. They rampaged through a whole set of funk and soul classics including The Commodores' "Brick House" and a tune I was very familiar with, "Do It Til Your Satisfied" and before we knew it the show was over.

I was hoping to meet the band members but they slipped out the back before we had a chance to say hello. They had another gig somewhere else. I later learned they had been the house band at Club Starlight every Friday, Saturday, and Sunday for over two years. And it showed in how tight they were and in the audience's appreciation and familiarity with their music. I also learned that during the week all the band members worked various daytime jobs. Tony the drummer was a bank teller; Robert the guitarist, a paralegal; the bass player Dennis was a school teacher; and the key-boardist, a cook at a local restaurant, was nicknamed Showboy. I never got to know his real name. I remember thinking later in my hotel room, how all that talent was just waiting to be discovered.

I had a rigorous schedule to keep, so unfortunately that was the end of the story, until the next year's tour took us through our nation's capital once more and I ran into Showboy at a local restaurant. I recognized him by his flashy personality, which judging by his star shaped glasses, he sported on and off the stage. Without revealing who I was, I asked if he was one of the members of SoulMan. He explained he had been a member of the group until about eight months prior, when the band had broken up. With a little more prying he revealed that he and the rest of the band had been hoping for a record contract that never happened, and he was under pressure from his family to get a "real job." Showboy had decided to go back to school and get a degree in accounting. Between school, studying, and his day gig as a cook there was little time left to rehearse with the band. The other members of SoulMan had gone their separate ways also. Tony had moved to Akron, Ohio and was playing with a local band there. Robert and Dennis went on to play with different house bands appearing at various nightclubs and hotels. I can remember the sinking feeling I got as Showboy told his story. I tried in vain to help by offering to see what I could do, but he was resolved to sticking to his plan; besides, he had seen one disappointment after another.

DIAGNOSIS

At first glance, one would think the frustration of not having any contacts in the record business, trying to get discovered, and the rigorous schedule of working during the day and playing three nights a week had proven too much and that was the cause of the group's splitting up. It wasn't because they were inactive, because they rehearsed and performed often. The problem was they had not pursued a specific course of action that would have guaranteed them contact with record labels and their representatives. They did what I have seen many artists and performers do, wait for the deal to come to them instead of taking action to bring themselves to the deal. That day left a lasting impression on me, one that would resurface time and time again.

REMEDY

The band could have recorded demos and hired a manager, or a lawyer, to shop them to record and publishing companies. A seasoned manager would have made it easier for them to get the attention of record companies and publishers. Establishing a relationship with publishers would have been a good idea, because publishers could have provided them with income that would have allowed them to quit their day jobs and concentrate on their music. Publishers, like managers, are also a link to record companies.

Scenario #2
THE SECRET SONGWRITER

I met Michael Cohen because he sold insurance and I needed to renew the coverage on my home recording studio. He had been assigned to me by the local Prudential office. I spoke with him by phone and we set an appointment for a Tuesday morning at ten. Michael showed up at ten o'clock sharp ready to take inventory and discuss the kind of coverage I needed. He was an odd sort of fellow. He did not exude much personality and his attitude was kind of short and straight to the point. Now, almost everyone is impressed when they walk into my studio for the first time, but not Michael. He just pulled out his paper and pen and got right down to business. I figured he viewed this as just another insurance sale and wanted to get the job over with.

When I began describing each instrument and device in my studio, he did something I found to be very strange. Without any expression or indication that he was impressed he would cut me off in mid-sentence and ask me what the next device was. I remember thinking, "Boy, what a weird character." I hurried the pace just so we could finish and I could get rid of him. But all was not lost, because as weird as he was, it was obvious he knew a lot about insurance, and before it was all over he had convinced me to double my coverage. Nonetheless, I was glad when he left.

Two days later, as I was leaving a local music store, I heard someone calling my name. I couldn't see who it was, but I was sure they knew me because they were using my first name and it sounded like they were happy to see me. To my astonishment it was Michael Cohen and a young boy of about eleven. I thought, "This is odd. What is he doing here in the parking lot of a music store?" Here he was greeting me like I was his best friend when just a couple of days earlier he was in my home being what I perceived as borderline rude. Anyway, I mustered up the best smile I could under the circumstances and said hello to Michael, who introduced me to his son, Michael Jr. Just as I was reluctantly about to join him in a conversation, a salesperson ran outside and called for Mr. Cohen to come back inside. He had forgotten to sign some papers. I figured he was settling some insurance claim for another musician or checking up on the prices I had given him regarding the instruments in my studio. Michael Sr. went back inside while his son stayed outside.

I was about to walk away when Michael, Jr. said in a friendly tone, "My dad says you have one of the best studios he's ever seen, and he's seen a lot." I smiled a half-smile and mumbled my thanks, wanting desperately to get on with my day. "My dad says you're a great musician and he's a big fan of yours" he continued. As awkward as the situation was, I was beginning to like this kid. Then he said something that was a real big shocker: "My dad's going to be a famous star too. He's got a studio just like yours only not as big. You wanna see some pictures?" And without waiting for an answer he pulled a load of pictures out of his backpack. I was floored. There were pictures of Mr. Cohen playing piano, pictures of Mr. Cohen singing into a microphone and strumming a guitar. All this in his own home studio. Then came the clinker. "My dad writes millions of songs and keeps them in a drawer at home," he said, displaying a picture of a dresser drawer filled with cassettes.

"Are all of these tapes your father's songs?" I muttered in dismay. With an eager look he replied "Yeah. Cool Huh?" Dumbfounded, I just sort of uttered "Yeah... Cool". Then the kid said "Don't tell my dad I told you, OK? He doesn't like me showing his stuff. He gets mad. I tried to send his tapes to the radio station but he said I couldn't. I asked him why and he said because they might not like them." At that instant we were both jolted by Mr. Cohen calling for Michael Jr., who quickly stuffed the pictures into his backpack as he went running toward his dad. They waved good-bye, got in their car and left. Then, it hit me like a ton of bricks. That's why Mr. Cohen had acted so strange at my house that day. He was familiar with studio equipment because he had his own home studio and didn't want to let on that he was also a musician and writer. I saw Mr. Cohen nine months later walking downtown. We were both in a hurry so we just sort of greeted each other as we kept walking in opposite directions. I did manage to ask him if he still sold insurance. He said yes, and was quickly on his way.

DIAGNOSIS

I never got to hear any of Mr. Cohen's songs but I'm willing to bet there were some good ones. He was his own worst enemy because of fear. He was aggressive and informed when it came to his insurance job, but timid and complacent when it came to his music.

REMEDY

Mr. Cohen may need to confront a fear of rejection. His son was a pretty good agent. Sometimes it pays to allow other people to showcase your work if you can't handle the direct contact with possible outlets and the possibility of being rejected. The moral of this story is, "**Never let an opportunity pass you by!**"

Scenario #3
THE SINGER WHO ALMOST BECAME A STAR

Nineteen year old Jennifer Carter is an A student who sings like an angel. In fact she's the lead singer in the church choir. Her mother, Ruth, is a social worker and also sings with the senior choir. Her father Jeffrey, a pilot for Delta Airlines, has been a deacon in the church for fifteen years. Both he and his wife have college degrees. Jennifer, filled with aspirations of becoming a professional singer, consistently works toward her goal by taking singing and piano lessons. Ruth is particularly proud of Jennifer and has supported her daughter's musical activities ever since Jennifer began uttering melodies as a toddler. There was a family joke that if you want to see the brightest smile in Cambridge you only had to go church on Sunday and watch Ruth as Jennifer sang in the choir.

One Sunday after Jennifer had moved the entire congregation to extreme emotional heights by performing a spectacular rendition of "Amazing Grace", she was approached by Tom Belsner, a successful concert promoter. Everyone in town knew of Tom Belsner Productions. Tom offered to sign Jennifer to a management and production contract. This was a once-in-a-lifetime opportunity, because Tom Belsner promoted all the big concerts that came to Cambridge. The excitement was almost more than Jennifer could bear. She poured even more of herself into her music by practicing every free moment she had. Everyone was excited. Jennifer was slated to become a star. The house was abuzz, Jennifer's school was abuzz. It seemed the whole town was abuzz about Jennifer Carter, Cambrige's new sensation. While Jennifer and her mother rehearsed for their Sunday church concerts, it was Jeffrey Carter's job to handle the business of finding an attorney to look over the contract that Belsner offered Jennifer. After a few days, Jeff Carter, as he preferred to be called, finally made the decision to hire a real estate attorney he had used many times before. The contract was reviewed and approved by the Carter's real estate attorney and the document was signed the next day. Jennifer was set, ready to work, ready to be a star. That night Jennifer, her parents and a host of family members and friends celebrated at one of Cambridge's swankiest restaurants. Everyone was there, that is, everyone except

Tom Belsner. He had to go out of town on business and would return in just a few days when he would make arrangements for Jennifer to have her first recording session. Jennifer continued her vocal and piano lessons, in fact she doubled up on them just to make sure she was ready. After a week went by without hearing from Belsner, although she continued to work hard, Jennifer began to wonder why she had not heard from Tom. After all, before they signed the contract and he left town he had called her every day. Sometimes even twice a day. Determined to remain positive she concluded that there was no cause for alarm. A second week passed without her hearing from Belsner and Jennifer's parents advised her to be patient. After all, Tom was a busy man and could not drop everything he was doing to concentrate on Jennifer.

Tom returned two and a half weeks later and called Jennifer to tell her she would be the opening act for the upcoming Boyz II Men Concert, which he was promoting. Everyone was ecstatic. "You see," her mother told her, "everything's going to be just fine." And it was, for Jennifer did open for Boyz II Men, and the crowd loved her. The celebrating and excitement was so mesmerizing that it didn't matter to any of the Carters that Jennifer was not paid for her performance. After all, how many people get to sing on the same show as Boyz II Men? Filled with the excitement and joy that came as a result of the audience's response to her performance, Jennifer was more ready than ever for her first recording session. But it wouldn't happen just yet because Tom had to go out of town again. He had to arrange for another big show to come to Cambridge. Everyone was still talking about Jennifers' performance, and how she wooed the audience of five thousand with her rendition of Whitney Houston's "I Will Always Love You." And while everyone else was in a celebratory mood, Jennifer felt anxious. Ever keeping her eyes on her goal of becoming a recording star, Jennifer continued to work hard while waiting for Tom's return. This time he was gone over a month before he returned with the good news that Jennifer was going to be his opening act for the upcoming TLC, Salt 'n' Pepa and Babyface Concert.

Again, Jennifer Carter captured the audience, only this time with a rendition of Anita Baker's "Just Because." She was so impressive that Babyface, a famed producer from California, visited her in her dressing room after the show. He asked if she was available to sing with his production company, and expressed disappointment when he was told that she had just signed with Belsner's company. The Carters were disappointed too, but they had Tom Belsner backing them, Cambridge's superstar promoter. As it turned out, Tom's pattern of leaving town continued for almost a year, always returning with a gift of a new concert for Jennifer to perform—with no pay of course. And although she enjoyed performing the concerts, Jennifer was becoming discouraged about her recording career. Exasperated, she insisted her father approach Belsner and tell him she would do no more concerts until Belsner made good on his promise of taking her into the recording studio. Belsner was mortified. How could Jennifer be this way, after all he had done for her and her family? Hadn't he made her a star in Cambridge, by putting her on every show he brought into town? That was true, but he also had not paid Jennifer a dime for any of those performances, Mr. Carter countered, and thus, their conversation soon escalated to a full blown argument, at the end of which Belsner proclaimed that he would do nothing else for Jennifer. Jeffrey Carter returned home with the bad news: Jennifer's contract with Tom was for two years and year two had just started. Although she was disappointed, she continued to take her singing and piano lessons. Determined not to be discouraged, Jennifer waited out the second year of the contract without hearing from Belsner. Fortunately for her she is still young, and still has a chance of realizing her goal of becoming a recording artist.

DIAGNOSIS

The problem started because neither Jennifer nor her family understood the music business enough to realize the difference between a production contract and a recording contract. Moreover, the family did not know the difference between a promoter and a producer. In this instance, as in many others just like it, a production contract does not guarantee a recording contract. Mesmerized by Belsner's local celebrity status, they committed their second fateful error by employing a real estate attorney to review Jennifer's contract instead of hiring an entertainment attorney, who could have clarified the situation. The Carters suffered from being uninformed and ill-informed. Uninformed because they knew nothing about the record industry and proceeded without the necessary caution one should use in these type of situations. They were ill-informed because they confused a promoter with a producer. They were right to hire an attorney, but unfortunately he was a real estate attorney who was not equipped to handle negotiations concerning the record industry. Fortunately, Jennifer's contract was for a short period of time, so by the time she was twenty-one she was able to terminate it and get on with the business of furthering her career.

REMEDY

It is important for Jennifer and the rest of her family to become familiar with the record industry via books, seminars and lectures. I also recommend they find a competent entertainment attorney to handle any future negotiations. It is always advisable to research the background of anyone, before entering into any contractual agreements. A key principle to remember here is to avoid making the common error of hiring an attorney who does not specialize in entertainment law. You would not go to an eye doctor for your foot.

CONCLUSION

If the three stories you've just read sound familiar, it's because situations like these are very common. Artists, songwriters, and producers, in small towns and large cities alike, are sabotaging their own careers, either by:

A) being complacent like SoulMan and the Funky Beat, and waiting for the deal to come to them, or

B) being complacent like Mr. Cohen because of fear of rejection, or

C) like Jennifer, proceeding without caution and the proper information.

Whether your goal is to become a doctor, a star producer, songwriter, performer, or artist, any one of these can keep you from getting there or make your road to success more difficult than it should be.

At first glance, you would think the members of the SoulMan band and Mr. Cohen don't stand a chance. But that is not true, because if they were to change their attitudes and become proactive they, like Jennifer, still have a chance to realize success. To do so, however, will take proper planning and putting that plan into action.

I have written this book hoping it will find its way into the hands of all the talented individuals who are looking for careers in the record business. Likewise, it is my sincere wish that this book will help those new to the recording industry find their way safely, and with less incident and misfortune. I also want it to help those tenured music veterans who have somehow lost their way to find it again.

Here's to a thousand and one happy endings and to all the SoulMen and the Funky Beats, Mr. Cohens and Jennifer Carters out there. Happy reading and good luck. Use this book and good old-fashioned common sense as your guide as you embark on what is sure to be an exciting journey into the wonderful world of the recording industry.

USING THIS BOOK

As songwriters, producers and artists, you and I have many things in common, one of which is an interest in the record business. Like me, I'm sure you have had dreams of stardom. Having a career in the recording industry can be fun, exciting and a great way to earn a living. But it also requires a great deal of planning. Most people I meet who want careers in the creative side of the music business, whether as artists, songwriters, performers or producers, focus much of their "dream energy" on how they envision life to be after they achieve star status. Yet when I ask these aspiring musicians, singers and music entrepreneurs what steps they think they will have to take in order to ensure success, outside of the obvious answers of recording demos, and hiring managers and lawyers, most are at a loss for words.

Not to worry, I was once there myself. In fact, I can remember a time as a young boy hearing a song being played on the radio and thinking the performers were actually down at the radio station singing the song live. To this day I wonder if my family ever knew where I was going, running off every time I heard a favorite song on the radio, only to return fifteen or twenty minutes later, with a slightly disappointed look on my face. I guess you could say I was wet behind the ears. But that's okay, because everybody has to start somewhere. I'm happy to say that I have grown in my knowledge about the business and I no longer rush down to the neighborhood station every time I hear my favorite song being played, in hopes of catching a glimpse of the star singing it.

While there have been numerous books written about the recording industry, few, if any, offer practical solutions to the everyday challenges that we as artists, producers and writers desperately need to address. They fail to answer questions such as "How do I get started?", "Where can I go for help?", "Who should I send my tapes to?", "How much will it cost?", and "How much money will I make?" These are just some of the smaller questions that make up the biggest one, "How do I get to where I want to go?" And that brings me to one of my favorite analogies about newcomers to the record business.

I OWN A PLANE, BUT I DON'T KNOW HOW TO FLY

Newcomers to the record business are like owners of airplanes who haven't attended flight school. The airplane is the equivalent to the equipment—keyboards, guitars, tape recorders—that most people amass in order to write songs and record demos. The artist is the equivalent of the owner who enjoys working on the airplane, who may even be able to start the plane and rev the engine, but who doesn't have the necessary skills to fly the plane safely or to navigate it to where he desires to go. The logical solution for the would-be pilot is to attend flight school. Likewise, the solution for folks new to the record business who wish to navigate safely to their destination of success is to properly educate themselves. Keeping this analogy in mind, I welcome you to Kashif's Flight School.

This book is broken down into four different categories, which represent my formula for success. They are: **"The Dream," "Your Dream Team," "Making The Dream Come True," and "Keeping Your Dream Alive."**

I think most of us would agree that dreaming is fun, because we can have the pleasure of living in our wildest fantasies. But at some point we need to get down to the business of organizing our lives and activities so they will support our efforts to make our dreams come true. That is what **The Dream** is about: identifying what facets of the music industry suit you best and planning a specific course of action to reach that goal. This includes understanding and organizing your thoughts as they pertain to the other three steps of action that I recommend. This section of the book contains the chapters: "Performers, Singers and Musicians," "The Complete Producer," and "The Songwriter."

Your Dream Team heads the group of chapters that will address issues that come into play as you begin to assemble your team which will include personal managers, booking agents, lawyers and accountants. In fact, your dream team may consist of all these individuals, with each one playing a key role in helping you map out your road to success. This section of the book contains the chapters "Choosing a Manager," "Choosing an Attorney," and "Business Managers & Accountants."

Making Your Dream Come True is about taking your life and career in your own hands. It gives examples of what artists and performers can do to become more self-sufficient and independent. It contains the chapters "Your Own Record Label" and "What Is Music Publishing."

Keeping Your Dream Alive deals entirely with issues such as running an audit and how to decipher legal agreements. It includes over one hundred and fifty pages of recording contracts which we explain in our easy to understand "Contract Explanatory Notes." This segment contains the chapters "Establishing Recording Budgets," "What Is An Audit," "Record Royalties," and "Contracts & Contract Explanatory Notes."

The final chapter, "The Future," speaks about the many changes and trends that are occurring in the record business. Some of these changes are technologically driven while others pertain to the changes in the way artists, songwriters, and producers will be doing business in the near future.

MUSICIANS & SINGERS ARE LIKE SMALL CORPORATIONS

One of the great myths about the recording industry is that a creative person should not be involved with the running of his own business. That the two don't mix well is a misconception shared by many. However, nothing could be farther from the truth. I often wonder whether this myth was created by dishonest managers who wanted their artists to remain in the dark about their own business so they could easily be taken advantage of. In fact, in order for an artist, songwriter, or producer to have a successful career, there must be collaboration between the artist and the various members of the dream team. Artists, songwriters, and producers are like small corporations, with themselves being both Chairman of the Board and Head of the Creative Department. The personal manager should be thought of as the president of the corporation. He is the necessary link to the other members of the dream team and is in charge of coordinating the activities of all parties involved with the artist. The other members of the dream team are in charge of their own departments, making regular reports to the Chairman and the President. Attorneys should be thought of as heading the legal department. Likewise, accountants are the head of the finance department and booking agents should be thought of as heading the sales department.

This structure is tried and true as most major corporations around the world are set up in a similar manner. I don't know about you, but I sure would like to enjoy the same type of success that some of those major corporations have.

I encourage every artist, songwriter and producer to get involved with his or her business from the beginning, and the only way to do that is to know as much as you can about the business. The best time to educate yourself is before you take that first step. The reason for this is, if you educate yourself before you take that first step you can avoid making costly errors that will cause you to lose time, energy and money. Now you might ask how can one learn about the business without actually being in the business. Or, how would one even know what questions to ask to get the right answers? Both questions are absolutely sound, but the answer is strikingly simple.

READ. Reading will give you a fundamental knowledge that will allow you to formulate an understanding of the business. Once you acquire this basic information you will begin to know what questions you should be asking yourself and the members of your Dream Team.

It's pretty easy to figure out what concerns most artists, producers and songwriters share. Put a group of them in a room and eavesdrop on their conversations. It doesn't matter whether they're established artists or newcomers to the industry, their wishes and desires are always the same as far as their careers are concerned: money, fame, respect, power and control over their artistry. Listen carefully and you will hear them seeking to answer such basic questions as: How much money will be made and who will benefit by it? Will I become recognizable? Will my peers respect me and my work? Will I be able to influence people and situations, both through my music and my popularity, and will I have control over my art? Listed below are more examples of some questions I am constantly being confronted with, and their answers. Read these and see if you share the same concerns as others who are interested in this business.

QUESTIONS & ANSWERS

Question: "I'm a new artist and have sent my demos to record companies but have not heard from any of them. What can I do to get their attention?"

Answer: Most record labels don't accept unsolicited material. They prefer to have an artist introduced to them through a manager or producer with whom they already have a relationship. This serves two purposes. First, record companies feel if an established manager or producer wants to introduce a new artist to the company, then this is an artist the manager must believe in. Otherwise, why would the manager or producer run the risk of jeopardizing his reputation with the label? Secondly, if a new artist comes in the door with a manager or producer, the record company feels it has less work to do because the artist already has some sort of organization behind them. Having a manager or attorney who is well connected is a good place to start.

Question: "I write songs and want to get them to artists who might record them. But I don't know how to get in touch with these artists. Who should I call or mail my songs to?"

Answer: Publishers usually have the inside track as to which artists are recording at any given time. They also have ongoing relationships with managers, record labels, songwriters and artists themselves. As a struggling songwriter your best bet might be to develop a relationship with a publisher. The best way to get the attention of a publishing company is through a lawyer or a manager who has an existing relationship with that publisher.

Question: "I'm afraid to send out tapes of my songs because someone might steal them. How can I market my songs and still be protected? Do I need to copyright them?"

Answer: This is a classic question and holds a lot of merit. Most people think they can only copyright their material by sending their songs to the copyright office in Washington, D.C. The truth is, however, your material is copyrighted the moment you finish writing it and put it into some type of material form, for example a cassette or sheet music. By sending your songs to the copyright office, you assure yourself the maximum amount of legal recourse should you ever have the misfortune of someone stealing your song. Yes, you should take every precaution, including registering your material with the copyright office in Washington, D.C. I recommend what is commonly referred to as the "poor man's copyright." Send yourself a sealed envelope containing your new material, via registered mail. Make sure it is addressed to you and when you receive it, do not open it! Put it in a safe place. The postmarked date will serve as proof to when it was written, and by whom, should the time come when you will need to prove that.

Question: "I've been under contract to a manager for three years but he has done nothing for my career, and I feel the need to move forward. There is a new manager and producer interested in me but I can't do anything until I get rid of my current manager. What can I do to remedy this situation?"

Answer: The first thing I suggest is that you talk to your current manager and let her know about your grievances. If the manager has money invested in you then that is an issue that will need to be addressed. The next step is to have your contract reviewed by an attorney to see if you have any grounds for breaking it. If you do, your attorney should carefully follow the guidelines of the contract as they pertain to remedies and notices.

If the manager happens to be a close friend, I recommend you tell them they will be receiving a dismissal notice in the mail. This could help preserve the integrity of the friendship. On another note, it is important to let the new manager and producer know what your current contractual status is.

Question: "I may be entering into negotiations with a publisher soon. Do I really need a music industry attorney or can I use my general counsel to handle the negotiations?"

Answer: Please use an entertainment attorney. I cannot emphasize enough how important it is to use the proper attorney for the job. A music attorney is a specialist in the area of entertainment law, particularly as those laws pertain to the music industry. A real estate attorney specializes in real estate law and while he will have a general understanding of the law, most likely he will not be as well versed in entertainment law as one who practices it full-time. Think of it this way: while a podiatrist and cardiologist are both doctors, you would not visit a foot doctor for a heart ailment.

Question: "How much money should I spend recording my demos?"

Answer: The amount of money you spend on recording a demo depends on a few variables, one of which is the type of music you play. For instance, if you are in a rock band, the amount of money you would spend on musicians would be less than the solo artist who did not play an instrument and therefore needed to hire a band. Another variable is whether the demo is intended for song writing purposes which would serve to solicit a publisher or artist, or as an artist's demo which would be used to shop a record contract. Generally, songwriter demos can be less detailed, with less production than artist and producer demos, and therefore should cost less. The cost for producing a demo of acceptable quality ranges from $500 to $1,500. Of course, if you have more, you can spend more, especially if you want to produce demo masters. Demo masters are demos that are intended to be used as masters once a contract is obtained.

Question: "How do record companies decide which artist to sign?"

Answer: Every record company has its own criteria for signing a new artist based upon company needs at the time and the type of music they specialize in. Record companies sign acts for two very simple reasons: 1) the act has the potential to sell a lot of records, and 2) the act fits in with the record company's needs. For instance, they may need a female pop singer. The most common deciding factor may be that the music is sellable and the image is marketable.
Question: "How difficult is it to start my own label?"

Answer: No more difficult than it is to start any other kind of business. Besides the normal procedures of registering a name, and obtaining a business license (which an attorney can do for a nominal fee), all that remains is to find acts to develop and have the resources to finance the recording, promoting and marketing of those projects. Because today's technology allows musicians and singers to do much of their recording in their own homes, the cost of recording a project has become much less expensive. Your biggest challenge will be to raise the money for promotion and marketing. I suggest that if you don't have the money to promote your product nationally, then start with what you feel will be your strongest market and work that market until you have made sufficient capital to expand.

Question: "A record company has offered me a contract and although I'm interested in signing with them, they also issued me a publishing contract that would take away one hundred percent of my publishing. Is it worthwhile to sign over all of my publishing rights to get the record deal or is there some way I can negotiate to keep my publishing intact?"

Answer: This was a tactic used by most record companies in the earlier days of the industry as a means of obtaining the publishing rights of artists. I am happy to say it happens far less frequently these days. However, there are still a few independent labels who continue this practice. I would shy away from a record company that demanded all of my publishing rights as a means for me to obtain a recording contract. Publishing and songwriter's royalties may be the only source of income due you if your record does not sell enough copies to recoup the recording costs but does sell some copies. That being the case, one must be very careful about signing away publishing rights without getting anything in return. However, sometimes this may be the only deal available and that must be taken into consideration. Use every means possible to negotiate a way to keep your publishing rights. If that is not possible here are a few rules to follow when signing a publishing contract with a publishing company that is an affiliate of the record company you are also signing with:

1) The recording and publishing deals should be separate but co-terminus. This means that a separate contract should be signed for the publishing portion of the deal, and it should terminate when the recording contract terminates.

2) An additional advance should be paid to the songwriter/artist for the publishing rights. This advance should be separate from the recording advance and should be comparable to what the artist/songwriter would receive from an independent publisher seeking to obtain the rights to that writer's songs.

3) The artist/songwriter should negotiate that only songs appearing on albums that are recorded for the label are included in the publishing portion of the contract. For instance, if one of the writer's songs is recorded by another artist that is not on the same label as the writer, then the record company does not share in the rights for that song.

4) The artist/writer should negotiate a co-publishing deal that allows him to retain at least 50% of the publishing rights.

5) The publishing and recording contracts must be non-cross collateralized. This means moneys earned from publishing and writer's income cannot be used against the unrecouped balances of the recording agreement and vice versa.

Question: "I have recorded a few albums with a major label but it seems like they never get behind my projects. How can I insure that they will promote my next project properly?"

Answer: Unfortunately, while superstars don't have this problem, artists who continuously sell three to four hundred thousand units (which, incidentally, gross record companies millions) often suffer from lack of attention and ill-formed marketing campaigns. Besides having your manager set up a twenty-four hour vigil in the office of the label's president, here are a few suggestions:

1) Try making members of the promotion, marketing, and sales staff feel included in the recording process by inviting them to visit you at some of the recording sessions.

2) Along with your manager, you should develop a marketing plan and present it to the record company.

3) You cannot rely upon the sole efforts of the record company to promote your product. An independent effort must be coordinated along with the label's efforts.

Question: "How much should I pay my attorney for negotiating a new recording contract?"

Answer: There is no real answer to this question since there are so many variables involved in negotiations. However, there are some guidelines that should help you formulate what is best for your situation. Depending upon the type of deal and the amount of time it will take to negotiate, attorney's fees vary in range from a few hundred dollars to tens of thousands. If the negotiation is a simple one that will only take a few hours of work, it is best to work out a flat fee with your attorney. Ask him or her to quote you a price on what it will cost to negotiate the deal at hand. If the negotiation is a complicated one, it will be best to have the attorney on a monthly retainer. Monthly retainers are based on the attorney's hourly rate and the amount of time spent working on the client's behalf. Attorneys' hourly rates range from $175 per hour up to $500 per hour. Retainers usually work out in the client's favor if there is a generous amount of work for the attorney. Some attorneys like to work on the basis of a percentage of the deal. This simply means that the attorney will receive a fee based on a percentage of the advance which is negotiated for the artist, producer, or songwriter. A typical percentage would be between 5% and 10%. However, an arrangement based on a percentage of the deal should be entered into with caution, because if the advance is a large sum, the attorney may wind up making an inappropriately large fee.

Question: "Is there any way I can break my recording contract without causing serious legal problems?"

Answer: Yes, if the record company is willing to release you from the label and you go through the normal legal channels. No, if the record company is not willing to release you from your contractual obligations. In that case, the best thing to do (with great care and caution) is to try and find another label that will buy you out of your contract. If your record company is in breach of your recording agreement then you may have grounds to put them on notice to either remedy the situation within an amount of time specified in the contract remedies section, or terminate the contract if that amount of time expires and they have not corrected the breach.

Question: "Early in my career as a songwriter I signed a bad publishing deal. Now my career has taken off. How can I negotiate a better deal for myself?"

Answer: This should be easily achieved if you have the right attorney. The publishing company has everything to gain by keeping you happy. The truth of the matter is the publishing company probably expects you to renegotiate your deal soon. Of course you must keep in mind, they too must benefit from their association with you. If your deal is where the publishing company has obtained 100% of your publishing, it might be wise to renegotiate that agreement into a co-publishing deal with larger advances. If you already have a co-publishing deal, then a larger advance and maybe an administration deal would be appropriate. Try to negotiate performance bonuses into the contract. That way, as your songs reach certain chart positions, you get additional advances.

Question: "I recently produced a few demos for an unsigned artist and there are a few labels interested, but I don't have a signed contract with that artist. Do I have any legal rights to that artist's services?"

Answer: This is a tricky one. If you can prove the songs you produced for that artist were used to solicit a deal with a label, you might be in a good position. There have been cases where courts have honored verbal agreements based on facts and evidence presented that proved the producer and artist did in fact have a binding agreement. However, it is best to avoid these situations by having a signed agreement before any work is begun. Sometimes it is not practical to draft and negotiate an entire formal agreement. In those cases, it is perfectly acceptable to draft and sign a one or two page letter of intent which states the most important terms of your agreement with the artist.

Question: "I'm a writer who writes lyrics and melodies only. I was given a track by someone who doesn't write lyrics and melodies. I completed the song and would like to know what is a fair split between myself and the person who wrote the track."

Answer: By law, the writer of the lyric and the melody is the writer of the song. But as you know in today's music world, sometimes the track is what makes the song a hit. Although to date, there is no law that addresses this issue, an agreement must be reached between you and the person who wrote the track. I too have found myself in this exact situation and my remedy was to split the song into three equal parts; lyrics 33 1/3%, melody 33 1/3%, and music 33 1/3%. Therefore, if you were to follow my example, you would be entitled to 66 2/3% of the song while the writer of the track would get the other 33 1/3%. Incidentally, by law, a track is considered an arrangement, not a song. Those of you who only write tracks may want to arrive at an early understanding with whomever you choose to write the lyric and melody before work on the song commences.

Question: "What is a realistic number of songs a publisher can demand from a writer in a one-year period?"

Answer: Depending on the size of the advance the artist receives from a publisher, between ten and twenty songs may be demanded of a writer in a one-year period and still be considered reasonable. Most publishing deals require the writer to hand in between six and twelve. Keep in mind, however, if you only write lyrics, melodies, or tracks (which may constitute only 50% of the song), the publisher will usually require twice the number of songs in order for the writer to fulfill his song commitment.

READ ON

While having the answers to the above questions certainly helps shed light on how the music industry functions, they alone don't embody a full understanding of its inner workings. Nor do they address the key issues that will make or break a career. My assessment of the music industry is, it's one where one either takes advantage of, or gets taken advantage of. Those who know are in a position to take advantage of those who don't. Here lies a chance to break that common and accepted belief, that in order to pay ones dues one must give into the misfortune of being ripped off. I challenge you to take the time to get to know the industry before you make costly errors. It is my further belief that we can change the way artists, producers, and songwriters approach their careers through education and education alone.

ATTITUDE ADJUSTMENTS AND PARADIGM SHIFTS

In the early days of the record industry the unfair conditions and terms most artist and performers were subjected to were the status quo, accepted as the normal way things worked in the business. Being ripped off was not only accepted but expected as normal everyday occurrences. But as musicians and performers are becoming more knowledgeable about the business, they are learning how the game is played. Thus more and more are avoiding pit falls they would have become victims to had they remained uninformed.

Musicians and performers are currently realizing a paradigm shift; this shift adjusts their attitude away from the "my job is to make music and I'll let my manager handle all the business" attitude which was prevalent up until the early 1990s, toward a viewpoint of "I must take full responsibility for my life and career." Of all of the changes the music industry has seen over the years this is by far the most important. The renewed self esteem that flows from the power of having control over ones own future is both invigorating and contagious.

As some of you may already know, trying to break into the industry on any level using traditional methods seems almost impossible. Between the Catch-22 of having to know someone to get into the business and yet not knowing anyone in the business, the horror stories of folks being taken advantage of, and the uncertainty of trying to enter into a field you know little about, it's no wonder so many of you are opting to take your fate into your own hands. And with great success, I might add.

I have one last note I'd like to share with you before we move on. It has occurred to me that through the facility of online services such as computer bulletin boards, and musician oriented events such as seminars and conferences musicians, performers, and music entrepreneurs are networking more than ever before. I would like to encourage all of you to continue to fellowship because it is through these connections that we are learning about each other. We are seeing how much we have in common and how much we differ. I believe as a result of this communication we are currently experiencing, we will find a collective voice, one which will undoubtedly continue to grow and speak to all our needs.

~ *The Dream* ~

The Songwriter

Performers and Singers

The Complete Producer

~

If you would like to attend one of Kashif's seminars or
participate in our talent searches, check out
Kashif's tour schedule at our web site on the Internet.

http://www.pacificnet.net/~kashif

THE DREAM

As I've noted in the introduction, **The Dream** is the first of the four step process I recommend to help you on your road to success. During this process you should enjoy fantasizing about your wildest dreams of stardom and identifying your goals in respect to where you are along that road to obtaining them. Some of you may be beginners or others of you may be established writers looking to transcend the next level. Some are producers and artists looking for the opportunity to break into the big time. Still others of you are starting your own record labels and publishing companies. The important thing to remember is although the actual steps that have to be taken in order to succeed in any of these areas may vary slightly, the principal steps remain the same. These principal steps are described and prescribed in each chapter. Some of you may have already progressed beyond the first few steps set forth in the chapters. If so, then use the information to evaluate your process and progress to date. Remember, to get the maximum benefit from the information contained here, it is best to read the entire book.

In this section you will learn what singers, performers, songwriters, and producers must do to obtain recording, production and publishing deals. We will identify the pitfalls of each area and offer practical solutions to those challenges. The chapters included here are: "Performers and Singers," "The Songwriter," and "The Complete Producer."

"The Songwriter" chapter gives practical solutions to the challenges faced by songwriters in today's marketplace.

"Performers and Singers" highlights the challenges that performers and singers face and offers practical solutions.

"The Complete Producer" is chock full of information concerning certain disciplines I have put into practice over the years that have allowed me to prosper creatively and financially as a producer.

THE SONGWRITER

The songwriter is at the heart of the recording and music industry. Without songs there would be no records, CDs, movie soundtracks, etc. Most people at one time or another have written a verse or two of poetry, and usually at the completion of their new work, can't wait to show it off to friends and relatives. This usually occurs at an early age and it often involves a school project. I would imagine these to be happy experiences that have the potential to one day blossom into writing careers. But as enjoyable as these experiences are, few people go on to become professional songwriters. They seem to think it's an impossible field to break into as a profession. Yet I have met few who would not jump at the chance to make a living writing songs. It is both fun and fulfilling, and there are a substantial number of people who make quite a living doing so. Those of you who only write lyrics, only music or who write both, are all referred to as songwriters. It helps if you are capable of both, but there are many successful writers who only do one or the other. If you write only lyrics, it helps to have a counterpart or partner who is capable of supplying the music and melody aspect of a song, and vice versa.

THE PRODUCER/SONGWRITER

The most valued breed of songwriters is the producer/songwriter. The value of a writer is determined by the marketplace, the marketplace being those who are interested in songwriters, such as publishing companies, record companies, artists, other songwriters, and the record buying public. The producer/songwriter is valuable to the publisher because if she is already established as a producer/songwriter, she can pretty much make the decisions about which songs will end up on a project she is producing. Thus, a publisher has less work to do in getting the producer/songwriter's songs recorded.

The producer/songwriter is an attractive consideration for record companies because record companies prefer to be able to find a songwriter and a producer at the same time. It's sort of like one-stop shopping. If a record company finds a song it thinks has the potential to become a hit, but it does not care for the production of the demo, the company will then have to shop for a producer. That additional effort requires more work and time on the part of the record company. The producer/songwriter represents the solution to that problem. Record companies know most producer/songwriters insist on producing their own songs, unless the song is a remake of one that was already recorded and released, and in that case the songwriter would probably be delighted someone else wanted to re-record a song they had written. The producer/songwriter's value to artists and other songwriters is similar to what it is for record companies and publishers. It represents a situation that requires less work on the part of collaborating songwriter and artist. Like the record companies and publishers, other songwriters and artists see the producer/songwriter as an opportunity to realize their goals. These songwriters look to collaborate with the producer/songwriter in hopes the songs they write together will find their way onto an album project.

THE ARTIST/SONGWRITER

The artist/songwriter is the second most valued breed of songwriter. They represent a chance for a record company to sign an artist and not have to search for songs. The more self-contained an artist is, the greater the chance a record company will be interested in that artist. This means less work for the record company, and less work means less money spent on searching for material and producers and more profit in the event of a hit. If the artist is also the writer and producer there will most likely be less paperwork as it pertains to the artist/songwriter's contract with the record company.

The artist/songwriter is of value to the publishers because if the artist lands a recording deal, the publishing company is sure to have a number of songs recorded and released that it publishes or co-publishes with that artist. Just as with the record company, this means less work for the publisher.

BEGINNER SONGWRITERS

Beginner songwriter simply means a writer who has sufficiently honed her craft and skills to a marketable degree but has yet to have one of her songs recorded and released. The beginner songwriter faces a number of challenges, none of which are insurmountable or terribly difficult if the writer is equipped with a knowledge of the business of songwriting.

MARKETING YOUR SONGS

There are several routes one might take in marketing musical compositions to prospective clients. Regardless of whether your interest is in writing musical scores for television, film, CDs, children's books and products, educational or documentary uses, symphony or orchestral music, the fundamental steps are the same. However, your contacts will be different in each case. Since this book is designed for the recording industry, I will concentrate on ways to market your songs in the recording industry.

THE RIGHT CONTACT AT THE RIGHT COMPANY

Those of you seeking to write songs with, for, or to have your songs recorded by a recording artist would send your material to either the record company, the producer, a publisher, the artist, artist's manager, or a representative of the artist.

RECORD COMPANIES

However, most major record companies do not accept unsolicited material. Unsolicited means material not coming from a source that has already had dealings with that record company. This does not mean that a beginner writer can't have songs reviewed and considered by a major record label, but instead means the beginner writer's material has to come to the record company through a source that is already established with the record company. That source could be a manager, lawyer, friend, associate, publisher, or anyone whose opinion is respected by the company. Record companies prefer to operate in this manner, because the number of tapes and solicitations they receive are overwhelming, and they need the insurance of having someone whose opinion they value act as an additional buffer for them. It is a totally practical and legitimate approach. Some smaller record companies do accept unsolicited material. In those cases you would send your material to a specific contact in the A&R department (the department within the record label or production company that is responsible for listening to new material and signing new talent). Independent labels seem to be more open to unsolicited material. Labels that release rap and alternative music are also more accessible than major labels. Currently the most efficient way to get your songs heard by record companies other than co-writing with the artist or producer is to have your songs peddled by a publisher. We'll discuss more about that later.

LABEL IDENTITIES and A & R DEPARTMENTS

Most record companies split up the duties of the A&R departments according to the type of music. For example most major record labels have a pop, urban or black music division, alternative and AOR (Album Oriented Rock), classical, and a rap division. Each of these departments has its own A&R personnel. A&R is the abbreviation for artist and repertoire. The A&R person's job includes finding artists to sign to the label, finding songs for all artists contained on that label (unless the artist is also a songwriter), making sure the other departments are kept abreast of the progress of upcoming releases, and assisting the artist in securing a creative direction.

Some labels also have gospel divisions, although they most likely would have an associated label that handles gospel music. Some labels have a reputation for excelling in different kinds of music. Geffen, for instance, has had tremendous success in selling rock and grunge rock music and has absolutely no success in the R&B, black music areas. In fact, they have no urban, or black music departments. Def Jam, on the other hand, has been the driving force behind rap music's development for many years, but has shown no interest in the rock and pop areas.

I only mention these facts because if you are going to solicit your songs to record labels, make sure you know what kinds of songs each record label is most interested in. If you are a writer who specializes in R&B you probably should not send your material to Geffen Records. Likewise if you write rap, you should probably send your material to Def Jam. The major labels RCA, Sony, Polygram, EMI, Capitol and Warner Bros., all do well in many types of music.

MANAGERS AND OTHER CONTACTS

Sending songs to managers and producers directly can also be rewarding in that managers and producers have a direct line to the artist they are working with. Again the problem of unsolicited material exists. The obvious conclusion here is getting in the front door of a record company, publisher, manager, or an artist is a most difficult step. If you can find some way to gain access to any of the above, and have them lend an ear to your music, you will be moving in the right direction. Your big break may not come directly from meeting or having contact with a record company executive, a publisher, manager or an artist, but it may come from people to whom they introduce you to.

PUBLISHERS & PUBLISHING COMPANIES AS CONTACTS

Another route to getting your material heard is the publishing route. The best way to get a publishers attention is through a manager or a lawyer. Publishers listen to your material and if they like it, you will be signed to a publishing deal. It then becomes the publishers responsibility to solicit your songs to record companies and other potential outlets. Even if you do sign with a publishing company, it still is important to remain active in creating your own contacts and following through on them. Publishing deals usually include advances that are paid to you by the publisher. What you will be giving up is part or all of the publishing share of the income generated from future earnings derived from the sale of albums, movies and T.V. shows, that contain your songs.

A publishing deal is an agreement made between a publisher, or publishing company and a writer. The publisher pays the writer advances against future earnings. The writer usually gives up a portion of his or her publishing rights in order for the publisher to make the advance money back along with a profit in the future. In other words, they will pay you to write songs. These deals range from just one song to an all out deal where they pay for the rights to publish and peddle everything you write over a specified period of time. Publishing deals usually last from one to five years. Anything past five years is probably not in your best interest. For more information refer to the chapter on publishing.

DECLINE OF THE SONGWRITER

In the music industry of the 1990s, the role of the songwriter who just writes songs and doesn't produce or is not an artist is diminishing rapidly. This is partly due to the popularity of rap music and its increasing share of the marketplace, and the increase in the number of artists that write their own songs. Most rappers write their own songs and therefore have a limited need for outside songwriters. Because of the increase market share of rap music and because rap music is relatively low risk for record labels (it doesn't cost much to produce) record labels are releasing more rap music each year. This means some labels are releasing less of other kinds of music such as R&B and Pop, which can cost more to produce. This in turn means fewer tunes are needed that are written by outside songwriters.

Country western, R & B, and pop ballads are the type of music where the traditional role of the songwriter remains relatively strong.

My advice to writers who only write and don't produce or are not also artists is, either become producers and artists or look for alternative outlets for your songs. These alternative outlets can be just as, if not more, financially rewarding as the record industry. There exist opportunities to write music for television, film, children's stories and books. There are far more opportunities to break into these fields than in the recording industry. Just think of the five hundred channels being developed for cable television and the fact that all of these stations will need music for their programming and promotions. Not to mention the spin-off projects like soundtrack albums.

MANAGERS WHO MANAGE SONGWRITERS

There are managers that specialize in managing songwriters and producers. They usually charge a fee of 15% to 20%. These relationships can also be rewarding because sometimes these managers represent big name producers and songwriters. The big name writers and producers are always in demand. Sometimes they are offered work they cannot accept due to prior commitments. If you are affiliated with the managers of these high profile writers and producers they may be able to use their influence to get that work passed along to you. These managers can also help you secure and negotiate publishing deals, and recording contracts.

YOUR SONG DEMO

The length of the songs you intend to solicit should be of acceptable duration. When sending songs to a record company or publisher never send more than three songs, each of which should be no more than 3:45 to 4:00 minutes in length. Put your best song first and the weakest song last. If you are a writer but not a singer be sure to have your songs sung by someone who possesses the proper feel for those particular songs. For instance, if a singer is at his or her best singing ballads don't try to force the issue by having this person sing an up-tempo dance track. It is obvious there are some singers that do both well and in those cases don't hesitate to hire them. The same goes for song style. If the singer's or player's forte is R&B don't try to force them onto a Rock & Roll track unless the song specifically calls for that marriage of styles.

SHOWCASES

In Los Angeles there is a songwriters' association that puts on a showcase for songwriters every Tuesday night. The showcase is sponsored by ASCAP. It is called The Los Angeles Songwriters' Association. The telephone number is (213) 467-7823. If you call, tell them you heard about them from me. It might be wise to contact BMI and ASCAP and ask them about songwriters' workshops and showcases they may be involved with in other parts of the country.

HELPFUL HINTS FOR THE SONGWRITER

Songwriters under contract to publishers can earn from $30,000 per year up to millions. It all depends upon your level of success. A hit song can generate a healthy income for both a writer and a publisher.

Publishers usually have established relationships with many producers, artists, and record companies. But be aware that in order for a publisher to be of help to you he will want something in return. That something will be the publishing rights to your songs. Don't panic — that is business as usual.

• Make sure your songs are original.

• Put your best song on the tape first.

• Send in no more than three or four songs.

• Use high quality recording equipment if at all possible.

• Whatever you do, do not sell your songs outright to anyone.

• Read all proposed contracts for what they contain as well as what they do not.

Here are some more hints to what all good publishing deals should contain:

• The writer should always get an advance against future earnings.

• The writer should be able to negotiate return of ownership of the copyright within a reasonable period of time.

• Make sure in foreign countries you are getting paid at the source of income. Ask your lawyer about this one.

• Demand stringent audit rights.

• If you are a songwriter and have no way of recording your demos, it might be a good idea to establish a relationship with a local band that plays your kind of music and is looking for songs to record.

• You can usually find free music publications at your local music store. They usually have classifieds relating to writers looking for bands, bands looking for writers, singers looking for songs, and more. This is a good place to start looking for songwriting relationships. Always use your common sense before entering into any relationship. Remember, if the deal sounds too good to be true then it probably isn't true. Be wary of advertisements that charge a fee to record your songs.

• Another reason to enter into a publishing contract is that publishers can make contacts with other writers who are looking to collaborate. The more collaborations you are involved in, the more you increase your chances of having a hit song.

• Remember, always have any contracts you are considering entering into reviewed by an expert music industry attorney.

• Purchase *The Craft of Lyric Writing* by Sheila Davis.

PERFORMERS, SINGERS, MUSICIANS & ARTISTS

Once upon a time there was a boy who dreamed of becoming a star. He played the piano, trumpet, he sang, and was the kind of kid who liked to tinker with electronics. He was born and raised in Brooklyn, New York and attended high school with a young girl whose father managed a band called B.T. Express. This girl told her father she thought the band needed the sound of a keyboard player, and asked him to consider a friend of hers from school. Now of course this friend of the manager's daughter was the same kid from Brooklyn that played piano, sang, and tinkered with electronics. The father agreed to at least audition the friend of his most beloved daughter and called the young boy to set it up. The boy was excited, because while he was known around the neighborhood for playing in various local bands, he had never met anyone who had made a record, and B.T. Express was known all over the world for their hits "Do It 'Til You're Satisfied" and "Here Comes the Express."

The audition went well and the manager asked the young boy to attend the band rehearsal the next day. All night the boy tossed and turned, too excited to sleep. The next morning he put on his best suit, took the braids out of his hair, and picked out his Jackson Five style afro to perfection. He arrived at the band's rehearsal two hours early and was greatly relieved when the first members of the band started to arrive. He immediately liked the band members and they liked him. He would do just fine. There were seven members in all. Six guys and one girl. The young boy was impressed by their shiny, matching outfits in all kinds of bright colors. They even had their own tour bus with their name on the front. The very next day they embarked on a world wide tour that paid $350.00 per week and the young boy has never looked back. And why should he? He was only fifteen years old and on the road with **B. T. Express!**

He stayed with the band four years, leaving to pursue a career as a solo artist. Well, that wasn't so easy. With little money and less experience, the road to success was proving harder than he thought. A young man now, he struggled for a few years with various bands and styles, but to no avail.

Two years later, a stroke of good luck again found him. An executive at RCA Records had heard one of the young man's demos and looked him up. The executive, Mr. Robert Wright, asked the youngster if he could write and produce a hit for Evelyn "Champagne" King. The boy said, "Sure," but he didn't know what producing was. The kind-hearted Mr. Wright replied, "Young man, just do what you do." Again too excited to sleep, the young man went home and wrote what was to become the first of a long line of hits.

I could go on but I thought I should tell you that the autobiography is yet to be written. The boy of course was me, and all other names and incidents have remained the same to respect the innocent.

Of course the story of my life does not begin where I started. I left out the parts about my personal struggles, the challenges that I faced as a young artist before I was inducted into B. T. Express. I also left out the parts about mistakes made and lessons learned.

In this chapter I have organized my thoughts and creative solutions to the problems I know a lot of you face today in your quest to become recording artists.

ARTISTS, BANDS, PERFORMERS AND SINGERS

Performers and singers looking for recording deals have a number of ways to achieve their goal, one of which is starting their own record label. Although I hope that is the way some of you will take, not every artist is equipped to do so. This chapter is for those of you who choose the more traditional route of acquiring a recording contract.

Before embarking on a mission to obtain a record deal, I recommend that artists spend time familiarizing themselves with the different types of recording deals that exist. This will allow them to conclude what type of deal best suits their needs.

Read everything you can get your hands on pertaining to the business. Read this book, magazines such as *Billboard, Musician, Recording,* and *Music Connection,* and any other books you can find on the subject. Attend the music seminars and conventions that are held as annual events each year. Colleges and universities also offer courses on the recording industry. The UCLA Extension program is an excellent source of education for those interested in the entertainment and music industry. They offer both creative and business classes instructed by some of the most celebrated personalities in the field.

Once you have a clear understanding of the business, you should begin your process of recording demos and distributing them to record labels for consideration. This doesn't mean you should not record demos while you are learning. It simply suggests that you should not attempt to shop a deal without a fair amount of understanding about how the process works. You may get lucky on the one hand and obtain a recording contract, but on the other hand without the right information you may end up with a recording agreement you will later regret.

WHAT YOU SHOULD KNOW ABOUT DEMOS

Demo tapes are used as a showcase for the audio performer's talents. If you are a singer or instrumentalist, and you are not yet signed to a record label, then most likely you will need to record a demo. Demo costs can range from a few hundred dollars up to whatever you can afford. In general, you won't need to spend more than $500 to $1,500 per song to record a professional quality demo.

Those of you who can't afford to spend your limited funds on demos need not fret. There's more than one way to skin a cat. There are thousands of up-and-coming songwriters and I would imagine quite a few in your general area. Try getting to know some of them. I'm sure you will find there are songwriters who are not singers and therefore are in need of someone to sing their song demos. That someone could be you.

These types of associations can open up all kinds of possibilities, the most obvious being co-writing, and the sharing of demo cost. I like this kind of networking because it gets the sometimes solitary creative types interacting. Those interactions can be rewarding in a number of ways. For example, if you are listed as the singer on the songwriter's demo, A&R executives, publishers, or producers who hear the recording will be exposed to your talent, and become aware of you. This could lead to your obtaining that record deal you've been looking for.

Word of mouth is the best advertisement anyone can get. Negotiate a deal with the songwriter to give you full credit as the artist appearing on the demo. Any pooling of resources is to your benefit. Not to mention it will also lead to more collaborations with songwriters and therefore increase your chances for success. For a singer, band, and instrumentalist it could mean the difference between success or failure. Oh, did I fail to mention the income you can earn performing another writer's demos? Get the picture? You can also use those same demo tapes to send to club owners and talent agents to secure live performance work.

HOW FAR SHOULD I GO WITH MY DEMO?

I receive hundreds of demo tapes every year from singers, bands, producers, and am amazed at some of the elaborate productions contained on some of these tapes. Others fall short of the minimum standards needed to show off an artist's talent. I've heard everything from demos recorded with full orchestras, to a single voice recorded on a cheap hand held recorder complete with background noises. Consequently, one of the most frequently asked questions regarding demos is how far an artist, producer, or songwriter should go or not go in order to impress someone with a demo. Should one record a piano/vocal demo or go all out with a full blown production? Of course, if you don't have the money that affords an elaborate production you probably won't be asking these questions. But sometimes there is a manager or an investor who can afford a full blown production, and is poised to spend the needed money on the project because he believes in the artist. While that may be a good situation, it still may not be a wise choice to spend thousands of dollars recording a such a big production. You may have to pay that money back someday. A full blown master demo can cost thousands of dollars, and an under-produced tape can be rendered for very little. Somewhere in the middle of these two extreme forms of demo production lies the right choice of how far you should take your demo project.

Demos are usually sent to A&R executives at record labels, and to producers, managers, artists, and creative directors at publishing companies. The bottom line is that no matter how much or little money you spend on your demo, it all boils down to whether the person the tape was intended for likes what they hear. In some cases a piano/vocal is appropriate. In others a full live band or demo utilizing midi instruments is the wiser choice. Some singers go as far as to have a full orchestra play on their demos, but unless you are auditioning for a job as an orchestrator, a demo containing a full orchestra is unnecessary. A well-crafted song, sung by a talented singer or played by a gifted musician is the most any executive should look for. Contrary to popular belief, A&R directors at record companies and creative directors at publishing companies could care less about the amount of money invested in a demo. They are looking to be impressed with the talent on the demo. Nevertheless, stylistic decisions have to be made about the kind of demo that is right for you. If you prefer dance music as an artist, a piano and vocal demo won't cut it. Obviously a dance song needs a beat and a beat requires drums, and a good arrangement of a dance song requires at least a rhythm section consisting of guitars, bass, drums, percussion, and keyboards. Likewise, if rock and roll is your thing, recording a demo with a marching band won't do you much good, unless you are making a unique artistic statement that requires a marching band to get your musical idea across. While observing the examples given in the last two sentences, also note that all rules can be broken when there is a reason to break them.

A demo should contain songs that are stylistically representative of where you see yourself as an artist. It is also important that a demo tape not contain songs that are too varied in their styles. For instance: if your demo tape contains a dance song, an opera, and a country and western song it will not work in your best interest to obtain a record deal. Demos containing too many different musical styles signal to the label that you don't know what style is best for you. If you're a rock artist and your demo tape contained an up-tempo rock and roll song, a rock ballad, and a pop standard, that would be more appropriate. Apply the old adage: **Keep it simple**.

With today's technology in keyboards, drum machines and se-quencers, musicians, writers, singers, and producers can achieve a full and elaborate sounding demo without spending a lot of money. In truth, a large number of demos that are used to obtain record-ing contracts actually end up being used as a part of the final mas-ter recordings. A&R executives and producers will be listening to the overall production and the artist's singing, playing and writing abili-ties, while listening for that special something that strikes their fancy and makes them feel the artist either has something unique or has a formula that has been proven and can be repackaged. For this reason, I say keep your demos relatively inexpensive. Great singers can be showcased with a piano/vocal if the song lends itself to a piano/vocal production. On the other hand if the magic of the music is in the arrangements and combination of band members, recording a live band is appropriate. In short, don't try to hype your music with dol-lars. It will be cheaper, and in the long run, if you are not picked up by a label you will not have spent unnecessary dollars. Even if you do get signed, there is no guarantee the songs contained on the demo will be used for the actual release.

A PRODUCTION DEAL VS. A RECORD DEAL

There are many ways to secure a recording contract with a record label. Direct contact with the label is one, contact through a manager, lawyer, or agent is another. But sometimes the only contact that an artist might have to the recording industry is through a record producer. There are probably more record producers than record companies, and hence producers are easier to make contact with than record companies. Furthermore, most producers are open to meeting new artists and have less rigid restrictions about whether or not they accept unsolicited material. Production companies and producers are also a natural go-between for record companies and artists because record companies hire producers on a regular basis to produce artists already on their label. In fact, there is a growing trend toward record companies' retaining producers to scout new talent. Record companies are also making label deals available to producers at an increasing rate. Producers, especially in the pop and rap music categories, have a pulse on the street that allows them to recognize what the record companies sometimes cannot—trends as they are developing. As stated earlier, hiring producers to carry out some of the functions of an A&R executive insures the record companies that when they find a new artist, that artist will have an association with a producer. And that means one less step a record company has to take in order to get the project started.

Basically, in a production deal, an artist signs an agreement with a production company and the production company agrees to either secure a record deal for the artist with a record label or, as in the case of many of today's producers, release the artist on the production company's own label. In the case where the producer secures a record deal for the artist with a label other than their own, the producer assigns (grants) the record company the right to release the artist on that label.

As stated above, one of the most successful routes an artist can take to acquiring a recording contract with a record label is to sign a deal with a production company. Although signing with a successful production company dramatically increases the possibility of a recording contract for the artist, it does not guarantee one unless the production company also owns a record label. When an artist signs a deal with a production company the upside is the producer usually pays all expenses for demo cost, pictures, and bios. The down side is the artist usually ends up with less percentage points than if he had signed an agreement directly with a record label. Record companies will only pay between 12 and 14 points to an artist and producer combined. If the artist is signed directly to the label, the artist is responsible for hiring the producer and the producer's points come out of the artist's share. Most producers receive 3 to 4 points as compensation for producing an artist. With that being the case, if the artist received 14 points and paid a producer 4 points, the artist would end up with 10 points. If the artist signs a deal with a production company and the production company is successful in convincing a label to sign and release that artist, the production company will receive the same 12 to 14 points. In that case, the producer pays the artist about half of the percentage points they receive from the label. That would amount to 7 points in this case. Although signing with a production company will result in the artist receiving on the average 3 points less than he would receive had he signed with the record label directly, the artist must weigh that against whether or not he stands a better chance at obtaining a recording contract with or without the producer. Each case should be assessed independently.

Any way you slice the pie, the artist's and producer's share combined will usually amount to 12 to 14 points, depending on the label. If the producer is a superstar she can demand a few more points. This does not mean the artist will receive a larger share, because you must remember it is the producer's credibility and track record that has influenced the record company. There are circumstances where a new artist can negotiate higher than the usual 12 to 14 percentage points, but in those cases there are usually two or more labels who have entered into a bidding war to obtain the artist. This is rare. If a bidding war does occur, you will find record companies are more willing to negotiate higher upfront dollars in the form of artist's advances and recording budgets rather than more percentage points on sales. (See the Recording Royalties chapter for more detail.) More upfront money in the form of advances is not always as good as it sounds because the more upfront money you receive, the more records you will have to sell in order to be in a position to receive producer's and artist's royalties. And that is precisely where every artist should want to be, in a royalty earning position.

Another key difference between a production deal and a record deal is when an artist is signed to a record company, he has far more control over the overall situation than when he is signed to a production company who then assigns him to a record label. All in all, it is better to sign directly to a record label, unless the producer is a hit producer and is willing to give you the attention that you deserve.

Over and beyond the normal concerns for an artist in any recording contract, the key issues concerning production deals are:

1) the length of the deal,
2) the amount of time the production company has to perform its duties before it is in default, and the contract is terminated,
3) who owns the masters,
4) who controls the budget,
5) "key man" and termination clauses.

I have definite opinions on these concerns and will address them one by one.

"HOW LONG SHOULD MY PRODUCTION DEAL BE AND HOW MUCH TIME SHOULD I GIVE MY PRODUCERS BEFORE THEY MEET RECORDING AND RECORDING CONTRACT REQUIREMENTS?"

Production deals can be tricky situations for artists. Besides having to make a decision to sign with a production company and receive fewer percentage points than when signed directly to a label, the artist also has to be comfortable with the fact that signing a production deal may not necessarily result in acquiring a recording contract. Although signing a production deal should guarantee at least that demos are recorded and paid for by the producers, artists need to be concerned about how long they are under contract to a producer or production company before the producer or production company must perform the duties of recording demos and securing a recording agreement.

Unfortunately, I have heard many stories of artists who signed production deals without stipulating the parameters by which the production company had to perform. Contracts that don't propose reasonable dates by which the producer must perform lock the artist into an unfair situation. For example: if the artist's contract with the production company merely states the production deal starts on date (x) and ends on date (y) the artist has no recourse if the producer fails to either record a demo or shop a recording deal. Let's assume the production deal in this case is a five year deal with no performance stipulations (like recording and paying for a demo and by what date these are to be carried out), then the artist is stuck in a deal for five years where she is not guaranteed anything other than a production deal. This situation of course would make any artist unhappy and should be avoided.

My suggestion is the artist should negotiate that the producer or production company has three months from the signing date of the contract to complete a three-song demo, and six to nine months from the completion date of the demo to shop and negotiate a recording contract with a label. If they fail to do either, the artist should have the option to terminate the contract.

The longevity of a production contract should be as short as possible. The shorter the contract duration, the sooner the artist is in a position to negotiate a better deal. If there is success, a new contract will bring fairer terms for the artist. In terms of the overall length of a production deal, three one-year options is a fair amount of time for a producer to prove himself. Producers usually want a minimum contract commitment of five one-year options and seven to eight albums. My opinion is that five years is too long. Trends change, people progress, and by the time five years roll around the contract is outdated and far more unfair than it was on its signing date. A commitment for seven albums can take up to ten years to fulfill and if five years is too long, then ten is certainly out of the question. Even if you do get a recording contract while signed to the production deal the record company will want a minimum of eight to ten albums, including a greatest hits album. That's a big chunk out of your life, so be careful. Think of it this way: the average life span of an American male is 72.5 years. If a record company or production company ties you up for ten years, that's almost one seventh of your total life expectancy.

REVERSION OF DEMO RIGHTS

In some situations where an artist signs a contract with a production company, the production company fails to meet the requirements of the deal and the deal must be terminated. If the production company has recorded demos, but has failed to secure a record deal for the artist in the allotted time, and the artist chooses to terminate the contract, there exists the issue of ownership and usage of the demos tapes. My opinion is the deal should be structured so in the event the production company does not perform its duties as required by the contract and the contract is terminated, the artist should, if she chooses, be allowed to at least use the demos recorded under the agreement to shop another deal.

The production company will have the right to own the masters, but should not have the right to use the artist's voice or, in the event the artist is an instrumentalist, his performance. If the producer is the writer of the track the producer should be allowed to erase the artist's performance and use the background track as he wishes after giving the artist first right of refusal to purchase those demos. However, the contract should require the producer to deliver a completed copy of the demo to the artist before erasing any of the artist's performances contained on those demos.

The artist should be sensitive to the situation, striving to part with the production company amicably. The artist should also have the first right of refusal to reimburse the producer for the cost associated with the recording of the demos at a price equal to the cost of recording those demos. All deliveries and first rights of refusal should be documented in the form of a 60-day letter. In other words, the artist has to send a letter to the producer after the termination of the contract, stating the artist has the first right of refusal to purchase the demos that were recorded under the contract with the producer. The artist then has sixty days to come up with the money to purchase the demo masters.

In some situations, the producer may have a good relationship with the artist and the artist may elect to continue the contract in good faith (the producer has not fulfilled his commitment). In this situation, the artist should extend the contract with an addendum, clearly stating what circumstances under which the contract is to be extended.

There should also be provisions within the contract that address the possibility that the contract might reach its termination date when the producer or production company is negotiating with a record label on the artist's behalf. In this situation the producer must be able to prove he is in fact engaged in good faith negotiations. Pending documentation of actual negotiations, the contract should be extended for a period of three months or until the artist feels the producer has exhausted his best efforts to secure the contract in question. If three months go by and the artist feels he is no closer to signing a record deal than before, the artist should have the full right to terminate the contract.

RECORD COMPANY DEMO DEALS

There are times when a record label will sign an artist to a demo deal. This usually happens when an A&R director at the label is interested in the artist but is unsure about wanting to make a commitment to the artist. There are also other reasons a record company would enter into a demo deal with an artist. For one, the artist may have piqued the curiosity of the record company but may have sub-standard demos. The record company may want to hear the artist under different and/or better circumstances. The label may also be undecided and want to take the artist off the market until the record company makes a final decision. Keep your senses sharp for this one.

A record company's seriousness about an artist will be reflected in the amount of money it is willing to spend on developing the demos. Record companies generally spend between $2,000 and $3,500 per song to develop artist demos. The same concerns an artist would have in a production deal exist when entering into a demo deal with a record label. However, the solutions should be different. A label should have the same three months to complete a demo, however, they should only have 30 days from the completion date of the demo in which to make a commitment to sign an artist to a full recording deal. If they fail to make a commitment within that time, the artist should have the power to terminate the contract and retain full ownership of the demo masters. In no case should the artist have to reimburse a record company for demo cost. The basic terms of the artist's deal should be negotiated, understood and contained in the demo contract. Most record companies will try to resist this but if they are genuinely interested they will concede.

KEY MAN CLAUSES

What happens if an artist signs with a production company and the production company succeeds in obtaining a recording contract and the original producer is no longer in the picture? This can become a seriously negative circumstance for the artist because her relationship in this case would have been established with a particular producer and not the record company. This particular set of circumstances can leave the artist in the peculiar position of not being able to move forward with her recording career. Here's why. The producer has met his commitment to record demos and secure a record deal for the artist and therefore has fulfilled all requirements of the contract. The artist would not be in a position to claim default on the part of the producer, yet the producer is unavailable. Therefore, the artist is left in a position of uncertainty.

A key man clause will give the artist recourse in the event the production company or producer cannot fulfill his duties according to the contract. Key man clauses specify that if a key person within the structure of the deal either is not available or unwilling to perform his duties, the artist would have the right to terminate the contract or pursue other remedies such as developing a relationship directly with the label.

KEY MAN CLAUSES AND LABELS HEADED BY PRODUCERS

Key man clauses are especially important these days when producers are also artists and performers. There is also a growing number of producers and artists who own record labels. That's great for the producer but can be a nightmare for an artist signed to a label where the producer is unavailable for extended periods of time, because the producer is touring or busy producing other artists. The manager and artist in these cases must pay close attention before signing an agreement with a producer who is also an artist. The contract must insure that the artist will receive the attention he deserves from the producer or the production company. If you sign a deal with a production company where the producer is also an artist or sign a deal with a label headed by a producer, assess the infrastructure of the production company or label, making sure they have the necessary personnel to get the job done in a reasonable amount of time.

WHO CONTROLS THE BUDGET?

When an artist is signed to a production company and the producer does have success in acquiring a recording deal, a budget will be issued. In most cases this puts the producer in control of the budget. However, when the producer is controlling the budget it leaves the artist vulnerable to the producer's whim as to how the money will be spent. For instance, what if the entire production budget for a record project is $200,000.00 and the producer decides he will only spend $50,000.00 on the actual recording and the rest will be spent on personal needs. This is unfair to the artist because he will actually be financing the producer's personal needs. **Remember, the full amount of the recording budget must be recouped before the artist can receive royalties.** (For more details on how royalties are paid see the chapter, "Record Royalties.")

Artists must be protected against these kinds of situations. Agreements with the producers or production company should contain three major points addressing the issue of budgets and how they can be used.

1)   The producer must submit a written budget to the artist that shows how he plans to use the budget. The artist must accept that budget unless he finds it to be unreasonable when compared to the normal way budgets are appropriated, e.g. if the budget contains items not directly associated with the recording of the project, or items that are priced higher than usual, or producers fees that are higher than the fees originally negotiated.

2)   In the event the producer or production company receives an all-in budget, at the end of the project, the producer or production company must share equally with the artist any part of the budget that is not spent on actual recording.

3)   The artist should also request a budget summary. The summary should include copies of receipts and purchase orders. A budget summary shows how much money was spent in each area, enabling the artist to detect discrepancies and misappropriations.

By functioning in this manner, the artist is sure to have a reasonable amount of control over how the budget is spent. And having this control is one of the reasons why it is better to be signed directly to a label rather than a production company.

PICTURES AND BIOS

There are elements other than the music that come into play when record companies consider whether or not they are interested in signing an artist. An important concern is their ability to market the artist's visual image. In the early days of the recording industry this was less important than it is today because more emphasis was put on the artist's musical abilities. Today we have MTV and the visual image is of utmost importance to record companies. For this reason having a flattering photograph of an artist as part of the demo package is important. These photographs probably should be a little more than a head shot but not a full blown photo session where thousands of dollars are spent. With the right photographer, two hundred dollars should get the job done.

A brief bio or resume detailing the history of the artist's musical experience is also necessary, but should not be more than one or two pages long. The cost of a biography written by a professional writer should be no more than $100.00. In fact, if you have a friend or family member who is a talented writer have them write the biography.

ALTERNATIVE METHODS

The reality for so many of you who are immensely talented is you have limited means for recording your own demos and you probably live in cities and towns that are not the musical hot spots. Those of you who fall into this category should try some of these alternative methods as stepping stones to achieving your goals. If all else fails you may have to pack up and move to where the action is or hire a representative that lives in the cities where they can have access to people that make the decisions.

There are countless local bands that need singers and instrumentalists to assist them in their demo making process. A demo for them is also a demo for you. Singing background vocals for recordings can also be a productive route to a recording deal. There have been many cases where producers have fallen in love with the talent of a background vocalist and assisted him or her in obtaining a solo recording deal. Classic examples include James Ingram and Patty Austin, both discovered and brought to the forefront by Quincy Jones. The same applies to instrumentalists.

Another thought comes to mind while pondering the many ways a performer or singer can record a demo, although this should be used as a last resort or just a practice demo (used for the purpose of becoming comfortable in front of the microphone). There are establishments that specialize in recording a demo and video for the cost of about thirty dollars. They are usually located in amusement parks. The upside is the cost is low and the results are immediate. The downside is there are no original songs and usually there is only a limited selection of songs to choose from. In most cases, a record company will want to hear original material when listening for a new artist. Nonetheless, if the talent is impressive enough it will not matter because the record company will want to get involved in the choosing of material you will record for their label. It might help to attend national and local music conventions, most of which are frequented by artists, producers, record executives, and radio programmers. Before attending, however, it is important to have a goal in mind. Network and try to make some contacts and set up a few meetings. These well-attended, festive and informal occasions offer outstanding networking potential.

Study the image and success of each record company. This will help you choose one that is best suited for your kind of music. In general, don't go for the ones that have too many artists similar to yourself. Avoid companies who don't have a history of selling the kind of music you intend to perform. Instead, try to find a home where you will be a unique and welcome addition.

The publications listed below can be found at most newsstands and will contain important information about the record industry. Two words of advice: Get them. They include *Billboard, Music Connection, Musician Magazine, Recording Magazine, Performing Songwriter.*

THE COMPLETE PRODUCER

A record producer has many responsibilities including but not limited to song writing, setting up recording budgets, finding creative solutions to budget problems, and keeping up with the latest technology. Producers are also required to make sure a song gets the proper rhythm and vocal arrangements, is recorded in a way that best suits the song (digital or analog, band, orchestra, or sequencer or some combination), and is somewhat responsible for whether or not the production becomes a musical hit. Whether or not the song becomes an actual hit is ultimately the responsibility of the record company. Although if the song does not become a hit, record companies will always blame it on the producer and or the artist. A producer must also be capable of balancing the relationship between the artist and the record company, while trying to please both.

I grew up playing music during a time when there were no synthesizers and drum machines, and one's musical ability was judged purely on whether or not you could play or sing. I was part of the first generation of musicians to embrace technology and utilize synthesizers, drum machines, and sequencers to help facilitate the recording process. Those producers on the cutting edge at that time were rewarded well because we were responsible for a new way of recording that was cheaper and faster. Of course record companies were delighted over the fact that records could be made in this fashion, and they encouraged the use of these new technological, money and time savers. The public also embraced these new recordings because the new music had a fresh sound that reflected the direction of American culture as it in turn embraced the new technological revolution.

During this time of technological exploration in the recording industry, not only did artists and musicians receive extensive publicity surrounding their new music, but the technology used in the recording process itself spawned an unprecedented amount of curiosity from the public. Every music magazine from *Recording Magazine* to *Rolling Stone* featured articles about computer based instruments and how they were changing the face of music. These articles further stimulated the curiosity of the public and musicians eager to learn about the new ways in which music was being made. I don't think any of us expected the kind of interest the public displayed. As I sit back now I can see how anyone interested in music would be fascinated by a keyboard that was capable of sounding like any instrument or a drum machine capable of playing any beat. All this was good. But we the producers and creators of music at that time failed to foresee how our use of this new technology would effect future generations of music makers. Unfortunately, every time we turned on a drum machine or sequencer, we were telling young musicians it was no longer necessary to spend long hours learning how to master a instrument and the basics of music. At the same time the message sent was, "you too can become an instant success by purchasing the latest drum machine or computer." The result is a new generation of musicians, not devoid of musical talent, but of musical skills. I cannot overemphasize the importance of old fashion study. Know your craft and know it well!

If you are a young up-and-coming musician or producer the next two paragraphs will be of utmost importance to you. You're probably gifted and have been for a long time. If you are like most gifted musicians, your abilities probably showed up early in life. You may remember your parents bragging to their friends about how you could listen to a song just once and afterwards are able to play it or sing it. I'm sure you cherished these moments of praise, as it set you apart from other children. Your musical talent made you special and that was good. My only questions are: Do you study music? Do you know the fundamentals of music? Do you know what an oboe is? A triangle ? A bassoon? Do you know how many flats are in the key of E Flat? If you don't know, then you could be limiting your career as a music maker. Understand, there are some producers who don't know music who have long and healthy careers, but they are the exception to the rule.

Your level of success at this point in your life is of no consequence because sooner or later you will not be as popular as you once were. Some of you are on your way to becoming the next Babyface, Trevor Horn or Artist Formerly Known as Prince, but the majority of you who do succeed in the music business will be talent-for-hire and will be judged on your latest accomplishments at all times. You may have a few hits if you're luckier more than most, but sooner or later the hits become far and fewer between. This doesn't mean you will have lost the touch, but simply that there is a new crop of music makers on the scene. What will distinguish you from other music makers of your generation is your true musical skills and your ability to adapt. Listen up.

INSTRUMENT GROUPS

One of the things I like most about being a producer is meeting different musicians from all over the world and listening to them play their instruments. Since each musician's approach to his instrument is different, I'm always amazed at how many different ways one instrument can be played. Musical instruments are to a musician what colors are to a painter. If a painter is not aware of all the colors and color combinations in the color spectrum she will most often use the colors that are most familiar. The result of which is repetitive art. Likewise, a musician who is not familiar with all instrument groups will not be able to create music that is varied in its texture and moods. Many of the young musicians and producers have not been exposed to the instruments of the symphony orchestra because their introduction to music came through synthesizers and samplers. Not knowing the full range of instruments and their capabilities severely limits a producer. These limitations can be overcome.

The easiest way to learn more about instrument groups is to listen to early recordings that utilize full orchestras and to attend classical and jazz concerts. The symphony is an exciting and entertaining way to learn all instrument groups. Ticket prices for symphonies range from $1.00 to $60.00 per seat. Most major cities have free outdoor classical concerts during the summer months. There are also a number of composers whose works I suggest you study. They include, but are not limited to: Tchaikovsky, Rachmaninoff, and Rimsky-Korsakov, who wrote "Flight Of the Bumble Bee" and was the instructor of Stravinsky, another influential composer. You can purchase their music at any record store that has a classical section. Of the modern composers and producers, George Martin, famous for his work with the Beatles, is a must-have in your collection of greats. Also listen to Stevie Wonder's "Songs in the Key of Life" and all the early Barry White recordings. Having an awareness of every instrument and instrument group arms a producer with the ability to manipulate musical moods at will. Having an extensive knowledge of all instruments is also the best thing short of being able to play them all. There is a CD-Rom called *"Musical Instruments"* by Microsoft that does an excellent job of demonstrating the sound of musical instruments from all over the world. If you have a computer with a CD-Rom drive I recommend its purchase.

There is no sound more beautiful than a full orchestra playing live. There is no better or enjoyable way to achieve a higher education about music than listening to classical and jazz. So I encourage you to take time on a consistent basis for continued education, because while in the process you will also be laying the foundation for a long and varied career.

FUNDAMENTAL MUSICAL SKILLS

Anyone who has a radio and reads knows most of today's music is either sequenced or sampled. Advancements in sampling technology and computer sequencing abilities has made it increasingly easier to arrive at musical arrangements that are acceptable in sound quality. The problem is some musicians that use sequencers never learn to master the fundamentals of music itself. Even fewer master a musical instrument. Instead, they learn to manipulate technology and in some cases, ignore the fundamentals of music. These fundamentals include, melody, rhythm, harmony, counterpoint, accompaniment, instrument groups, and basic theory. By understanding the fundamentals of music, musicians and producers will have a better chance at having prosperous careers in the music industry. As cultural trends and social conditions change, so will the public's taste in music. If you are limited as a producer because of the lack of fundamental skills, your career as a music maker will be limited.

There are literally thousands of music schools around the country with programs aimed at teaching adults the basics of music. Taking advantage of these opportunities can only help you. They are relatively inexpensive considering the amount of knowledge you will gain by attending. No matter where you are in the development of your career, there is no better time than now to expand your education. No matter how successful you are as a musician or producer, if your skills are limited, it will limit the kinds of success you will be able to enjoy. If the above has not been enough to convince you that your career as the young trend setter of today will be limited no matter what you do, try asking yourself what you will be doing for a living when you turn fifty. If you think you will still be cranking out the latest dance hits or be on the cutting edge of pop trends, chances are you're wrong. There will be a whole new army of youngsters that will have those jobs. If not that, then what? Will you be able to lead the Tonight Show orchestra, or music conduct a television special, or score a movie? If you don't know the fundamentals of music you will not be able to effectively do any of the above and more than likely you will be one of many to say they used to be in the music industry.

THE PRODUCER'S JOB

There are a number of responsibilities and skills directly associated with being a producer. I will list some of them below and will discuss them in detail. All of these responsibilities should be taken very seriously as they will determine your value as a producer in the long run. If you can afford it, the administrative duties should be handled by someone you trust. This will take the pressure off you to do the office work. However, the creative responsibilities are all yours.

Creative responsibilities:

• Song writing and co-writing songs with the artist
• Becoming familiar with the artist's past work
• Researching the artist's musical preferences
• Musical arrangements
• Vocal arrangements
• Recording

Administrative Responsibilities:

• Creating recording budgets
• Creative budget solutions
• Scheduling sessions
• Hiring personnel (singers, musicians, engineers, arrangers)
• Arranging for guest artist
• Paperwork (I9s, W4s, union forms, album credits etc.)
• Mailings (ruff mixes and final product)
• Printing and distribution of lyrics
  (to engineer, artist, assistant, engineer and label)
• Album credits

THE PRODUCTION PROCESSES BROKEN DOWN

Pre-production:

• Song writing
• Song selection
• Key selection
• Tempos
• Demo if necessary
• Band rehearsal if necessary
• Getting music from home studio to recording studio
  for over dubs and mixing (transfers)

• Bad song great record
• Good song, lousy record

Production:

• Basic tracking
• Overdubs
  (If more than one song, save overdubs till you can do
  multiple songs that require that type of instrument.
  It will save money and time.)
• Background vocals
• Lead vocals
• Track organization and mix preparation
• Ruff mixes
• Mixing

Post-Production:

• Editing and overlays
• Remixing
• Mastering

GAINING THE TRUST

Over the years the most important thing I've realized about artists is they are people first. Most artists when viewed away from the spotlight lead the same kind of lives most non-entertainers lead. Some artists may make more money and lead a fancier lifestyle than the average person, but their hearts and souls remain surprisingly similar to Joe Public's. I find most artists have a strong need to be appreciated and they have their own set of problems, wishes, fears, hopes, and dreams. Just like most average everyday citizens they have to make adjustments and sacrifices that are unique to their trade. These sacrifices, include late nights and rising early in the morning to catch trains, plains and automobiles. Entertainers suffer under the constant scrutiny of the public and critics; this often produces stress. Each artist has his own way of dealing with these stresses and it's part of the producers job to recognize the stressful moments. One of the recognizable signs of a seasoned producer is his ability to deal with artists and their emotions effectively.

In order to fully understand an artist it is important that a producer get to know the artist's previous work and history. Getting to know the artist will give the producer a foundation of information that will be useful in picking the right songs and charting the best musical direction. It also gives the producer a good indication of the artist's strong and weak points.

I like to find out what kind of music the artist likes other than the kind of music they perform. One question I frequently ask an artist I am considering working with is, what song she has heard recently she wishes she had recorded. The answer is usually a strong indication of where the artist sees herself musically.

Of all the challenges I have faced as a producer, none is more demanding than working with an artist who has had a recent bad experience with another producer.

I once worked with a famous female vocalist who had worked with a producer on her previous album and had a bad experience. She felt the producer had been indecisive, making drudgery of work that should have been enjoyable. The project took longer to record than it should have, and ended up costing the artist more money than necessary. On top of that, the project was not received well by the public, therefore, sales where not what the artist and the record company had anticipated. Because of this the singer felt insecure and was unwilling to let go and allow me to do my job as her new producer. When we had our first meeting, although she said she wanted to work with me, she seemed stubborn and closed to almost any suggestions I made. I sensed this would be a difficult project. My first instinct was to pass on producing it, but as I thought more about the situation, I felt I might be able to restore the artist's security.

Our second meeting was spent listening to recordings of Aretha Franklin and Chaka Khan, two of the artist's favorite singers. I learned this during our first meeting. I watched as we listened to these two divas. The artist began to loosen up as I pointed out my favorite parts of those records and she followed suit. Before the evening was over we were a team. I had gained her trust by showing her I had a little class and a musical education. The latter part of our meeting turned into a laughter filled jam session as I played piano and she sang songs from the recordings we had listened to earlier. We went on to record a song that hit the top of the charts. By the way, I now do listening sessions with every artist I work with before we actually start our recording sessions. This technique has never failed to promote a harmonious relationship between myself and the artist. This is just one of many ways to gain the trust of an artist.

If the artist has made a few records that have not achieved the success he expected, find out from his view point what has gone wrong in the past. Determine if you agree with his point of view or whether you can offer another light. Even if you disagree, it is important to show the artist that you are sensitive to his issues.

Most artists take direction well and don't mind the producer telling them what to sing or play, and how to sing or play it. But every once in a while I run into a musician or performer who is unwilling to give me a chance to help them realize their goal of recording a hit. I once worked with a singer who liked to slur her words. Every word was an extension of the word before and after, so the vocal performances sounded like a run-on sentence. Her style of phrasing did not fit the style of the song we were to record and no matter what I did or said she continued to sing in this fashion. Finally, I stopped the session so we could talk. I asked why she wasn't following my directions and she replied that she already had her own style and did not need me to tell her how to sing. I respected her answer and responded accordingly. I told her that part of my job as the producer was to pull things out of her vocally that she could not do herself. She replied once again that she had her own style and that the style was fine. At this point I knew I had to give in a little. Although I knew I was right, there was no point in trying to prove it at the risk of alienating the artist. I then had what I thought was a great idea. I asked the artist if she were hungry. She replied no and she wanted to continue with the recording session. I told her I was hungry and would like to stop for a while. I also told her I had come up with a compromise that would make her happy. The compromise was that I would go to lunch and she could continue to record with just the engineer and herself present. I would allow her to sing in any style she felt was right for the song and I would provide as many tracks as she needed. She could also take as long as she needed. In return, all I wanted was for her to take my direction for a few hours after she finished and I would only require two tracks. She agreed and off to lunch I went.

I returned in two hours to a smiling artist. We laughed and talked about things other than music (I knew this was important because I could sense she was nervous about whether I would approve of her performances). When the time was right we listened to what she had recorded with the engineer and I made sure to note the highlights of her performances. There were quite a few. As I observed her I could sense her self esteem rising with each of my compliments. She was happy and so was I. She couldn't wait until we were ready to do the next part of the session. We then began to record her vocals on two separate tracks. I gave her explicit directions on what to sing and how to sing it. The funny thing is, the instructions were the same instructions I had tried to give her earlier in the day. The difference was, my new found friend was now more than happy to follow my instructions. She began to help make suggestions that took her performance further in the direction in which I wanted it to go. She had made a 180 degree turn for the better. After we finished I complimented her on her ability to follow instructions. Again, I paused to give us both a rest as we laughed and joked. I then asked the engineer to play back the tracks she had done with him one by one. Afterward I asked him to play back my tracks and the artist was quite impressed. I made no suggestions and just watched as she listened to each track she had recorded. Before long she was asking to hear the tracks I had produced over her self produced tracks. What I had succeeded at doing was giving her the respect she needed by allowing her to express herself and at the same time prove I could be of assistance to her. In the end, she hands down preferred the vocals tracks I had produced. So much so that she wanted to erase what she had recorded herself because she was afraid I would use some of it. Again, we had a number one hit.

The moral of the story is, you as the producer have to be willing to demonstrate a little patience and understanding in the studio in order for you to get the performances you desire out of an artist. You do that by gaining the artist's respect. The way to gain an artist's respect is to show respect.

Not all of my escapades go as well as the above. Every once and a while I run into a tasmanian devil and the only thing for me to do is either take myself off the project, which I don't like doing, or use a combination of painstaking editing and other advanced recording techniques to coach the desired performances out of the artist.

The Producer's Mind

KEY SELECTION

Choosing the right key for every song is one of the more important early steps in the recording process. It is essential to the artist and the song because if the proper key is not selected, you will either not be able to finish the song or the song will take longer to finish because it will be more difficult to perform. Obviously if you get halfway through recording basic tracks and discover the key is two high or low for the artist, you will have wasted a great deal of time, energy, and money. Selecting the right key is subjective and depends upon the mood you are trying to achieve. The process of choosing the key is rather simple. I will outline it for you.

A)   Have a cassette or DAT ready to record multiple performances in various keys. I prefer using a DAT recorder over a cassette machine because DAT machines don't vary in speed from machine to machine the way cassettes and other analog machines do. DATs are controlled by an internal crystal that regulates the speed at which the motor winds the tape around the reel. But, for those of you who don't own a DAT machine, a cassette will do, just as long as it is relatively near to the correct speed of 7 1/2 IPS and you record and playback on the same machine.

The accompaniment can be done with a sequencer or a simple guitar-vocal or piano-vocal approach. At this point we are only trying to identify the proper key, so an entire ensemble is not that important.

Have the performer state verbally each key before he proceeds to perform the song in that key, e.g., "This is the key of B flat." This technique will allow you to easily identify the keys as you are listening back to the recording.

B)   Starting in a lower key, have the singer or instrumentalist proceed to perform the song up until the part of the tune where the highest vocal note is hit. This is called the emotional high point. It is very important to be sure the DAT or cassette is recording both the accompaniment and the lead performer.

C)   Once the singer or performer has reached the emotional high of the song or the highest notes for the lead performer are reached, stop. You have just completed recording the performance requirements of the first key signature. Repeat steps B and C one half step higher than the previous one.

D)   Repeat steps B and C until you are well above what is a reasonable performance key for the lead performer.

E)   After you have reached the highest possible key, start at the original key again, but this time you are going to repeat steps B and C one half tone lower than the original key until you reach the emotional high point of the song.For instance: If the original Key is C then a half tone down would be the key of B.

F)   Continue to record the song in progressively lower keys until you have reached the key where the performer can no long sing or perform the notes in a reasonable fashion.

G)   After you have finished recording the different keys, rewind the tape and listen to each performance. Note the subtle changes from key to key. Pick the key that best sells the artist and the song. Be sure to make a written note of the key you have chosen. That note should appear on lyric sheets, track sheets, and the master tape box.

That's it. It's a simple but important step in the recording process. Pay close attention to how the mood of the song changes as you make key changes. Remember to take your time in making your decision as this is a very important step in the production process. A mistake in key selection can be costly.

STRETCHING THE ARTIST'S CAPABILITIES

Another important responsibility of a producer is to stretch the artist's creative boundaries. Striving to pull something out of the artist that they would not have been capable of without you will make the artist's experience with you unique and will keep the artist from becoming boring to the public. New influences both vocally and musically can add a great deal of excitement to a project.

GUEST APPEARANCES

Guest appearances of other artists can bring not only creative excitement but also marquee value—the value a performer has to an audience. If you get someone with a stronger name than the artist you are working with, you will be adding much value to the project.   It's the old two-for-one concept, which is tried and true. Of course this will not make up for a weak song or a weak project, but it will help if the project has its own merit.

RECORDING

I like to break down the recording process into nine categories. They appear here in order of occurrence: pre-production, basic tracking, overdubs, background and lead vocals, track organization and mix preparation, "ruff" mixing, overlays and editing, and mastering.

Pre-production includes song writing, song selection, key selection, sequencing, rhythm arrangements, and tempo selection.

The next step in the recording process is called **basic tracking**. Basic tracking is the actual recording to tape of the rhythm section and/or sequenced music. Key and tempo selection should be completed prior to this step. There are usually live musicians to pay and therefore, if a mistake is made in this process it can be very costly. If you're using a sequencer and midi instruments, the midi instruments must be recorded to tape. This part of the process is called **transfers**.

During the transfer process it's extremely important that the engineer pay close attention to synching both the sequencer and tape properly. This is done using a SMPTE code generator and a SMPTE code reader. SMPTE code is a tone which is recorded onto the tape that allows either two tape machines or a tape machine and a computer to lock together. This produces more tracks and greatly facilitates the number of instruments and voices that can be used. Two 24-track tape machines locked together by SMPTE allows 46 tracks for recording. Two of the tracks are taken up by sympte. It should be noted that most engineers like to use track 24 because it is at the edge of the tape and will not be affected by cross talk from other tracks except track 23. Recording SMPTE on any other tract other than track 1 and track twenty four will run the risk of having cross talk from two tracks instead of just one. Whatever is recorded on track 23 should be low enough in volume so as not to affect the SMPTE tone on track 24.

Very often a SMPTE code generator and a SMPTE code reader are the same device. Again, special care should be taken to record the SMPTE tone to tape properly because if a mistake is made the tape machines and sequencers will not lock properly. A properly recorded SMPTE tone can be a life saver in many instances. For example, if the key chosen for the song to be recorded in turns out to be the wrong key and you have already added drums and percussion to the recording, those tracks can be saved because the sequencer will lock to the tape and the instruments that were generated by midi instruments can be recorded again with ease. This will save you from having to record the percussion and drums over and therefore minimize the financial ramifications of having recorded the song in the wrong key.

After your basic tracks are completed you can proceed with **overdubs**. Overdubs include guitars, keyboards, live percussion, drums, and vocals and is usually the step following basic tracking. At this point I prefer to record a guide lead vocal track. Some overdubs like horns and strings should not be recorded until you have recorded at least ruff lead and background vocals because their function is to complement the lead vocalist or solo instrumentalist. If you do horn and string arrangements before recording a guide vocal or guide lead instrument you run the risk of having strings and horns in places they are not needed, or worse, in the way of the vocals. I like to record overdubs on three or four songs in one day. For instance, if I know I will need percussion on three songs, I wait until I am ready to record percussion on all three songs and then hire a percussionist. This saves on studio setup time because every time a setup is required for additional overdubs it requires additional time and money. The exception would be if you wanted one percussionist on a particular song and another percussionist on other songs. The same goes for all overdubs including lead and background vocals. In short, to save money on overdubs you should wait until you can record like overdubs on several songs in the same day.

You should only commence recording **background and lead vocals** after you are sure the basic tracks have been recorded in the proper keys and the tempo is to your liking. Usually the lead vocalist or instrumentalist will record a guide track so the vocal arranger can arrange background vocals. Background vocals should complement the lead vocal or instrument. Lead vocals should take anywhere from eight to sixteen hours to complete. Background vocals should take between three to six hours to complete.

Singing for more than eight hours can put a strain on the singer so it may take two days to achieve the desired result from a lead vocalist. Variations in the amount of time it takes to record lead and background vocals are directly related to the singer's and producer's abilities. After you finish recording vocals you should make a safety copy of the vocal tracks in case they are erased by mistake from the original masters. This should never happen but it is better to be safe than sorry.

Additional overdubs like horns, strings and keyboard can be recorded after the lead and backgrounds vocals are finished.

After all the vocals and instruments have been recorded it is important to take a day and prepare for the next step, which is mixing. I call this process **track organization and mix preparation**. In this phase the engineer rearranges the order of recorded tracks so the mix will be as easy as possible to accomplish. By arranging instruments and vocals in groups the engineer will be able to easily locate any instrument or vocal during the mix. I have seen few producers use mix preparation and track organization, but I highly recommend it.

The **ruff mix** is needed so the producer can make copies of the recording in order for the record company to hear the songs before they are fully mixed. This is advisable because an A&R executive may need to use these ruff mixes to act as a teaser to motivate the rest of the record company and to give them a taste of what is to come. This process also allows a producer to hear the song after all overdubs have been completed and to formulate a mixing concept. I like to have a day or two to study the completed song before I begin a mix.

Mixing can make or break a record, so special attention should be paid to who is chosen as the mix engineer to mix each song. Sometimes the mix engineer is the same as the recording engineer, other times he is different. There are some engineers that specialize in mixing and others are more known for their recording abilities. Before choosing a mix engineer make sure you have a chance to review his prior mixing work.

For every song there should be several mix versions. Each of these versions have a different purpose. The versions are: full mix, TV track (which is the full mix without the lead vocal or lead instrument), and an instrumental version which has no lead or background vocals. All these versions will come in handy when it's time to edit your recordings. The TV track can also be used for the artist's television performances when a live band is not available. That's why they are called TV tracks. Additional mixes can be arranged according to what the producer or record company's needs are.

One of the more frustrating things about being a producer is finishing a final mix and realizing you have failed to record all that you had wanted to. Fear not, all is not lost. Out of my own frustration for the same reasons, I developed a process that allows me to keep my final mixes and add the additional instruments and/or voices I deem necessary. I call the process **Overlaying**. This is achieved by recording the final mix back to 24-track tape and overdubbing the additional instruments or vocals. The additional tracks and final mix tracks are then blended together for a final-final mix. This process works better if the original mixes are digital because you will not be adding tape hiss to your mixes and overlays. Unlike analog tape, one of the qualities of digital tape is it generates no hiss.

After the mix is complete you may want to shorten or elongate a section of the song. Or you may simply want to rearrange the various sections of the song and that is where **editing** comes in. **Manual editing** is when the engineer cuts and splices the physical tape until the desired result is achieved. **Hard disk** or **digital editing** is easier and quicker than manual editing and is usually done on a computer. Before manual editing begins it is imperative that safeties (copies) are made of all the mix just in case the engineer has to attempt the edits a second, third or fourth time. I make all my safety copies on DAT so I will always be able to return to the original version should I need to.

Mastering is the final step in the recording process and can either be handled by the A&R Director for record company or the producer or both. The producer should always be present for at least the mastering of the songs he produced on a project. This will ensure that the final quality represents what he had in mind. An entire album project can be mastered in five to six hours or less depending upon the final mixes and how meticulous the producer or mastering engineer wants to get. As in final mixes, it is important that you hire a mastering engineer who is familiar with the kind of music you have produced.

USING THE COMPUTER IN PRODUCTION

Computers can be very helpful, if not essential, to the production process. Everything from scheduling and budgeting to sampling and editing can be done on a computer. The Macintosh computer is probably the most frequently used computer for music. While they are generally more expensive than IBM computers they more than make up for the price with ease of use and practicality.

The best Macintosh for the job would be anything from a Mac II CI and up. Anything below this model would be too slow and have limited capabilities. Exclude the Quadra 840 av and Quadra 700 because they do not work well with music applications. A computer for office needs would be different from one you would use for musical needs like sampling and sequencing. If you think you might do both office work and music on one computer I suggest a model that has at least three nubus expansion slots. Nubus slots allow you to expand your computer's capabilities by adding nubus devices, including sampling cards and disk recording. Nubus cards with reverb, effects and mixing capabilities are also available. The Quadra 950 is a powerful machine and has five nubus slots which means it has plenty of room to expand. The other considerations when shopping for the right computer are RAM (random access memory) and hard drive size.

It would be wise to spend a fair amount of time deciding what your computer needs are. Visit a Mac dealer or local music store to find out which Macintosh computer best suits your needs.

Programs & Books for Administrative Needs

PRODUCER'S PHONE BOOK

The organized phone book is the most useful tool of the complete producer. Keeping a detailed listing of phone numbers, addresses, and pager numbers makes getting the job done a cinch. I usually organize by instrument and skills. For instance saxophonist will appear under the letter S, arrangers under the letter A, guitarist under G, and so on. I prefer a electronic phone book because it's easier to use and the information is more permanent. In an electronic phone book it is easy to mark each persons file with the particulars of their talents. This makes it convenient to search by category. Searching for tenor singers becomes a single key stroke on your computer. I collect new phone numbers and enter them into my database once a week. Always have an additional copy of your phone book which you update frequently and keep in a safe place. If something happens to the original you will be able to replace it without a substantial loss.

There are numerous programs designed for scheduling and organizing your contact list, but one I prefer is Touchbase by Aldus. The manuals are well written and are easy to understand. Included in Touchbase is a list of the most commonly used 800 numbers that will be useful in any line of work. Touchbase is easy to use.

DATEBOOK PRO BY ALDUS

Using Datebook Pro for your general scheduling is just one of the ways it can be of help to organize the recording process. It contains a to-do list and memo list. It is also capable of sounding alarms when you need to be reminded of important events that are coming up.

For the producer creating a different project for each song or production, Datebook Pro is the best way to keep up with your busy schedule. Datebook Pro can list everything that needs to be done for that particular song in the calendar as a to-do list or memo, and as you decide to execute an event it can be moved onto your general calendar. In the general calendar you will be able to view and organize events so they don't conflict with your other engagements and activities. One of Datebook Pro's special features is the way it allows the user to create a list of custom categories that correspond to their lifestyle and work habits.

Touchbase and Datebook Pro also allow you to use a special find function. This one step function allows you to view all of a particular kind of contact in a listed format at once. For instance you could ask it to find all the saxophonists in the 213 area code or all your contacts that are guitarists. Again this just speeds up the process of finding the personnel you need when you need them. Whatever your preference for databases and calendars, the techniques described in the last few paragraphs should work well in that program.

Programs for Financial and Budgeting

QUICKEN

Quicken is the quintessential financial and budgeting program. In the world of production where every penny counts, it is most important to keep abreast of every cent spent on your productions. You must always know where you are in order not to go over budget. In the long run staying within budget will help keep you in good standing with record companies. If you are fortunate enough to develop a reputation as a mega hit maker, record companies will be less concerned about over budgets. Quicken can be used to keep a running tab and at any time will give detailed reports on how money is being spent.

FILEMAKER PRO 2.0 AND UP

Filemaker pro by Claris is an excellent program for creating custom databases. A database is a file that organizes and contains a list of contacts and important information concerning them. It is perfect for both mailing list and creating budgets. I suggest this as a must have in your software library.

SONGTRACKER BY WORKING SOLUTIONZ

SongTracker is a program developed by a company called Working Solutionz out of Simi Valley, California. It facilitates the tracking of your songs as a songwriter and publisher. It keeps track of who you sent your song to, what their response was, what your follow up action should be and when. It categorizes your song by style, keeps track of who the collaborators were and what their percentages are and much more. Most importantly, once your song is recorded it keeps track of your royalties. It has a check list that you can consult for plugging your songs. SongTracker can generate over 40 different reports concerning your songs and related subjects. SongTracker is the most useful non-musical computer program ever written for musicians. It is easy to use and understand. It's one of those once in a lifetime programs that has the uncanny ability to give the user a great deal of confidence and sense of accomplishment while using it. It is available for both Windows and Macintosh. My hat goes off to the developers. It can be purchased by simply calling (805) 522-2170.

Programs for Your Musical Needs

SEQUENCING AND DISK RECORDING

Vision and Studio Vision, both sequencing programs by Opcode, are the programs of choice for your computer musical needs. Others to be considered include Cubase by Steinberg and Performer by Mark Of the Unicorn. But the beauty of Vision and Studio Vision is they interface with other computer programs that make recording and sequencing easy. This is important because you don't want your technology to get in the way of your creative process. Companies like Opcode offer above average customer service and tech 800 numbers. One of the most impressive things about Opcode is they open up their software and hardware to third party developers, allowing them to develop new programs and hardware to work with the Opcode line of products.

SYNTH PROGRAMMING AND LIBRARIANS

Galaxy Plus Librarians by Opcode is the choice here hands down. This program allows the user to edit sounds inside synthesizers and samplers from your Mac computer. The obvious advantage to this is you will only have to make limited trips over to the actual synthesizer keyboards and modules in your studio setup. Again you must be aware to pick programs that simplify the technical part of the creative process. Hardware or software that gets in the way is a hindrance.

Creating libraries of sounds and being able to find the sounds you need at any given time is a must in any synth and computer rig. Again Opcode wins. Sure, there are other programs like Mark Of the Unicorn's Unix, but it falls short of working with other products not made by Mark of the Unicorn. When organizing your sounds with a librarian program, think of the librarian as a database. You should be able to search and sort your sounds just like you can an electronic phone book. Keep the saxes together and the trumpets in one spot. Arrange keyboard sounds so that similar sounds are grouped together.

HARD DISK RECORDING & SAMPLING

Digidesign, a relatively young company based in the Bay area, makes great products to facilitate your hard disk recording needs. The range in track configurations goes from two tracks to sixteen. Call your local music store and ask for a brochure of the Digidesign line of products. You won't be sorry. These devices also interface well with Opcodes products. Don't forget to ask for samplecell Digidesigns sampling modules for the Macintosh.

There are other hard disk recorders and samplers, but remember, right now we are referring to just the devices directly related to using your Macintosh computer for these purposes.

As with any purchase, remember to shop around for the best price. You will be surprised at the savings you can realize by shopping around. Talk with friends and other producers to get their opinion about certain products.

EQUIPMENT RENTAL

Many of you may already own a four track recorder, keyboard, guitar, and a microphone, which is enough equipment to sketch out a rough idea for a song. But in today's market, record and publishing executives are used to hearing demos of professional quality. The difference in cost of purchasing a professional quality home studio and what has just been described is probably four or five thousand dollars. Some of you may not have that kind of money at your disposal, and if you do, are obligated to spend it reducing your already towering debts. Fear not, there is a solution that works and is easy to achieve. There are companies that specialize in audio equipment rental. Up until a few years ago they rented mostly to recording studios, but with the number of home recording studios on a sharp rise, they have ventured into renting to the independent musician. These companies will rent you anything, from keyboards, samplers, bass guitars, guitars, recorders, microphones, to pre-amps. You name it, they have it. The icing on the cake is that they will deliver right to your door step, and usually at a reasonable rate. One such company, Design FX Audio specializes in renting Multi-track recorders, microphones, and eight different types of hard disk recorders, including Pro Tools and Sonic Solutions. They can also provide mixing consoles. If you are a cost conscious producer or musician, and would rather leave the shopping to someone else, (not to mention that when you purchase a new piece of recording equipment, you need only wait a few months before there is a even newer device designed to do the job better) give Design FX Audio a call at 800 441-4415 or 310 838-6555. When you call don't forget to ask for a menu. Oh and as always, tell them that Kashif said hello. Think of the money and time you will save.

PRODUCER ROYALTIES

After you have mastered the above mentioned skills and technologies there is only one other thing to worry about, how you are to be paid as a producer. Producers, for the most part, are hired by either the record company or the artist. In the past it was always the record company that hired the producer. In the early 1980s record companies started hiring multiple producers for a single album project. Album projects have been known to have as many as six or seven producers. Besides the various creative ramifications of having multiple producers on one project, the trend also created paperwork nightmares for record labels. Instead of having to negotiate with one producer, record companies found themselves having to manage multiple contracts. The trend today is to have the artist hire the producers and therefore shift the paperwork and the expense of the paperwork onto the artist's shoulders. Artists and artist managers should be aware of this.

In all cases a producer is entitled to a producer's advance. This advance, along with the entire artist's recording budget, must be recouped from record sales before the producer realizes producer's royalties. At the point the entire recording expense has been recouped the producer gets paid retroactively from the first record sold. Sometimes I elect not to take a producer's advance and will build it into what is called an all-in recording fund. (See the chapter on record royalties.) What this means is I will request an all-in recording fund and within that fund there is enough money for me to record the songs and keep an amount equal to a producer's fee when all recording is finished. Remember with a recording fund, the producer is allowed to keep what is left over after recording expenses. By doing this I have put myself in the position where a producer's fee does not have to be recouped before I can earn producers royalties, thus allowing myself to be in a royalty earning position sooner than if I had taken a producer's advance.

Most producers today are hired by artists and their managers. Unless otherwise specified the producer will be paid by the artist. I recommend the producer be paid by the record company. To accomplish this, I recommend a letter of direction, which we will discuss in the next paragraph. Producer royalties start at three points (3%) and can go up to 6% and 7%, if the producer is of superstar status. These percentages are paid to the producer by the record company. In most cases producers enjoy better deals than recording artists, and end up earning royalties before artists do. In these cases the producer has been clever and has enough clout to negotiate responsibility only for the amount of the budget that directly corresponds with the songs they are involved with. If there are numerous producers on a project, and each producer is in control of whether or not he goes over budget, why should producer (a) be responsible for the over budgets of producer (b), especially when producer (a) has no control over how much producer (b), (c) or (d) for that matter, spends on their portion of the project. Furthermore, the more money spent recording a project the more sales have to be realized in order for the producer to be in a royalty earning position. Also a producer's involvement is considered work-for-hire and this being the case, why should a producer be responsible for any of the recording budget? Recording budgets should be the responsibility of the record company. It should be the price record companies are forced to pay for doing business.

The good news for the producer is that once the entire recording budget has been recouped the producer gets paid retroactively from the sale of the first record. This is an important issue because a producer needs to be aware of the entire budget in order to properly assess what position he will be in to realize royalties. If an artist takes a large cash advance as part of the recording fund, that puts the producers on the project at a disadvantage because before the producers can realize producer royalties the entire recording budget must be recouped.

If a producer is involved with more than one project on the same label, we must be careful not to allow the record company to cross collateralize royalties between the projects. What this means is if a producer has produced a record for artist A and sales of that project put that producer in a royalty earning position with the label but another project he worked on (project B) for that label remains unrecouped, the label should not be allowed to apply royalties that are owed to the producer on project A to unrecouped balances on project B. In other words, the label should have to pay you the royalties that are owed you for participation in project A.

LETTERS OF DIRECTION

Even if a producer is hired by an artist or artist's manager it is imperative that he insist upon being paid directly by the record company. This can be accomplished with a letter of direction. This letter should be drafted by the artist or artist's manager and sent to the record company instructing the record company to pay the producer his royalties directly. The most important reason for this is the ability to track down the record company should you find you have not been paid royalties owed to you. Record companies also have a reputation to uphold and in most cases will make at least an attempt to do so. Make sure you receive a copy of the letter of direction before you start any project. There should also be a specific reference to the letter of direction in your formal contract with the artist.

Increases in the producer's percentage are commonly tied to performance thresholds. This means that producer royalties increase as sales increase. For example if the producer's share starts at 3% the producer's royalty rate should increase by either 1/2 % or a full 1% for every 500,000 units sold. These increases are referred to as performance bonuses.

PRODUCER ADVANCES

Producer's advances can range from $1,500 to $30,000 or $40,000 per song depending on the status of the producer. The more successful a producer is as a hit maker, the more he is able to charge as a producer's fee. Smart producers don't ask for astronomical producer's fees because they know these fees have to be recouped against their account before they will receive any royalties. Instead they should negotiate higher all-in recording funds which will allow them to keep whatever they like after the recording expenses have been paid. This puts the amount that a producer can realize as the producer's upfront payment in the producer's hands.

PRODUCER BUDGETS

Producer budgets are as varied as artist budgets. The status of the producer will dictate what a record company is willing to pay to have that producer involved with a project. Producer budgets can range from $15,000 per song up to $75,000 per song if you are a superstar producer.

NON-RELEASE OF MATERIAL & RE-RECORD RIGHTS

Record companies on occasion, for various reasons, elect either not to finish a project or not to release it when it is finished. When this happens the producers and the songwriters are left in a peculiar position. In some situations songwriters have either specifically written songs for that project or have pulled songs from their catalog (songs that have already been written and are waiting to be recorded by an artist). Either way the writer and publisher are now left with unreleased material. The same goes for the producer who may also be the writer, but in the case of the producer the most important issue in this situation is the contents of the re-record clause in their producer's contract.

A re-record clause usually states that the producer cannot re-record any of the songs they produce on a project for five years after the release of the project. What if the album is never released? Does the record company expect the producer to never use those songs again? Effectively the answer is yes. There have been cases where this has happened and the producer had to go to the record label and ask permission to re-record the unreleased material on another project and was granted the right. In that case the producer was lucky because I have heard of other cases where the record company has asked the producer to reimburse them for recording expenses associated with the original recording of the songs in return for the right to record them again.

I suggest the producer protect against this by including a contractual clause which states if the record company elects not to release the project and has no intention of releasing the project the producer has the right to re-record the song that they originally produced with no restrictions. Songs are the lifeblood of the songwriter and producer and they cannot afford to spend valuable time and effort writing and producing, and have the projects that contain their songs go unreleased. Therefore, if a record company chooses not to release a project they should at least allow producers and writers to get on with the business of having their songs recorded and released. Don't forget to ask your attorney about this matter.

HELPFUL HINTS FOR PRODUCERS

1. Co-writing songs with the artist is one of the best ways to insure your involvement on a project.

2. Always create a recording budget if not for the record company, then for yourself. This will let you know when you are spending too much money in certain areas.

3. Always insist on a letter of direction that states that you are to be paid royalties directly from the record company if you are hired by the artist or the artist's manager.

4. Always include increases in points for the producer as the sales increase.

5. Ask for B side protection. If you are a hit producer you don't want producers of lesser status benefiting from the sales of hits you produce. This means if your song is chosen as a single, another one of your productions or an instrumental of one of your productions will be on the B side of that single. This will increase your

writer's royalties if you are also the writer and publisher. If you are both the producer and the writer of both sides of a single your writer's and publishing royalties will double.

6. After a project has recouped recording cost, producers should always receive royalties from the first record sold.

7. Royalties for home videos should be based on at least one-half of what the producer is getting for the sales of CDs, cassettes, and records.

8. Try to get the record label to pay you royalties after your portion of the recording budget has been recouped as opposed to having to wait until the entire artist's budget has been recouped.

~ *Your Dream Team* ~

Choosing a Manager

Choosing an Attorney

Business Managers & Accountants

YOUR DREAM TEAM

I remember watching the United States Basketball Team during the 1992 Summer Olympics. All year long I and millions of other basketball fans waited in anticipation to see "The Dream Team" defeat team after team of able opponents. Michael Jordan, Magic Johnson, Charles Barkley, Karl Malone, and Scottie Pippin were on the same team proudly representing their homeland, the USA. Each member of "The Dream Team" defended his country's reputation for having the best players in the world by recognizing and exploiting the angles and opportunities that arose during each game. Each victory served to further substantiate America's leadership in the field and the sport itself.

As music makers each of you must find and select the individuals who will comprise your own dream team, one made up of the most talented and hard working people that you can find, individuals who will be willing to work toward a common cause: our success. Like the members of the "Dream Team" that represented America during the 1992 Olympics, your dream team must be able to recognize and exploit the angles and opportunities as they arise in your career. Your dream team must also be able to create opportunity where there is none. The members of your team will include a manager, music industry attorney, an accountant or business manager (I prefer the former and will explain why in the accountants vs. business manager chapter). In this group of chapters, I address the everyday issues that pertain to dealing with the members of your dream team. How do I find a good attorney?, How do they get paid? How do I recognize the right manager? What is the difference between an accountant and a business manager? These are just some of the many questions you will find answers to in this group of chapters. Read carefully. These individuals will be your lifeline to the industry and it is of paramount importance that you understand how to handle your relationship with each member of your team if you're to maximize the return on the work they do on your behalf.

Choosing a Manager

Choosing a manager is one of the most important decisions you will make in your career. There can never be too many words of advice given concerning the caution one should take in making such a decision. Many bright careers have dimmed and been cut short due to mismanagement. Likewise, there have been many moderately talented individuals that enjoy long and healthy careers that can be attributed to the guidance of effective management. I have heard amazing stories of how some managers have gotten into the business, such as the guy who was a limousine driver one day and the next day was managing the artist he had chauffeuring to and from the airport the day before. I certainly am not saying that driving a limousine is not hard honest work, because it is, but one must be sensible in assessing the qualities that are necessary to effectively guide careers in the entertainment industry.

I have mulled over whether or not to write this section for fear of offending some artists and their managers. As you can tell from the previous chapters in this book, I consistently voice my allegiance and dedication to the well being of artists and the creators of music. My concern stems from the knowledge of a large number of artists and musicians who are managed by friends or relatives. Some of these managers are strong in their skills and others are weak and therefore detrimental to the artist's career. Understanding the dynamics of these kinds of relationships and why they happen from first hand experience gives me an acute awareness and sensitivity for both the artist and the manager. However, one of the duties I have in writing this book is to tell the truth no matter what. So with all due respect, here we go.

RELATIVES AND FRIENDS

Being an artist can sometimes be a lonely affair. I know because I am also a recording artist. Although I spend the majority of my time writing and producing for other people, when it comes to recording, promoting and marketing my own albums, I switch into the artist mode, wherein excessive demands are made on my time and emotional space.

Because of the travel that is necessary in order to record and promote a record I'm always finding myself in unfamiliar surroundings. These unfamiliar places and faces leave me with a sense of longing. I need a familiar face that somehow connects me to my friends and family; a face that can fill that role when it is needed. This person needs to understand me, my thinking, my moods and personalities, and help bring about the warm and fuzzy emotional environment that only friends and family can provide. Besides, the number of people an artist can meet in a day is astounding. Not to mention the pressure to be at your best whether recording, performing, doing an interview or just being out in public. One might think these pressures only exist for the accomplished and celebrated artist but this is untrue. How many times have you been to a party and someone has asked you to perform? While the pressures I'm referring to are felt by well known performers much more than they are by up and coming artists, nonetheless, they still exist and will grow as that artist's career grows.

Most artists usually have a close friend or relative that hangs with them most of the time. It is this individual's role to provide a familiar and trusting variable to the complicated and sometimes taxing life of the artist. They usually become inseparable because the artist needs consistency in his life and that consistency often comes in the form of this longtime friend or relative.

Sometimes during what is the normal course of business for the recording industry the artist becomes frustrated with the complexities and up-and-down nature of the business. He may become disenchanted with a manager and other representatives. Those relationships may be dissolved, leaving the artist with the responsibility of managing his own career. Having travelled this road I can understand why after a few repeats of promises, negotiations, bad deals and unfulfilled dreams an artist may feel better off doing the job himself. The artist is frustrated, concerned about who to trust, and is at the same time in need of help to keep his career moving forward. If the friend or relative closest to the artist is privy to these frustrations and is concerned for the artist, in most cases this person will try to find a way to help the artist. In this case it is absolutely logical that the friend or relative end up becoming the artists' manager. In some cases this may be the appropriate solution to what has been a frustrating issue for the artist. Especially if the friend or family member has the wherewithal to grasp the necessary skills needed to be an effective manager. In fact, some may already possess skills that make them well suited for such a position, but too often others are not at all qualified, and should remain in the role of friend and confidant.

I have had friends and confidants who have contributed to my overall well being, but never have I put one in a managerial position. There was no question they were good friends but they were also not qualified for the job. I must say I was tempted a few times during one of those frustrating moments, to manage myself along with a friend but decided there were too many decisions that needed an expertise that neither I nor my friend could bring to the situation. I had to make a hard decision to hire a professional manager.

Making a wise choice in a professional manager has not always worked out for me either, and not always because they were not skilled managers. Quite the contrary, the problem was they just were not interested enough to spend the necessary time to do the job. Others I have hired to manage me were no more capable than the average citizen in the street for the job. What they had was an impressive office and a large staff which impressed me. The lessons from these incidents have been well learned. It is because of these adventures and journeys in the search for the perfect manager that I share with you what I have come to know about the relationship between manager and artist.

BE CAREFUL

In all honesty, the life span of the average artist in the nineties is about two albums, three at the most. If they are to make the best of this once-in-a-lifetime opportunity they had better have adequate management. If managers were required to have a college degree, it would prove they have at least had some formal training in the area of artist management. If that were the case there would be a greater number of successful artists. There are probably hundreds of managers who can't even spell artist and certainly can't manage one. It is mandatory that a doctor have a minimum amount of training to practice medicine and a lawyer is required to spend a great deal of time developing her skills and legal mind. Why should an artist manager be exempt from the same type of rigorous training? You wouldn't think of hiring a lawyer if you knew she had never attended law school, would you? It is a well know fact that most artists make inappropriate choices in management and get ripped off and the little money they make often goes to paying a lawyer to clean up the aftermath of mis-management.

CHARACTERISTICS: WHAT TO LOOK FOR

There are many styles of management and many facets to management duties. Most managers in the music industry do not start out as managers. They usually start out as either road managers, artists, agents, or record company executives, friends or relatives and at some point in their careers decide to make the transition into becoming an artist manager. Because of this there are several different styles of management. The manager who is an ex-talent agent might excel in getting you bookings. The manager who is an ex-record company official should be able to help guide the record company into making the proper decisions concerning marketing and promotion. Some managers are also attorneys, they should be adept in negotiating deals.

Finally, there is the person with none of the above backgrounds but possesses that get-up-and-go-for-it attitude. He or she is willing to stay up all night on your behalf and willing to go through thick and thin to see you through. This kind of manager obviously has merits. One thing is for sure, one cannot be an effective manager without possessing some degree of all the above mentioned skills. It is rare to find someone equally talented in dealing with labels, legal matters, touring, and management, but you should try to find someone with a clear understanding of the many facets and duties of management. It is just as important to find someone with a special interest in your career who also has the energy and resources to implement a program designed especially for you.

PROVING IT

The single most important thing in choosing a manager is that he demonstrates a genuine belief in you as a talent and as a person. Hard work on your behalf as the artist is a good starting place. Honesty is another quality high on my list of must-haves.

MANAGEMENT FEES

Managers earn between 15 percent and 20 percent of the income derived from an artist's entertainment activities. However, there have been deals where a manager received less. If your career is already in full swing and you're looking for someone to stay the course, then a lessor amount might be appropriate. In no case should a manager demand more then 20 percent. There are also arrangements where the more successful the artist becomes and the more money they make touring, the smaller the percentage taken by the manager. This is called a sliding scale arrangement and is designed so the manager does not make an inappropriately large amount of income compared to the amount of work involved with managing an artist's career. As the artist's career reaches new heights it becomes easier to realize additional income as a result of that artist's efforts. Thus the manager has to do less work to achieve the same income. This decrease in the amount of effort required to manage an artist at that level is reflected in a decrease in the percentage of the income the manager is entitled to.

PAYING YOUR MANAGER ON THE NET INCOME OF LIVE PERFORMANCES

Contrary to what occurs 90 percent of the time concerning live gigs and concerts, a manager ought to get paid on net profits, not on the gross income. I urge this because, when a manager is paid on the gross, her share of the income is calculated before the necessary expenses have been accounted for by the artist. This is unfair to the artist because if there were no expenses their would be no gig. So, why should the manager take a percentage off the top as if there were no expenses?

AN EXAMPLE OF MANAGEMENT FEES BASED ON GROSS

In this case the artist has set himself up as a corporation. That corporation pays the artist what ever income is left over after expenses including all fees. Taxes are computed on the amount of monies that the artist actually receives. Keep in mind that if the artist is not set up as a corporation the taxes will be computed on the full amount of income. Also note the corporation has to pay taxes also, but the IRS guidelines for corporations are different than they are for individuals. My advice is to always consult a qualified tax accountant on these and other tax matters.

Let's say that you, the artist, have earned $100,000 touring. Let's say the manager is getting a high end range fee of 20 percent. This means that twenty thousand dollars goes to the manager straight off the top. Let's assume that there was an agent involved who is getting paid at the suggested agent fee of 10 percent. (Of course the suggestion is made by agencies who employ agents.) That's another 10 percent off the original $100,000 you no longer have. The remaining amount is $70,000. Deduct your travel and band expenses, crew salaries, band salaries, road manager salary, gas, tolls, meals, and lodging—that totals about $25,000 and you end up with $45,000 for yourself, until your favorite Uncle Sam comes by for an unwelcome visit. Maybe he doesn't really come by, but he's one of those relatives that lives nearby and there is always a chance of his just stopping in without calling. If you live in Los Angeles making this kind of money we must assume you're in the 50 percent tax bracket. (38 percent federal tax and eleven percent state tax equals 49 percent. For ease of math, I rounded it off to 50 percent.) 50 percent of $45,000 is $22,500, $45,000 minus $22,500 is $22,500. The dollar amount you end up with is $22,500 out of the original $100,000. If this sounds a little unfair, it is!

Management fees based on net profits and agency fees deducted after expenses are fairer to the artist. Right about now I have managers and agents picketing my house, shouting slogans like "unfair education" and keep the artist ignorant. But not to worry, I have a stereo capable of mega decibels. I'll just face the speakers out the window and blast back, "We Will, We Will Rock You."

MANAGERS' AND AGENTS' FEES BASED ON NET

Anyway back to the computations. Remember this is the same tour with the same $100,000 earned as before. In this case your manager and your trusty agent get paid on the amount calculated after expenses. Travel and band expenses are still $25,000. Deduct $25,000 from $100,000 and the remaining amount is $75,000, which by the way is called "net after expenses". Deduct the manager's share of 20 percent from $75,000 which is $15,000. This represents a full $5,000 less than if the manager were paid on gross receipts. Now deduct 10 percent of $75,000 for the agent's fee which amounts to $7,500. After all is said and done you are left with $52,500. Of course you know Uncle Sam just pulled up in the driveway and is threatening to come in for a lengthy visit until you nearly break your neck running out the door to give him his hard earned share of 50 percent of $52,500 which amounts to $26,250.

At this point the artist is left with $26,250, instead of $22,500 which is what the artist would have if the manager and agent had commissioned the gross. Hold on I need to run to the window and wave to my captive audience of agents and managers. It seems to have grown to thousands waving picket signs and screaming unmentionables. Oh well, guess I'll just sleep with a pair of head phones.

WHAT A MANAGER SHOULD
AND SHOULD NOT COMMISSION

As I mentioned above, a manager is paid on a commission basis. However there are certain monies that an artist or producer receives that a manager should not commission because those monies are not actually income for the artist or producer. If an artist or producer is having any level of success there will be expenses that are associated with doing the job. A clear example of that is a recording budget in which an artist advance is included. If the entire album budget is $150,000 and the artist advance is $15,000 the artist manager should only commission $15,000 of that total album budget. One of the best arguments that I can give for this is the remaining $135,000 is not income to the artist but it is merely the budget within which the artist must work to record the album. To further substantiate that fact we must remember the entire album budget is recoupable by the record company from the artist's account and therefore must be looked at as an expense of the artist and not income.

Unfortunately most artist and producers are not aware of this and end up allowing managers to commission money that is not income. In a sense, this issue is related to the issue of getting paid on net as opposed to gross income. Other areas in which a manager should not participate on a commission basis are tour support, demo cost, and, if you're a headlining act, monies paid to an opening act. A manager should also not expect to receive a commission on uncollected monies owed to the artist or producer.

MONIES EARNED AFTER YOUR
MANAGEMENT AGREEMENT HAS EXPIRED

Just as every contract has a starting date, there is also a termination date, a time at which the contract itself expires. The manager and artist, producer or songwriter at that time agree to go their separate ways. But the projects that were recorded during the term of the contract sometimes continue earning income and what happens to this income as far as the manager is concerned has to be addressed. The manager's position will be that he continue to commission that income. The artist's or producer's position is most likely to be that the manager should not get any of that income. What happens 90 percent of the time due to the artist's, producer's or songwriter's lack of experience is the manager continues to receive a full commission on that income for as long as there is income. To a large degree this is unfair to the artist, producer and songwriter, whose contract with the manager has terminated, but the manager is continuing to receiving income without having to do any work to earn that income.

While I do agree that if a recording contract was entered into during the term of the management contract, the manager should continue receiving commissions on income derived from the sale of those recordings, the commissions that are earned after the management contract has terminated should be paid at a reduced rate. That rate should be one-half of the rate that was being paid during the term of the management contract, or be based on some type of sliding scale.

Another solution would be to limit the amount of time a manager is allowed to commission income derived from recordings that were made during the term of the management contract when the income is earned after the management contract has terminated.

Although these issues will not arise before the termination date of the contract it is important that they are negotiated and written into the contract before it is executed.

It is a good idea for an artist, producer or songwriter whose management contract is close to its termination date, to refrain from signing any new recording, production, and publishing agreements until the termination date of the management contract has passed.

I do realize that managers will be unhappy with my suggestion of delaying the signing of contracts that may fall near the termination date of a management contract, but I'm sure they will agree that it makes good business sense for the artist, producer, or songwriter.

In general, as an artist, producer, and songwriter you should try and limit as much as possible the amount of income that a former manager can earn from your activities after your contract with that manager has terminated .

ENTERTAINMENT ACTIVITIES ONLY

A manager should be paid on your entertainment activities only. If you are fortunate enough to have other incomes not derived through your work in the recording industry, your manager should not share in the income derived from those activities.

MANAGER'S RECOUPMENT OF DEMO & OTHER UP-FRONT COSTS

It is customary for a manager to be reimbursed for their expenses, and advances to the artist, off the top of any income earned from the artist entertainment activities. For instance: it is not unusual for a manager to pay for demo costs. Remember this is a time when the artist cannot afford to pay these costs herself. If a manager were to invest $10,000 to develop a demo and to secure a record deal, she would recoup that investment as soon as the record deal is inked. If you add that together with the management fee of 15 percent it could leave the artist with much less money with which to record the album. What if your record deal is for a total of $100,000 (low by most standards except jazz, but for ease of demonstration lets use these numbers). If your manager recouped her $10,000 off the top plus the 15 percent management commission of $15,000, that would leave you with only $75,000 to make an entire recording probably consisting of ten songs. If you divide $75,000 by 10 each song would have a budget of $7,500 which is unrealistic. This is the old way of doing business. The new way (the way I'm suggesting) is to have the manager only commission the artist's advance.

What the manager needs to demonstrate here is a commitment to this project for the long haul, and recouping all of her expenses immediately may not be the best thing for the artist. It would impact the project too negatively. In a case such as this, a manager would have to use discretion in deciding how she would impact the entire project by demanding full recovery of the demo cost up front and off the top. Spreading recoupment of demo and other up front costs over time is a show of good faith by a manager and is to be commended. If I were an artist I would look at that as a sign that the manager really believed in me as a talent.

MANAGER'S PERFORMANCE

Managers in general are a dime a dozen in the recording industry, but a manager that is honest, fair, and talented is a rare find. Part of a manager's job is to promote the artist within the industry itself. In order to be able to do this a manager must be a good salesperson. If a buzz develops about an artist that is unsigned, they are sure to receive phone calls from various managers, each of which will give the artist his or her pitch about what they can do for the artist that other managers can't do. The best advice that can be given about choosing a manager is to make a decision based on facts. What has that manager done that is outstanding? Who else does he manage? Is he well respected within the industry? Is he willing to give you references of long-standing relationships?

Artist and producers, be aware that a manager looking to pick you up as a new client will in some cases make all kinds of promises about what he will do for you if you hire him as your manager. Be prepared for these kinds of conversations but at the end of the day when you do make a choice, make sure your contract with the manager states that your manager will be held accountable for certain promises that have been made to you as a client. In other words, get those promises in writing. For example if a manager promises that you will earn $150,000 within the first 12 months, make them put it in writing, and at the end of the first year if you have not earned that amount you have the right to terminate that contract. This is the only protection that you will have from being under contract to a manager that is not effective.

Other issues that should be addressed in your contract with a manager include helping to acquire a record deal, a publishing deal, production work if you are a producer, and live performances. There should be a clause in the contract that addresses each of these issues and a time line by which the manager must perform all of these duties.

MANAGEMENT COMPANIES & WHO OWNS MY CONTRACT

Sometimes a producer's, writer's, or artist's management contract will be with a management company. If that is the case the issue arises about who is really the artist's manager. Here's why. If an artist signs with a management company and that company is sold and the person that actually signed that artist to that company is fired by the new owners, that artist could find herself doing business with a complete stranger.

An even more likely set of circumstances would be if an artist were signed to a management company and the manager were to become ill and was not able to perform his duties as a manager. The artist would still be under contract to the management company. What rights should the artist have given this set of circumstances? It is obvious that the artist should have some rights and those rights must be spelled out in the management agreement.

First, the artist is protected by the performance clause that we addressed earlier in this chapter. Secondly, the artist should negotiate a key man clause into her contract. A key man clause simply states that although the artist, producer, or writer is entering into an agreement with a corporation or partnership that artist expects their services to be rendered by a particular person either employed by that corporation or one of its key executives. If for some reason that person becomes unavailable the artist can terminate the contract.

Key man clauses are difficult to obtain if the contract is to be with a larger management company and therefore may require some negotiation.

Assessing where you are as an artist will play an important role in both who you choose as a manager and determining what is fair as compensation for that manager's contributions. I have listed below three types of artists.

THE BEGINNING ARTISTS

You may or may not have recorded demos. You've never had a record released but you have done live shows around town and are looking to expand your career to include recording and touring.

You're a touring musician looking to become a front man. You have plenty of experience on stage as a back-up musician and feel you have what it takes to be a successful solo artist or member of a recording band.

You sing all the time and your friends tell you that you should pursue a career in the record business, but up until now you have not had the courage to get started.

ALREADY ON YOUR WAY

You've recorded albums and they have sold well, but not enough for you to realize any royalties and you are concerned that your current manager does not have the skills that are essential in helping you reach the next level.

YOU HAVE A PUBLISHING DEAL
BUT NO RECORD CONTRACT

You are in between managers. New prospects continue to approach you about management but you sense that they see you as an immediate meal ticket.

You have toured as a solo artist and done well, but have never made a killing from your live performances.

THE ESTABLISHED ARTIST

Gold and or platinum records are to your credit. You consistently can command $50,000 and up for each night of live performances.

Your album budgets are a minimum of $500,000.

You have enough experience as an artist to manage yourself but you need some one to help you do the day-to-day work.

BE CLEAR ABOUT WHAT YOU NEED

Be clear about what you need a manager to achieve for you. For instance, if you're a club singer you might want a manager to find work for you in respectable establishments, or get more money for your performances.

A manager should be able to help you to determine where you are in the development of your career, as well as identifying future goals. He or she should be able to help plot a course of action designed to achieve these goals.

Think of a manager as a head coach of a basketball team. While there are other coaches including the fitness coach or trainer, it is the head coach who coordinates the activities of the team to ensure success in the game. A good manager will have contacts within the industry. A good manager is well organized, and will recognize the artist's weaknesses and make suggestions on how to improve them.

If you don't understand the above paragraphs, read them again, maybe with a friend to help clarify the idea. I am not suggesting that you are having trouble but, instead I am hell-bent on relieving you of any uncertainties you may have concerning what I have written. If I could explain it to you in person I would. Who knows? Maybe someday I will get that chance.

HELPFUL HINTS FOR DEALING WITH MANAGERS

• It is my opinion that a manager should never make more money on a specific job than the artist.

• Never give a manager, or person posing as a manager, money to get involved with your career.

• At no time should your manager also be your attorney. That is a conflict of interest.

• Your manager should never be your business manager. If you do allow this, I can assure you that it will lead to an unhappy ending. A smart and honest manager would never jeopardize the relationship with a client in this way. Your accountant or business manager will be giving you advice that should be in your best interest. That advice sometimes means the manager may make less money on a deal. If your manager is also your business manager there can exist the strong potential for a conflict of interest and the manager may not be able to resist the temptation to take advantage of the situation. Read the chapter on business management, and you'll find that they have a limited use in most situations. I prefer accountants. Likewise, your manager should never be your accountant, nor should anyone else in your manager's office.

• When interviewing a manager ask specific questions about what he plans to do for you.

• Ask what he sees as your strengths and weaknesses and what experience he has in dealing with situations such as yours.

• If a prospective manager is living and working in a different city than you are, find out how they intend to stay in touch with you and your needs, and decide whether or not the plan is practical.

• Ask about the proposed manager's staff.

• Find out how long he has been in the business.

• Know what you need before you begin the interview

• Use your common sense and a good attorney before signing any contracts.

• Set up your own management company and do a co-management arrangement with a manager. Split the responsibilities and the fee.

Choosing an Attorney

I have met more people who would rather have a tooth removed without Novocaine, than sit in the same room with an attorney. Satan himself could not intimidate more than a visit to an attorney's office. While I must admit I've met a few lawyers that leave burn spots wherever their cloven hooves land, I have far more often met and had dealings with attorneys I found to be straightforward and honest.

People get intimidated by attorneys because they feel inferior. They feel vulnerable because attorneys know more than they do and therefore they are at their mercy. While these fears are common and are a hindrance, they are not insurmountable. In this chapter I list and demonstrate some guidelines that will give you a point of reference when working with attorneys. This chapter should help take some of the guess work out of your attorney-client relationships.

I've heard many stories of folks being taken advantage of by attorneys. This is particularly sad because we usually hire attorneys so we don't get taken advantage of. Nonetheless, there are a few unscrupulous individuals masquerading as attorneys. In most cases when folks are taken advantage of by attorneys, or anyone for that matter, it is always partly due to their own inexperience. The more you know, the less likely you'll get taken advantage of. No matter what line of business you're in, the results of your relationships with lawyers would be far more satisfying if you were to take the time to familiarize yourself with the fundamentals of that industry. Some clients, rather than participate in the process of negotiating, assessing and determining what is best for themselves along with the attorney, elect to drop a project or negotiation in the lap of the lawyer and hope to have satisfactory results. This approach, while it may lead to satisfactory results some of the time, is not the most effective approach to deal making. Instead, I endorse a hands on approach, where the attorney keeps the client informed on a continuous basis.

Engaging in an ongoing dialogue concerning your legal matters will cost more in the beginning because it requires more time spent consulting your attorney, but what you gain and pay for along with the attorney's services is an informal education. As you reach higher levels of awareness concerning deal making and the music industry as a whole, you will require less time of your attorney because you will have a built-in knowledge of what is fair and makes sense in any given situation. You will also gain greater insights into legal ideas and concepts.

ASK FOR REFERENCES

Attorneys or law firms being considered for your employment should be happy to provide you with a list of references. This list should include distinctly different client assignments, including a recording artist, songwriter, production company, publishing company and record company. Each client on the attorney's reference list should have had a business relationship with that attorney no less than three years. Inquire about what other clients they represent and their experience in the entertainment industry. Although who is represented by the attorney will play a limited role in what he will be able to achieve for your situation, having that information will help you establish an overall opinion of the attorney or law firm. That information will also serve as an indicator as to how well the attorney is connected within the recording and entertainment industries.

Steer away from lawyers whose main concern is when they will be paid. It is extremely important to align yourself with legal counsel that not only sees you as an opportunity to make money, but also believes in what you are trying to achieve. Every triumph you claim in your career is also a triumph for your attorney. Those lawyers who take pride in their work are more likely to pay attention to small details. Those just looking to make a quick buck won't. It's as simple as that. I suggest that you shy away from the quick-talking, deal-guaranteeing types, who seem to have just the right combination of gab and sleaze. If your instincts tell you no, then I recommend no.

WHAT YOU'RE PAYING FOR

In general, what you pay for when you hire an attorney is expert advice on how to obtain the best deal, advice on how to remedy legal problems, his or her connections within the industry that might benefit you directly or indirectly, career direction and planning and legal protection overall. Some attorneys will also take on the responsibility of shopping demo tapes to obtain recording and publishing deals.

The value of an attorney is determined in a number of ways, the most visible of those being the attorney's image or reputation within the industry. Part of an attorney's image can be his or her association with a law firm. If that law firm has a high profile, any lawyer that is an associate or partner within that firm will benefit from the firm's image and reputation. The advantage of working with an attorney associated with a prominent law firm is that he will be well connected and should be able to gain the attention of record industry executives. Such an attorney also has valuable resources in the other attorneys in that office. For instance, if your attorney is negotiating a publishing deal, he has the advantage of reviewing the most recent and successful negotiations carried out by attorneys in his office. This gives your lawyer a good idea of the parameters in which certain publishing companies prefer to work. The same goes for all types of deals that a client may be interested in, whether television, film, recording, live performances, etc. Attorneys that are well known in the business also enjoy the asset of having an extensive negotiating history. This history says to the client that the attorney should have a firm grasp on how specific negotiations should be handled, as well as an above-average understanding of negotiations in general.

While high profile law firms and well known attorneys tend to attract the most clients, a glossy image does not always translate into the desired results for the client. Sometimes a client can get lost in the shuffle at a large law firm. For those of you who fear this may happen to you at a larger firm or with a more prominent attorney, there are many low profile lawyers with modest office accommodations that are more than capable of handling any type of negotiation. The same considerations must be taken when interviewing lawyers with a high profile as with lawyers who are not as well known. Considerations and steps for interviewing potential legal counsel are listed later in this chapter.

Although an attorney is often looked upon as a non-creative member of the team, I tend to think differently on this matter. I believe it should be a largely creative function, because in most deals there are issues that each negotiating party feels strongly about that differ from the opinion and practices of the other party. During these times you want your attorney to be a creative thinker and not just a clerk negotiating the same deal time and time again. In fact, having a creative attorney can make the difference between a successful or a broken negotiation. Obviously it is at these times that devising creative solutions to deal-breaking points is probably one of the most important functions of a negotiating attorney. The more creative the attorney the better. This is also one of the things you're paying for when you hire an attorney.

Unlike an accountant or business manager, an attorney's function is largely one of negotiating and negotiations are largely affected by trends in the business. Attorneys who are in small cities may not be as well informed as those who practice law in cities where the music industry is in prominence. This is not an indictment of small town attorneys but rather a factor to consider when interviewing an attorney. It is important to find out how informed any attorney is overall and a consideration of greater importance if the attorney practices in a small town.

THE RIGHT KIND OF ATTORNEY FOR THE JOB

Make sure any attorney you consider employing has experience in the area in which you need her services. It makes no sense to employ a banking attorney for entertainment matters, unless she has extensive knowledge in both areas. There are several types of attorneys. Litigators are appropriate for court cases and lawsuits. You may not want to hire one to negotiate your recording contracts, but you may want to in a situation that involves a law suit.

THE VALUE OF THE DEAL

It is important for you, the client, to be clear about what is fair in any given situation. Ask friends and acquaintances about the structure of deals they have been involved in that may be similar to yours. There is no greater strength in negotiations than to know the strong points and pitfalls of a deal before committing. It is equally important to know your true value and worth in any potential deal. Your attorney needs to know vital facts about your life philosophies, and how far you are willing to go.

Some attorneys, because of their stature and relationships in the business, put more value on themselves and their abilities than they put on the artist or client for whom they are working. While having an attorney that is well respected and well informed can result in better deals, always remember it is the value perceived in you as the artist, not in your attorney, that will most affect a deal.

HOW IS THIS ATTORNEY GOING TO GET PAID?

One of the more dreaded fears concerning working with an attorney is discussing how they will be compensated. If this is your first time approaching a lawyer, feeling a little uncomfortable is understandable. But think of it this way: most people when buying cars want the most economical price available. Even after narrowing their choices down to the brand and model car they want, they will continue to negotiate the price of the car to get the best value for the dollar.

The same approach should be taken when shopping for an attorney. Your mission should be to find the best attorney for the dollar that will give you the highest quality legal services. One that will show a special interest in your career. One that will demonstrate an understanding of your financial status and go that extra mile to insure your success.

FIVE WAYS OF PAYING

There are five ways attorneys can be compensated for their services: By retainer, by the hour, by the flat rate option, by a percentage of the deal, or by a deferred payment arrangement.

RETAINERS

A retainer means the client guarantees the lawyer or law firm a fixed amount every month whether you use them a little or a lot. Paying this way can be to your advantage if you foresee needing an attorney's services frequently. Retainer fees can range from $500 per month up to thousands of dollars a month. The larger the work load an attorney anticipates the higher the amount of the retainer. The retainer amount should still be less than if you were charged an hourly rate for the same amount of work.

HOURLY RATES

Hourly rates are expensive, and most attorneys prefer retainers because a retainer guarantees a set amount of income each month. The reason attorneys set their hourly rates so high is to force clients into a relationship based upon a retainer. The going rate for most attorneys if paying by the hour is from $175 to $400 per hour. Anything above $200 per hour is excessive and inflated. Attorneys ask for what they know they can get. I find it hard to believe any attorney is worth $400 an hour, especially if what they are doing can be done by other attorneys that charge less and are just as effective.

Like accountants, business managers and practically everything else, the cost for services are always higher in the larger metropolitan areas than they are in smaller cities. Attorneys fees in small towns should range from $125 per hour to $200. In the larger cities such as New York and Los Angeles the costs tend to start at $175 per hour and can go up to as much as $400 per hour.

Remember these attorneys are in the entertainment industry and a big part of the entertainment industry is hype. Need I say more? Ask what the estimated amount of time the attorney anticipates spending on your project. You must do this knowing that sometimes unforeseen variables will come into play and therefore affect the amount of time a negotiation might take. This can work in your favor, where things go smoothly and therefore take less time, but works against you if the negotiations get complicated and end up taking longer than expected. In any case, staying abreast of the situation can only be to your advantage.

Be aware that in most situations when paying by the hour, every time you talk to your attorney by phone you are being charged. My advice is to know what you need to talk about before you pick up the phone and keep the preliminary conversations short and to the point.

FLAT RATES

Of all the ways an attorney can be compensated for time and expenses, a flat rate fee is the simplest and most desirable. A flat rate in this case is when an attorney charges a flat fee for his or her services on a project by project basis. The beauty in these type of deals is that a rate is negotiated for that particular job and when it's finished the attorney gets paid and that's the end of story. Flat fees are based upon the amount of time an attorney feels he or she will spend working on a project and are usually given in a case where the attorney is willing to give a client a break in pricing. Flat rates can range from $175 which represents about an hour's worth of work up to thousands of dollars depending upon the amount time the attorney anticipates they will have to spend on a project. The more time the project will require, the more it will cost. However, a flat rate should still work out to be a bargain for the client.

DEFERRED PAYMENTS

In some instances, attorneys will work on a deferred payment plan. If there is a deal to negotiate, or a situation to resolve, and the client can't afford to pay up front, or on an hourly or retainer basis, the attorney has an option to work out a deal where he is compensated as soon as the deal closes. While this type of arrangement serves the immediate needs of the client, the down side is that usually the client will end up paying more for the services in the long run than they were actually worth because the lawyer feels he is taking a risk and that justifies a premium fee. To a great degree that is a fair arrangement. However, the client should make sure she knows what the attorney's services would have cost if she had been able to pay up front.

In addition, the attorney may ask for a percentage of whatever deal is being negotiated, again with the justification being they are taking a risk and should be compensated accordingly. However, the percentage should only apply to the advance that the client receives and not the value of the entire deal. We will discuss more about percentages in the next paragraph. Attorneys willing to work on a deferred payment plan will defer payment only up to a certain point. For practical purposes they cannot afford to defer payment for an indefinite amount of time, nor can you expect them to let your tab run into very high numbers. If an actual negotiation is being engaged in, the attorney will feel better about taking a chance on deferred payments and will generally not be as uptight about getting paid. If the work they are doing on your behalf is purely speculative, expect them to limit the amount of time and energy they are willing to spend to a reasonable amount. I have found most attorneys, if they believe in a project, are willing to defer up to $7,500 with no problem.

PERCENTAGE BASIS

Some attorneys, particularly those that spend most of their time negotiating deals, like to work on a percentage of the deal basis. Five to ten percent is the usual fee. If the percentage is fair and the negotiation takes a considerable amount of time, five or ten percent of the advance might turn out to be a bargain considering the number of hours the attorney has spent working on this negotiation. This may be especially true when compared to the attorney's hourly rate. However, there are some situations when paying a percentage of the deal would not be fair to the client. Keep in mind that what is fair and what is not depends upon the amount of time the attorney has to spend negotiating the deal, her fee, and the percentage amount. If the percentage of the deal the attorney is asking for does not reflect the amount of work required, the percentage is too high.

Here is how it should work. If your advance is $250,000 and your attorney demands 10 percent of the deal to handle the negotiation, make sure the amount of hours the attorney proposes to spend negotiating the deal is equal to or less than the amount of hours multiplied by the attorney's hourly rate. As mentioned above, an attorney being paid on a percentage basis should only receive a percentage of the advance received by the client. In this instance, that would mean if your attorney's hourly rates were $250 per hour, the attorney would have to spend close to 100 hours negotiating and putting your deal together in order to justify her $25,000 fee. A more appropriate fee would be 5 percent which would amount to $12,500. Most record deals should not take anywhere near 100 hours to negotiate unless you're a superstar.

CHANGE OF RELATIONSHIPS

Sometimes an attorney will give a client they believe in a preferred rate based on that client's ability to pay. However, when that client reaches a point of financial stability, the attorney may want to change the financial arrangements with the client. The client should be emotionally prepared for these changes and understand the nature of the past and present relationship with the attorney.

WORKING WITH YOUR MANAGER
AND YOUR ATTORNEY

If you know enough about the music industry and what is going to be acceptable in a particular negotiation, you might be able to hash out most of the deal points with your manager acting as a go-between for you and the other negotiating party. A note of caution: before working in this manner you should make sure your manager is well-versed in the area of negotiations and is capable of providing the guidance that is necessary to insure the best outcome for you. Taking this approach just to save money with a manager who is not knowledgeable might prove detrimental to the overall deal and to your career. If you feel confident enough in your manager's abilities to take this approach, much of your attorney's participation and work load will be limited to what's termed boiler-plate and legalese language. If you achieve a successful negotiation in this manner, your manager has done well by you and has earned his or her keep. The manager will have saved you money on attorney's fees and stayed in the information loop knowing all the details of your new deal. This is an economical approach simply because, if the lawyer gets involved with the actual negotiations, naturally the charges increase. This is just another reason to stay aware of the latest trends in deal making and contracts.

If you have a friend that is an attorney take her out to lunch and ask questions. Be candid about your purpose for meeting. Let your friend know upfront that you are seeking to gain information that will help you get a firm grip on how the industry works.

THE LACK OF NERVE SYNDROME

I have in the past worked with lawyers that I felt lacked nerve and backbone. I have also encountered disrespect and egomania when dealing with some attorneys. I don't tolerate either. I have never appreciated the I know-it-all and you-stay-out-of-your-business attitude that some attorneys seem to sport as if it were some Olympic medal. Whose business is it anyway? The fact is, if your attorney is not willing to listen to your point of view, then he or she isn't worth the effort.

The other end of the spectrum is an attorney that lacks self-confidence and cowers at the first sign of an altercation or sticky situation. Unwillingness to fight for what is fair and equitable for all involved is never acceptable. Knowingly entering into a deal when you know you are being taken advantage of can only lead to total disenchantment between the two parties making the deal. Doing so on the instruction of your legal counsel can only lead to more income for your counsel.

3. An attorney's position, statur
should be a consideration whe
best attorney.

4. If your attorney does not pro
move on to another attorney.

5. Your lawyer should never be y

6. If your manager is an attorne
sure deals are being made for
have a separate entertainment
review every document.

, and reputation is important and
it comes to deciding who is the

nptly return your calls you should

our manager or business manager.

double check everything to make
your benefit and not his. In fact,
attorney acting on your behalf to

BUSINESS MANAGERS VS. ACCOUNTANTS

Business manager, what a cool phrase. It's such a hip thing to be able to say to someone, "I will have to check with my business manager." It might be hip, it may even be true, but it may not always be smart.

After all, your finances, personal or business, are what support your art and other life activities. If at some point in your career you experience financial problems due to a lack of knowledge about your financial affairs, you would eventually be forced to take time away from your art and other activities to attend to those complications. So, why not attend to them in the first place before any problems occur? By doing this you will be able to address any and all matters as they arise, positive or negative, and therefore avoid even bigger financial trouble down the line. While this can be time consuming, taking this approach will afford you an invaluable education about how money is made and should be handled in the recording industry. I strongly suggest that you do not try to do everything yourself but to hire seasoned professionals to help you do the job. Before I tell you how you should go about acquiring professional financial help, I'd like to share with you some of my experiences that lead me to the conclusions I express in the paragraphs above and below.

MY STORY

I've had the experience of dealing with quite a few business managers, all of them upright, honest law abiding citizens. Most of them were paid 5 percent of my gross income for the time period in which they were employed by me. The problem was that the first business management firm I retained was not qualified for the job, and I was inexperienced in the area of finances. Unfortunately, this firm did not keep records that were up to professional standards, and I soon caught on to that fact. Soon after my awakening, I made a decision to part ways with the firm. After severing my relationship with them, I realized my financial records were in such disarray I had to spend extra time and money having them deciphered and brought up to professional standards.

I then hired a second business manager. After the affair with the first business manager, I was understandably nervous about my financial affairs. Sure enough, one day while I was reviewing my statements, I found a discrepancy. After that incident, I needed to make another change. Again, I had to spend more time and money employing yet a third business management firm to enter my records into their system, only to find this third company was overcharging me for time spent working on my books. They were hitting me with surprise bills every month. Needless to say, it didn't take long for me to fire them.

Once financial record keeping is not correctly done it is a mess to fix and more than likely you will be dealing with the ramifications for many years. It is extremely important that you make the right decisions when selecting a firm to handle your financial affairs. My affairs were finally cleared up by an accountant who took a special interest in my financial well being and he has recommended that I do as I will suggest to you later in this chapter.

During those short stints with various business management firms my professional activities fluctuated between recording and producing my own albums, producing other artists, and concert tour-ing. At times, there may have been moderate amounts of work for these firms on my behalf, and sometimes when I was in the studio recording, activity was very slow. But at all times, these firms charged me 5 percent of my gross income. I mention this because it took me a while to come to the conclusion that the cost of a ser-vice should be directly related to the amount of time and effort a service organization has to put in to perform the service it offers and it is not at all related to that firm's ability to market and hype its image. I would very much like for all of my readers to under-stand and use this reasoning when choosing any third party ser-vices. If you do, your earnings will stretch further and last longer. All too frequently a business manager is paid five percent of an individual's gross income as compensation for spending a few hours each month working on that individual's account. Fortunately, it was not long before I learned my lesson and ceased my association with business management firms until I found it absolutely necessary to employ them.

GIVING UP THE CONTROL

I have a basic problem with the idea of relinquishing total control of one's finances to anyone other than a spouse, trusted family member or someone you have known for many years who is trust-worthy and qualified for the job. Call me old-fashioned, but it just doesn't sit well with me. I think it is safe to say that the above does not describe the majority of business management-client relation-ship histories.

I am not at all suggesting that business management is not a need-ed function, but merely stating that in many instances artists and producers enter into relationships with business managers sooner than necessary. I believe that as your career grows, so should your knowledge of financial management. By allowing someone else to control your financial situation, you inhibit your ability to have a clear picture of your finances at all times; you are ensuring that you will not be getting the benefits of the on-the-job training that other, more traditional relationships will allow.

The proper time to hire a business manager is when you have investments that require more time and energy than you can provide. All other resources and alternatives such as accountants and business consultants should be thoroughly investigated prior to hiring a business manager. You should not hire a business manager because you suddenly find yourself with more money than you ever have had. This is the case much of the time in the recording industry. Hiring a business manager should not be a stroke to your ego either, but should insure a healthy financial future. Business managers, if hired, should be an unavoidable addition, not a luxury.

Anytime an individual is earning more than $200,000 annually, I strongly recommend a relationship with a financial advisor. A financial advisor is someone who can help make the most of your hard-earned money and can work with you on an hour-by-hour basis. There is no need to have the advisor on retainer unless a serious problem requiring a substantial amount of their time exists.

YOUR FINANCES ARE YOUR RESPONSIBILITY

I am an advocate of self-business management in the beginning of one's career. I don't mean to suggest that you should handle everything that has to do with the money. Instead, what I am trying to get across is that ultimately you will have to take full responsibility for your business and the rewards or consequences that result from getting things done properly or improperly. Your tax returns should be handled by a qualified tax accountant, because the Internal Revenue Service frequently audits companies and individuals in the entertainment field. This is not to say that business managers are not qualified tax accountants, because some are. Instead, what I am trying to convey is that in most cases having a business manager is overkill. What you should have is an accountant. You should write and sign your own checks. You should keep every receipt, no matter how small, and organize them by category. The gas receipt goes in the gas receipt folder, the food receipts in the food receipt folder, and so forth. At the end of the year (or each quarter), all of that information, along with your bank statements, should be mailed or better yet taken to your tax accountant. I would suggest your tax accountant be someone whose specialty is the entertainment industry. By having a tax accountant that specializes in the entertainment industry, you insure yourself every deduction that can be taken will be taken, and should a problem arise with the IRS, that accountant will be more than capable of handling it.

BOOKKEEPERS, ACCOUNTANTS & BUSINESS MANAGERS

Business managers usually ask 5 percent of gross income as compensation. In most cases all they are doing is signing checks, and computing taxes, thus I believe 5 percent of gross income is overcharging. Consider the musician who earns $100,000 a year. Five percent of $100,000 is $5,000, and a gross overcharge for writing checks and computing taxes. Furthermore, business management firms sometimes have hundreds of clients, and there is no way they can keep up with the details and paperwork necessary to effectively manage each client's full financial affairs. Business managers and business management firms consist largely of accountants and bookkeepers, and it is these accountants and bookkeepers who do the bulk of the work. If you employ a business management firm and you're one of its larger clients, your finances may be handled by one of the partners of the firm. If you are one of the lesser clients, meaning you have less money to handle, your account will be assigned to a bookkeeper. With a business management firm, the bookkeeper assigned to your account will work on your account part-time. If your account is being looked over and handled by a bookkeeper at a business management firm, why not hire a bookkeeper in the first place on a part-time basis? Bookkeepers get paid by the hour and if your business is not time consuming it makes sense to pay a bookkeeper an hourly rate instead of the five percent demanded by most business management firms.

There is nothing mysterious about bookkeeping. Bookkeeping is bookkeeping whether the bookkeeper is working for a business manager, an individual, or a record company. The bookkeeper's duties include reconciling bank statements, organizing accounts payable, and accounts receivable, assisting in forecasts of cash flow, and setting up various budgets. The bookkeeper should also be responsible for organizing your financial records so your tax accountant can have the easiest job in computing your taxes.

Bookkeepers earn around $75 per hour. Accountants start at $100 and can earn up to $200 per hour. Bookkeepers and accountants will cost more if they are located in Los Angeles, New York and Chicago. In some instances, if you live in either Los Angeles, New York or Chicago, it might prove wise to work with an accounting firm that is located in a city other than where you live. Accountants and business managers located in the larger metropolitan areas such as New York, Chicago, and Los Angeles charge a premium rate for their services. The only reason they can charge what amounts to exorbitant fees is the fact that there are enough people who can afford to pay them in the big cities. If those same accountants and business managers were to set up shop in smaller towns they would not be able to charge as much for their services. It's really a case of what the market will bear. As a rule, the bigger the office and staff, the more you will have to pay for their services. In the larger cities rents and salaries are higher and the accounting firms and business managers will pass these expenses along to you in the form of higher fees for services rendered. The service you will receive from an accountant in a smaller city should not be any different than the service you would receive from a big-city, fancy-office accounting firm. The difference is a small town firm will cost considerably less. There is one consideration you should take into account when hiring a small town accountant and that is to make sure they are a specialist in the entertainment field.

FEAR OF THE UNKNOWN

Very few business management firms, given the volume of work most have, can afford to take care of your money the way you will if you know how to interface with an accountant and tax adviser. This is assuming, of course, that you have an interest in your own affairs. Some people have no interest at all in their own affairs and feel compelled to hand over the responsibility to someone else. Sometimes I have found that those handing over their financial responsibilities to business managers do it simply because they think it is what they're supposed to do when they reach a certain level of success. The thing to remember is that when an artist reaches that first big milestone in her career, she suddenly finds herself in uncharted territories. Uncharted, in the sense that no one has written a book on how to manage success itself, and believe me, success does need managing.

It is my belief that unless success itself is managed, it will breed non-success. Most artists, singers, producers and musicians, upon reaching that first level of success, begin to feel lost and long for trustworthy guidance in their decision making. Some are smart enough to reach out to the resources that are available and take advantage of those opportunities to learn. Others may not have resources or know where to look for them, so it is understandable that they get taken advantage of. Still others are drunk with their own success and not of sound mind to make any decisions concerning their financial and business well-being. These are some of the reasons why creative types, when they reach the slightest level of success, are eager to hand over their financial matters to a business manager. They are afraid, and it is this fear that makes them willing to believe a large business management firm will take care of them.

If it's absolutely necessary to have someone else handle your hard-earned money, then at least you should sign the checks. You can assign the responsibility of handling the paperwork to the business management firm, then weekly or twice monthly visit their office or have them visit your home so that you can sign the checks. This method allows you to maintain the financial control by at least keeping up with your bank accounts. Subscribing to this methodology also allows you to see where you money is going. It is easy to spend foolishly if you never see the books or sign the checks.

If you're lucky and have real estate and other investments you're the exception rather than the rule in the recording industry. If your day-to-day activities are so numerous and their importance is truly high-ranking, then business management might be the right route to take. In all other cases, accountants and bookkeepers are more than qualified for the job. The challenge is not to let your ego get the best of you. Thinking with your mind and not with your ego will probably keep any fantasies and unrealistic notions in check.

HELPFUL HINTS ABOUT DEALING WITH BUSINESS MANAGERS

• Business managers should provide you with an easy to read, detailed report about your accounts on a monthly basis.

• Any business manager you are considering should be a CPA (Certified Public Accountant). Licensed CPAs have had special training in financial matters, including taxes. They should also have a specialty in dealing within the entertainment industry or better yet, the music business.

• Make sure you know how much a business management firm charges for its services and find out if that charge includes doing your taxes.

• Find out if their fee includes consultations on new deals and re-negotiations of existing contracts.

• Find out if they have experience in dealing with international financial matters. You may tour or work in foreign countries and your financial representative will need to understand the tax laws that govern those countries.

• Ask if they plan to invest your money. If so, where? And will you be notified prior to their doing so? Ask whether they plan to invest your money in deals they are involved in and if so, will this constitute a conflict of interest? Insist that they inform you before making any investments with your money.

• Find out if they see any conflict of interest in dealing with your finances.

• Ask how long they have been in business.

• Require five references that have been with the business manager or accountant for at least five years. These accounts should be of varying sizes and types.

~ *Making Your Dream* ~
Come True

What is Music Publishing

Your Own Record Company

Making Your Dream Come True

Making your dream come true almost sounds like it's too good to be true. The way I intend making your dream come true to be interpreted is more like, knowing and doing the things that will lead to your reaching your goals, becoming pro-active in your quest, and taking full responsibility for your actions or non-actions. I can remember a time when I felt helpless in the pursuit of my goals in the music industry. There was almost no written information available that could help me formulate a course of action that I could take, and that would guide me toward my dreams and aspirations. I can also remember that being the most frustrating of times, because I had no way of gauging if I was actually making progress or not. There was no step-by-step process that I could follow, so my approach was catch-as-catch-can. Needless to say, I was spinning my wheels and going nowhere fast. If some of you share or have shared some of these same feelings, I understand completely and would do anything in my power to help guide you to where you want to go. This next group of chapters is designed to give you a course of action you can easily follow and put into practice. It is my hope that after reading these chapters you will understand the steps that must be taken in order for you to take your life and career into your own hands.

One of the first steps an artist can take to make themselves more self-sufficient is to become a songwriter. The obvious reason is if you are an artist and also a songwriter you won't have to depend upon anyone else to write songs for you. And if you acquire a recording contract you will get to keep a lot more of the money that results from record sales. An intermediate step for a songwriter is to obtain a publishing deal, thus the "What is Music Publishing?" chapter. "Owning Your Own Record Company" is one of my favorite chapters because it encourages music makers to take their fate fully in their own hands by establishing their own record companies. More and more artists and producers are finding that starting their own record companies, while providing an outlet for their music, also relieves them of that "I'm not in control of my own destiny" feeling. Enough said. Find a comfortable chair and dive in. I'm sure you'll find all sorts of treasures that will enrich you.

WHAT IS
MUSIC PUBLISHING?

When a song is released and sold in any format — CD, record, or cassette — there are two incomes that are derived from that sale as far as the songs are concerned. They are called the songwriter's and the publisher's share and are of equal proportion. This income is referred to as *mechanical royalties* and is paid by record companies to the publisher, who in turn pays the songwriter. We'll talk more about mechanical royalties below.

Income is also generated when a song plays on the radio, television and from other public performances. That income is referred to as *performance royalties* and is collected by performance societies that in turn pay the publisher and writer an equal split. You will learn more about performance societies in a later paragraph. There are other incomes that can be derived from your songs that include sync licenses and printed sheet music sales. I will address those in this chapter as well. It is important to note that sometimes artists and producers are also songwriters and publishers. Let's look at what a publishing deal is and how it works.

MECHANICAL ROYALTIES

Mechanical royalties are royalties paid to publishers by a record company for the right to use songs contained on albums and singles released by that label. Writer royalties are also referred to as mechanical royalties. Mechanical royalties are based on whatever licensing rate is negotiated with the record company by either a publisher or the producer, if the producer is also the writer.

Although these licensing fees are compensation for the uses of songs contained on a project that is released by a record company, they are not paid upfront. These fees are calculated according to the number of units that are sold. These fees are paid on a fixed schedule that starts after the release date of the project that contains the songs.

A PUBLISHING DEAL

Beginner writers barely make it by from week to week financially unless they have a paying job. Believe me, I've seen enough starving songwriters in my time. I know because I was one once. A songwriter's work goes unrewarded financially until one of his songs is recorded and that song generates record sales, or contact is made with a publisher who believes in his writing abilities and is willing to invest in him so that he can become a full time songwriter. If the songwriter has a song released and has not yet signed with a publishing company, he is considered to be his own publisher.

If a songwriter signs a deal with a publishing company, the publisher pays the writer advances and thus becomes entitled to part or all of the publisher's share of mechanical royalties resulting from record sales. In some instances the publisher also becomes entitled to the publisher's share of performance royalties that are generated from airplay and public performances of that songwriter's songs.

The publisher will pay a songwriter an advance because he believes the writer will eventually write a song or songs that will become hits that will generate money for both the publisher and the writer. The publisher also believes the amount of money generated by the writer's songs will be enough for the publisher to pay the writer, the writer's royalties and pay himself publishing royalties that amount to substantially more than the initial investment in the writer.

Publishers also share income made when a song becomes part of a TV series or appears in a film.

There are many types of publishing deals, including deals between writers and publishers, publishing companies and other publishing companies, administration deals, and foreign publishing. Each type of publishing deal has characteristics that are similar.

Remember, mechanical royalties are paid by the record company to the publisher, who in turn pays the songwriter. Also remember, the publisher's share and the writer's share are equal.

THE PUBLISHER'S JOB

A publisher also has duties that are directly related to the well being of both the publishing company and its relationship with the writers signed to the company. A publisher's job includes finding artists to record songs written or co-written by writers signed to the company, issuing licenses to individuals or record companies who wish to use songs written by its writers, and ensuring that if income is derived from songs published by the company it is properly collected and the writer is paid.

Along with these administrative duties, publishers also are responsible for administrative paperwork such as copyright and licensing forms. Some publishing companies also help their writer further develop their writing skills by encouraging and securing collaborations with other writers. Of all the responsibilities of the publisher, none are as important as marketing the writer to the rest of the recording industry.

THE STATUTORY RATE

For every record, CD or cassette sold, the writers and publishers of the songs contained on them should receive a set amount of money from a record company, called mechanical royalties. In 1976, Congress invoked legislation aimed at regulating the amount of money earned by songwriters and publishers. More precisely, its goal was to structure a payment calculation system that was fair to songwriters and publishers. This system of calculation is called the statutory rate and is paid by the record company in the form of mechanical royalties (publishing royalties) to publishers, who in turn pay the songwriters. The rate is based on a formula of 1.32 cents per minute or fraction thereof. Subsequently, if a song is 3:02 seconds it would be calculated as if it were a four minute song, and if a song is four minutes and forty five seconds the statutory rate for that song would amount to 6.6 cents. Most songs recorded today are at least four minutes in length and are usually less than five. Thus, the most common statutory rate that should be used is 6.6 cents. But, most labels don't like to pay the full rate. We'll talk more about that later in this chapter.

Record companies pay publishers a set amount per song for every record manufactured and distributed. In most cases the amount is 75 percent of the statutory rate and sometimes it is the full statutory rate. There are also some cases where a set amount of cents per album per song is stipulated.

As previously noted, most record companies will demand a rate that is less than the full statutory rate. I have been successful in negotiating deals for my songs where the rate was adjusted in my favor at certain levels of sales. For instance, if the recording sold 100,000 copies or less I would receive a 75 percent rate, but if the record sold over 100,000 copies, I would receive the full statutory rate for every record sold over 100,000 copies. As in all negotiations, if the record company insists on a reduction in the statutory rate make them pay for it in some other way.

By law, the statutory rate only applies to songs that have been recorded and released at least once. In other words, if a song has not been released, the publisher can charge whatever rate he chooses. In theory, this gives the songwriter and publisher the upper hand. The problem will be finding a label that will pay even the statutory rate. Therefore, the assumption that you can charge whatever licensing rate you choose is strictly theoretical and not practical. I will discuss the first-time-released song in more detail later. Record companies commonly insist upon a licensing rate that is less than the one required by law because to pay the true statutory rate obviously means less profits for them.

Songwriters and publishers often have no recourse because beginner writers are eager to have their first song recorded and released and publishers want to recoup advances and other expenses incurred on the songwriter's behalf. Therefore, publishers and writers, more often than not, will be forced into giving record companies concessions on the statutory rate. The most common of theses concessions is accepting 3/4 of the statutory rate.

Because of the way the statutory rate legislation is structured, the amount of money per minute per song paid to the publisher and songwriter by record labels increases every few years. This is to compensate for inflation and to allow the system to become even more fair to the creators of music. Again, in theory, this should work to the advantage of the songwriter and publisher, but record companies won't allow it. Instead, record labels almost always negotiate the rate by which a writer and publisher will be paid and stamp a date on it that says you will always be paid that set amount regardless of how the statutory rate increases. By doing this, they are insuring themselves that no matter what the increases are in the statutory rate, they will only be obligated to pay writers and publishers what their contract with the publisher says they are obligated to pay. In others words, if the rate today is 1.32 cents per minute but the rate goes up to 1.67 cents per minute between now and the time a project is recorded and released, the rate stated in the contract will remain 1.32 cents per minute.

While fairness to writers and publishers is increasing and that does make a difference in the amount of income a writer and publisher can earn, the untold stories of countless writers and publishers who continue to suffer because of the lack of regulation on songs recorded before 1976 is depressing. Repackaging and rereleasing albums that were recorded and released before 1976 has become the industry standard, especially if the songs contained on those recordings were hits when they were first released, or the artist contained on those packages is rediscovered by a younger generation or if there is a resurgence in the artist's popularity. There are hundreds of new box sets of old recordings that are governed under the old rates. The rate prior to 1976 was two cents per song no matter what the length of the song. This means the new sales of those old recordings render the same unfair profits for the songwriters and publishers of those songs as they did before 1976. Sounds to me like our legislators should get to work on this one.

CANADA AND FOREIGN TERRITORIES

Most major U.S. publishers like to include Canada in any deals with writers and other publishers. The rest of the world is referred to as foreign territories. Canada has its own version of the statutory rate, which is 6.47 cents per song that is five minutes or under. For each additional minute of recording over five minutes an additional 1.29 cents is added to the base statutory rate.

FIRST USE OF A SONG

The first time a song is released is called first use of a song. As mentioned above, for the first use of a song, record companies are theoretically at the mercy of the publisher of that song concerning the licensing rate the publisher is to be paid. By law, the statutory rate—the licensing rate set by the United States Government—only applies to songs that have been previously released. The reality of first time use of a song, and what rate a publisher can charge for the use of the song, is that it is almost impossible to get record companies to pay the statutory rate and absolutely impossible to get a label to pay more than the statutory rate.

The publishers of a song that has never been released can withhold the use of that song. That does give them bargaining power, especially if the song is written by a known hit maker. For subsequent releases and re-records of a song, a publisher must grant anyone who wishes to record that song permission to do so, and this is when the statutory rate comes into play.

This means that the most a publisher can demand for the second time and subsequent use of a song is regulated by government standards, the statutory rate. The truth is there are no above the statutory rate benefits for first time use of a song. The real benefit for the writer and publisher of an unreleased song is that the publisher can control who gets to record that song. That bargaining chip sometimes can get the writer and publisher the full statutory rate.

CONTROLLED COMPOSITION CLAUSES

A controlled composition is a song that is owned and controlled by the artist that records it. Owning a song means you either own part of the song as a writer or publisher, or you are the controlling administrator. A controlled composition clause is a specific paragraph or phrase in a recording or publishing contract that addresses the issues of controlled compositions. These issues include how many songs can appear on an album, what the licensing rate will be on those songs, whether or not the songs are written by the artist that is recording the album, the maximum amount a record company will pay for the licensing of songs on that album and what the remedies will be should the artist decided to record more songs on the album than the record company is willing to pay for.

What this really boils down to is, record companies put a cap on how much money they are willing to pay to songwriters and publishers for licensing (mechanical royalties) no matter how many songs are contained on an album.

Basically, controlled composition clauses are designed as a way to force artists to pay the licensing charges on albums that are in excess of what the record company is willing to pay. Controlled composition clauses are never to the advantage of the artist because if the combined licensing fees on an album exceed what the record company is willing to pay, the excess amount gets deducted from artist royalties if the artist is not a songwriter on the album.

If the artist is also a songwriter on an album and the combined licensing rates amount to more than what the record company is obligated to pay as per the artist contract, the songs that are written by the artist will be calculated at a reduced rate where publishing and songwriters royalties are concerned. Remember, the record company pays the publisher who in turn pays the songwriter.

Artists who are also writers and/or producers that have publishing deals should be wary. If your contract with the publisher is based upon all songs authored by you receiving full statutory rates, and you settle for less on your album or any other album your songs end up on, this will result in reduced income for the publishing company. The publishing company will then deduct the reduced amount from your publishing and/or writer's royalties.

Artists can control songs they write and sometimes songs they co-write concerning the licensing rate. But an artist cannot guarantee a rate that is less than statutory rate on songs written by other writers that may appear on their albums. If an artist records a song written by another writer, which is published and controlled by someone other than the artist, and the publisher of that song demands the full statutory rate, there is nothing the artist can do except agree to the full rate or not use that song. If an artist chooses to use a song that requires the label to pay the full statutory rate, more often than not it will result in lower mechanical royalties for the artist's publisher and the artist.

Artists can also be publishers or owners of publishing companies that own songs they do not write. If an artist is the publisher he usually can negotiate a lower licensing rate. However, this is never to the artist's advantage because it will ultimately lead to less income.

Sometimes a record company will encourage or even insist that an artist record certain songs. If that is ever the case, and the publisher of that song demands the full statutory rate and the combined licensing fees exceed what your artist contract permits, don't allow the record company to deduct those excess fees from your artist's or publisher's account. The company is responsible for the excess licensing fees that are incurred on the song since it insisted that you record it.

In my honest opinion, none of the issues concerning controlled compositions would be a problem if record companies would pay full statutory rates. I do, however, understand a record company's needing protection on how much they can afford to spend for licensing of songs contained on albums. If record companies did not put a limit on how much they were willing to pay for licensing on an album, the artist who is also a songwriter could record as many songs for an album as he chose, whether the songs added value to the album or not, and the record company would be obligated to pay the licensing fees. It's easy to see how these fees could add up. This can easily be remedied by limiting the number of songs that an artist can have on an album.

Overall, the controlled composition issue is a complex one that, if not monitored by either a manager, publisher or attorney, can end up costing the songwriter, artist and publisher dearly. Be diligent in your efforts and stay aware of this issue.

LET'S DO A LITTLE MATH

Let's do a little math so you can see how much money is generated by a hit song where publishing and writing is concerned. For ease of math, we will calculate the number of units sold as 6,000,000. Remember the statutory rate is 6.6 cents per song, for songs of 5 minutes. If there were ten songs on that album, the writers and publishers would equally divide 66 cents per album. Sixty six cents times 6,000,000 units equals $3,396,000. Nice number, huh?

If each song were written by one writer and each writer received the same licensing rate of 6.6 cents per song, $3,396,000 would be split ten ways. When you divide $3,396.000 by 10, you will see each writer is due $300,396. Remember, the total income gets divided into two equal parts. Half goes to the writer and half to the publisher. In this scenario each publisher and each writer will ultimately earn $198,000. If the writer is also the publisher then he gets to keep the full $300,396. If the publisher is not the writer, the publisher will deduct expenses from the writer's share.

PERFORMANCE ROYALTIES & PERFORMANCE SOCIETIES

Songwriters and publishers also earn money each time a song plays on the radio, television or during any public performances. These earnings are called performance royalties. These royalties are collected from radio and television stations, bars, night clubs, and movie theaters by organizations called performance societies.

The most noted performance societies are BMI (Broadcast Music Incorporated), ASCAP (American Association of Composers, Authors, & Publishers), and SESAC (formally Society of European Stage Authors & Composers). SESAC used to represent predominantly European writers but is now considered as viable a performance society in America as BMI and ASCAP. These companies track and calculate how many times your songs are being played on the radio, television and in public places. There is a set performance fee that each venue pays to the performance society. Again, there is a 50-50 split between writers and publishers. Before a writer has a song released, played on television or in a movie, the publisher of that song must register as a member of either BMI, ASCAP or SESAC. If the publisher is already a member of a performance society, he must at least register those new songs with the performance society. That registration will include the writer's information so the writer can receive his share of public performance fees. If you, your publishing company and your song are not registered with a performance society you will not be paid for public performances of your song.

BMI's telephone number is (212) 586-2000.
ASCAP's telephone number is (212) 621-6000.
SESAC can be reached at (800) 826-9996.

In some cases, the publishing company will have the right to collect the writer's share of performance royalties and apply that income against the songwriter's unrecouped advances. A writer should make every attempt to negotiate an exclusion clause that exempts performance royalties from the income that the publishers have a right to collect.

WHAT IS LICENSING?

Before a song can be released in any format, whether CD, cassette, television or commercials, the user must get permission from the owner of that song. The user is usually a record company, television production company or film company. The owner of that copyright grants the user the right to release that song. This is commonly referred to as granting a license. Licenses are usually granted or issued by publishing companies. However, in the case where the writer is also the publisher and is not affiliated with another publishing company, the writer's publishing company issues the license. Keep in mind if the song has been released at least once before, the license is automatically granted. I'll talk more about that in the paragraph entitled "First Time Use of a Song."

TYPES OF PUBLISHING DEALS

When a writer enters into a deal with a publisher that grants the publisher 100% of the writers publishing rights, the writer is in fact giving up 50% of the total income generated by his songs. While this kind of deal is not all bad, a writer should carefully weigh whether or not the amount of advances received from a publisher will be more than the amount of income the song will generate. Of course, there is no way for a writer to know that unless he has songs that are in the process of being recorded for release and can estimate how many records are likely to be sold on those projects.

The other issue to consider is that publishing advances are guaranteed income and getting any of your songs recorded and released is not guaranteed unless you are a star writer. If you are a star writer chances are you won't need the advances publishing companies offer. Even in a situation where songs are being recorded by an artist with an established track record, it will be difficult for the songwriter to figure out the earning potential of those songs without accurate sales figures regarding previously released product. Writers should try to retain at least fifty percent of their publishing rights. Keep in mind that the more a publisher pays a writer in advances, the larger the percentage of the publishing share of income the publisher will demand. The larger the amount of the advances negotiated for the writer, the more guarantees in the form of songs written, and more importantly, songs recorded and released, will be demanded by the publishing company.

Remember the $198,000 that went to the writer of one of the songs on the album that sold 6,000,000 copies? That was the writer's share and represented one half of the income derived from that song. The other $198,000 was also paid to the writer because the songwriter was also the publisher. That represented the other half of the income that was derived from the same song. If the writer had signed a publishing deal, the publishing company would get part or all of the $198,000 that accounted for the publisher's share. The publishing company may have paid the writer $30,000 or $40,000 or less in advances, but it is still entitled to the full publisher's share unless the writer's attorney negotiated a co-publishing deal. In that case, the publisher would only be entitled to the percentage of the publishing income that was negotiated.

For example, if the writer was successful in negotiating to keep 50% of the publishing rights, the publisher and the writer would split the publisher's share of $198,000; with $99,000 going to each. Keep in mind that the publisher would also get to recoup any advances that had been paid to the writer. In this case, lets assume that the publishers has paid the writer $30,000 in advances. That amount would have come out of the writer's share of $198,000 leaving the writer with $168,000 plus the writer's publishing share of $99,000.

If a writer has received $30,000 in advances, that amount must be paid back to the publisher before any writer's royalties are paid. Let's use the same scenario that we've been using and let's say the publisher has paid the writer $50,000 in advances. The record has sold six million units and the writer has negotiated a full statutory rate. Remember, the writer's share of the total income was $198,000 and the publisher's share was equal to the writer's share. In this instance, the writer has granted the publisher 100% of the publisher's share. The publisher, in return, has paid the writer $50,000 in advances. The publisher is now entitled to the full publisher's share which is $198,000. In addition to that, the publisher is also entitled to recoup the $50,000 paid to the writer as advances. That amount would be deducted from the writer's share. As a result of that deduction, the writer is now entitled to $148,000 instead of the original $198,000. At this point, the publisher would have not only made back their original investment of $50,000, but also would have made an additional hefty return on his investment.

You may ask why someone would give up that much money as in the case described above. Remember, most beginning writers are struggling and would welcome someone believing in their future. Especially if it is someone who is willing to pay the writer upfront money against future earnings. The benefit to the writer is getting much-needed cash. The benefit to the publisher is sharing in the profits derived from publishing income. The objective for a writer negotiating a publishing deal is to retain at least half of the publishing rights.

CO-PUBLISHING DEALS

A co-publishing deal exists when there is more than one publisher involved with a writer or writers. The most common co-publishing deals occur when a writer signs a deal with a publisher to split the publisher's share of income 50-50. There are co-publishing deals where the publisher's share is not split 50-50, but theses deals are still referred to as co-publishing deals. For instance, the split could be 70-30 or 60-40.

Co-publishing deals can also exist where a writer owns their own publishing company and splits the publisher's share of their songs with other publishers. The biggest concerns in a co-publishing situation will always be who will own the copyright and who controls the administration of the copyright.

Administration of the copyright includes collecting mechanical royalties and collecting performance royalties from performance societies. The controlling administrator is also responsible for paying the writers and other publishers.

Publishing Companies

MAJOR PUBLISHERS

There are different types and sizes of publishing companies. The major publishers are large in size and own a large number of copyrights. They also have a larger number of writers under contract. In addition to having writers under contract, they also have smaller publishing companies under contract. Some of these deals are co-publishing deals and others are administration deals where the larger publishing company is the administrator of the copyrights.

In an administration deal of this sort, the major company receives a portion of the entire income derived from sales of records and videos. In almost all cases like these, the major company funds the association in the beginning. This means that the major company is supplying advances against future earnings to writers and/or publishing companies under contract to them. The major publishing companies include MCA Music, Warner Chappell, and BMG Music.

THE NEXT RUNG DOWN

The second largest type of publishing companies include Jobete and SBK. While they have a full staff of writers, administrators and creative personnel, they still are smaller than the larger companies such as Warner Chappell, Sony Music, MCA Music and BMG Music. A characteristic they do share with the larger companies is that they also have smaller companies that they administer and fund.

SMALLER YET

Publishing companies that are independent but are administered by the major publishing companies are called major affiliates. These include companies such as Rondor Music ,which is administered by Irving/Almo. It is not uncommon for these companies to be owned by artist and producers. I own a company called The New Music Group that was once administered by MCA Music. We at one time published the talented writer LaLa, the writer of "You Give Good Love," which became Whitney Houston's first hit record.

THE SUB-PUBLISHER

One thing I like about owning a publishing company is that I can make deals with the larger companies to administer my copyrights in America and make independent deals with other publishers everywhere else in the world. Each time I make an independent deal with another publisher around the world, I receive an advance against future earnings from that publisher. Deals made to operate in foreign territories with foreign publishers are called sub-publishing deals. A sub-publisher's share of monies earned in territories where they operate ranges anywhere between 10 to 50 percent. Because of additional fees the sub-publisher charges the original publishers, most sub-publishers end up earning between 15 to 25 percent of the total income earned in their territory.

OTHERS

There are other publishing companies that have no affiliation with any other publishers. They do all of the work themselves. In my opinion, these are the true independents. Some record companies also have their own publishing companies. In the early days of the record industry it was almost mandatory for an artist to sign away their publishing rights in order to secure the record deal. The most famous of these was Motown and Jobete. Motown was the label and Jobete was the publisher. While some record companies continue this unsavory practice of both deals or no deal at all, most labels treat recording and publishing deals as independent of each other.

Any competent lawyer can overcome these tactics today. However, if you find yourself in this kind of situation and decide to take the plunge, make sure the record portion of the deal is not cross-collateralized with the publishing part. This means the label can't recoup money from the publishing side of the deal to pay unrecouped amounts on the recording side, and vice versa.

Also, make sure the deal is co-terminous. This means that both deals are of the same length. You must insist that if the record deal is terminated the publishing deal is also terminated. This is important because if the recording agreement is terminated and the publishing agreement is not, then the company will still make money on your songwriting and publishing.

If at all possible, I recommend that every writer and artist avoid any deals where a record company insists that the writer also sign with its publishing company. Such deals are restrictive and unnecessary. It is like putting too many eggs in one basket. One of the main reasons I don't care for them is that if your relationship with the label goes sour and your recording contract is terminated, you are forced to deal with the record company's publishing wing because they will continue to have a publisher's relationship with you as a writer, unless the publishing portion of the deal is also terminated.

WRITERS WHO PUBLISH THEIR OWN SONGS

Some writers, as we discussed earlier, are their own publishers. In fact, all writers are their own publishers at first. That is until they affiliate themselves with another publisher. The writers who are most likely to publish themselves are the more successful writers who don't need the cash advances that publishing companies offer.

ADMINISTRATION DEALS

Administration deals are made between a writer and publisher, or the copyright owning publisher and a second publisher, to administer one or more copyrights for a limited period of time. The original publisher or writer still retains the copyright. The administrating publisher is usually required to handle all administrative duties including collecting monies owed, paying the writers and other participating publishers if there are any, and issuing licenses.

Administration fees range between 5% to 25% of gross income. The administrator first deducts this fee and all expenses associated with the administrative process.

RE-RELEASES
(YOUR SONG AS A REMAKE)

If a song is recorded and released once by one artist, and then recorded by another artist at a later date, and income is derived from these subsequent releases, the writer and the publisher of that song are entitled to the writer's and publisher's share of income derived from that release. Of course, the amount they would be paid would depend upon the sales of the subsequent releases and has nothing to do with prior releases of that song. No matter how many times a song is recorded and released, if it creates income, the writer and the publisher are always entitled to their share. This is one of the reasons why publishing is valued so highly in the recording field. The writer and publisher of a hit song can have pay day after pay day, depending upon the popularity of the song. Consider for instance, " White Christmas" or "Bridge Over Troubled Waters." They have been recorded and released many times and have generated millions of dollars of income.

WHAT IS PUBLIC DOMAIN

A composition exists in the public domain when the copyright has expired or never existed, and therefore, it has no protection under copyright law. Anyone is free to use a public domain composition without permission. Both BMI and ASCAP pay performance royalties on public domain compositions, but the amount paid is not the same as that paid on controlled compositions. Record companies also routinely enjoy reduced mechanical rates on public domain compositions recorded by artists on that label.

PUBLISHING ROYALTIES ON FREE GOODS

Just like artist royalties, publishing royalties are affected by free goods. Mechanical royalties are generally not paid on free goods. New artists don't stand a chance of negotiating payment on free goods but an established artist might negotiate a fifty percent payment of mechanical royalties on free goods. (See Record Royalties Chapter for more information on free goods.)

SYNCHRONIZATION LICENSING

When a song is used in a movie or on television the producer of that television show or the producer of that film must get permission from the publisher to use that song. If the publisher and the producer can negotiate a financial arrangement the producer will be granted a license. This is commonly referred to as a sync license. The rate of payment for a sync license varies and is totally arbitrary, depending on what the publisher feels the song is worth. If the song has already been a hit then its value is higher. Different rates are negotiated depending on how many uses of the song are required and if it will be used as a theme song and how many times the song will be used in the film or TV show.

SHEET MUSIC

Sheet music sales are another source of income for publishers and songwriters, especially if the song has become a hit or a repeated theme of a popular TV series. The publisher makes arrangements to have the music transcribed, printed and distributed to stores. There are usually clauses in publishing contracts that address sheet music issues. The publisher's royalty rate for sheet music is 20% of listed retail price for a single song. Single song means that the sheet only contains one song as opposed to folios that contain multiple compositions. Royalty rates for folios rage from 10% to 13% of the listed retail price. Publishers earn between 70 and 80 cents per copy of a single song sheet music, while they pay an inappropriately small percentage to the writer. Usually the writer earns between 5 and 6 cents per copy.

SAMPLING

Advancements in technology have made it possible for a musician to take audio snapshots of records and CDs, and use those snapshots in new musical compositions. This process is called sampling.

Unlike in the early days of sampling, permission to use parts of those recordings must now first be cleared by the original copyright holder before the new uses of the recording can be released. A fee is negotiated between the original copyright holder and the new user that is based upon how prominent the original recording stands out in the new track. That fee is also based upon how many seconds or minutes of the original recording the user intends to consume in the new composition. Sampling time can range from a few seconds to an entire background track. Sample use fees start at $2500. If the recording being sampled was a hit, the original copyright holder will most likely also request percentage points on the new recording. Percentage points for sample usage range from one to five points.

When a new composition is created using samples, sometimes the original composition is used so prominently in the new creation that the original copyright holder demands a percentage of the new copyright. In those cases, it is not uncommon for an original copyright holder to demand up to fifty percent of the new creation.

FOREIGN MECHANICAL ROYALTIES

In some countries publishers have no way of collecting mechanical royalties earned in those territories. In these territories government agencies collect mechanical royalties for the publishers. The publishers must make sure they file a claim for that song with the government collection agency. The publishers claim can be for the whole or part of a composition and must be accompanied by proof of truth. The best proof is in the form of a contract with the original publisher or songwriter.

HARRY FOX

Harry Fox Agency is an independent company that will handle all of your administration needs for your publishing and songwriting business. They do so for a small fee of 4-1/2 percent. They also collect foreign royalties. They are often the desirable alternative to using a major publisher. They boast a clean reputation and are easily reached by phone. There is a great deal of paperwork and expertise needed to do the right things at the right time to collect your publishing and songwriter royalties. Consideration must be given to these activities and who is going to do them for you.

One of the key functions that Harry Fox Agency offers is that they will audit record companies for you. Again, the charge is 4-1/2 percent of what they recover from a label on your behalf. Harry Fox does such a good job that some of the larger publishing companies also use them to do their administration.

ADVANCES

A writer who is signed for the first time to a major publisher will usually receive an advance of around $30,000 for the first year. Each year the advances should increase enough to at least keep up with the rate of inflation. Advances for established successful writers often reach $150,000 or more per year.

Remember the higher the advances, the more guarantees the publishing company will demand in the form of songs written, recorded, and released.

RENEGOTIATING YOUR PUBLISHING DEAL

When renegotiating a publishing or co-publishing agreement it is important that the writer or co-publisher know the amount of pipeline income. Pipeline income is income that is due the writer or publisher under a current deal but has not been paid to them. What this means is that the publisher may have already received that income but has not yet passed it along to the writer or co-publisher because they are between royalty periods.

One of the most common practices of publishing companies is to use monies that are already owed to a writer or co-publisher as advances on a new deal that is being negotiated with that writer or co-publisher. For example, when a writer's publishing agreement comes to an end and the publishing company wants to negotiate a new deal, that writer should ascertain that any royalties that are due to him under the current deal be paid under the current deal. Any new advances paid on behalf of the new deal should be accounted for under the new deal. For the writer this obviously makes sense because he can allow the current deal to terminate and still receive all royalties that are due under that contract. However, if he were to renegotiate the current deal and receive new advances, those advances could actually be income that is already due. In that case, the publisher would be using the writer's own money to advance on a new deal.

WHAT ALL FAIR PUBLISHING DEALS SHOULD CONTAIN

The writer should always get an advance.

The writer's contract with the publisher should be negotiated so that the ownership of the copyright reverts back to the songwriter in ten to twelve years.

Make sure in foreign countries you are getting paid at the source of income. Ask your attorney about this one. (See the explanatory notes of the publishing agreement.)

Ask for the most stringent audit rights possible. Ask for the life of the deal and back to the beginning rights. This one will be difficult but have your attorney try to negotiate more than the standard two years.

Avoid signing publishing deals that have a minimum record and release clause. They are usually unfair and can lead to problems of suspension until you reach you required number of releases. Instead try to negotiate for a minimum amount of songs written and delivered per year.

The more success you have, the better deal you and your attorney can negotiate. Once you have a hit, you can climb into the driver's seat, if you know what you are doing.

YOUR OWN RECORD LABEL

Well, well, well, so you're feeling brave, like a maverick, huh? You're ready for the long hours, the intense concentration and the all-around stamina it will take to run your own record label.

Congratulations. You have finally come to your senses. You have finally figured out that you will make more money as an artist selling 50,000 records on your own record label, than selling 500,000 units as an artist signed to a major record label. As stated in the chapter, "Record Royalties", an artist will receive between 12 percent and 14 percent of the the suggested retail price of cassettes and albums and about 10 percent of the cassette royalty rate on CDs as compensation for their efforts of recording the album. In my opinion, these percentages are too low and you should explore the possibility of starting your own record label.

THEIR RATIONALE

Record companies blame low royalty rates on the non-success of nine out of every ten records released. That's a ten percent success rate, one that would be poor performance by any standards in any other industry. Take General Motors, for instance. If they designed and manufactured ten new cars, and only out of those ten new designs sold and was profitable, they would be out of business.

MY RATIONALE

Record companies do take most of the risk in the beginning. So it seems only fair that they enjoy the lion's share of the profits. The operative word here is *seems*. If the artist's time, energy, and emotions mattered to labels, they wouldn't feel that they were the only ones taking risks. But in all fairness, the record company, by signing an artist, is in a sense giving the artist an unsecured loan. Both artist and record labels devote their time, energy, and resources to record, promote, market, and sell music. The label has money as their most valuable resource; the artist brings talent and creativity as a most valuable contribution. Which is more valuable? I say the artist, because artists can exist without record companies, but record companies need something to sell. That something is the artist's product.

Most record deals are negotiated so that the artist gets 12 to 14 percent of the profits and the record company gets the remaining 88 percent. The 12 percent an artist receives is just not representative of the amount of effort an artist puts into recording an album. It becomes blatantly apparent when compared to the 88 percent of sales the record company gets to keep. This is all the more reason to start your own label and release your own records. I think it's safe to assume that most of us feel we have the same one in ten chance of success as a major record label.

The only difference is that unless you are independently wealthy or have investors willing to invest in you, record labels have more money available to get the job done. From my perspective, they also have more money to waste. While money is a major concern when putting together an album, it is not the be all and end all. Money problems can be overcome. At that point, the only thing a major label has over an independent is if a record is a hit, they can sell more because of their distribution network. The flip side of that is even if that same record were released on a major label and sold more, you would still make less than if you released it on your own label. With all things being equal, you'll make more money from the sales of your record released on your own label than you would if that same record were to be released on a label other than yours. That is, of course, unless your record is a flop. And in that case, no one makes any money.

STARTING YOUR OWN BUSINESS

Starting your own business is an exciting and challenging affair. Every detail, from naming your new business to choosing the legal setup of the business, will be governed by you and your team of associates. The legal setup will determine the form in which you do business, such as sole proprietorship, corporation, partnership, S-class corporation, etc. Other considerations are what state your business will be registered in, how many officers are in the company, and who will be the president, treasurer, secretary, and CEO.

Different states have different tax laws that can affect how much money you will have to pay in taxes. In the state of California, state income taxes can be as high as 11 percent, but in the state of Nevada and Florida there are no state income taxes. Each state also charges a different fee to issue business licenses. In the state of California the fee can be as high as $1,500. In the state of Arizona the business license fee is only $50. Obviously, when you are starting a new business every dime counts, so saving on your start-up cost will be a consideration. Be sure to ask your attorney about the state in which you should set up your business.

FICTITIOUS BUSINESS NAME (D.B.A.)

One of the first things that must be done when starting up a new business is coming up with a name for it. The name has to be one that is not yet filed with the secretary of state and used by someone else in the same line of business. It should also be easy to remember. The first thing that is usually done is a search to see if the name you are proposing is already in use. Each state has a different but similar method of applying and receiving a license to use a name, so check with your attorney. It is wise to select three names when doing the search just in case your first name choice is already in use. In the event that name is already in use, they will automatically search the availability of the second and third names you have submitted. Fees for the name search vary, although it is not expensive. If you want to save money I recommend you do the search yourself. If you want to save time have your attorney do the necessary paperwork.

BUSINESS PLANS

A business plan will play an important role in planning your label, for two reasons. It will be your financial road map from the startup to the point where you are making substantial income from the sale of your product. If you are looking for financial investors, they will need to see a business plan that shows how solid an investment your record label will be.

Business plans should include historical information about the company, biographical information about the executives of the company, description of the kind of acts that you plan to sign and release, description of the market you intend to sell your product to and financial spread sheets, including profit and loss projections, five year financial plan, and startup requirements.

I know that sounds like a lot of information, and it is, but any investor who is willing to invest in your new record company will require this information. There is a computer program that can assist in creating your business plan. It is call BizPlanBuilder and sells for $69. Basically it is a generic outline of a business plan. It provides templates and you fill in the blanks. It should be easy to find in most computer software stores. I highly recommend hiring an accountant to help you with the financial information.

THE EXPENSES

The first consideration when starting an independent label is the expense involved and where you will get the funding. The expenses include recording, manufacturing, union fees, marketing and promotion, distribution and office expenses. While there are certain hard costs that remain pretty much concrete no matter what your approach is, there are no set rules as to what will lead to success. I'm sure you have heard of how "Whomp! There It Is" was recorded on a shoestring budget and went on to rack up one of the most successful sales records in the history of the recording industry. Congratulations are in order for both the artist and the independent label. I commend the fact that they were willing to take the chance and make success for themselves.

There is no magic in this or any other kind of success. Research the market, make a good product, distribute it, make adjustments to accommodate the marketplace, work hard and you'll eventually succeed. Believe it or not, it can be done for a fraction of what the major labels spend.

YOUR LABEL & RECORDING BUDGETS

Most acts signed to major labels record on inflated budgets. Some of you who will start your own label cannot expect to compete with the $200,000 recording budgets that major record companies offer. There is no reason you should have to compete with those type of numbers. One reason recording budgets are so large at major labels is that artists need to make money on the recording of the album, because nine times out of ten they will not make money from sales. In all likelihood, most recording artists will never see a royalty check in their name. Most artists take their recording budgets as a recording fund. (See chapter on budgets.) The reason they do this is because they are able to keep whatever is left over after recording expenses. Rap albums can be recorded for as little as $15,000 while R&B and pop albums can be recorded for as little as $30,000 to $60,000. At major labels these same acts receive recording budgets as high as $300,000.

MAKING A DEAL WITH A RECORDING STUDIO

With the ongoing surge of high quality, low cost musical instruments and recording devices, there is now a diminishing need for major recording studios. With this decreased demand comes an increase in the number of studios that have a substantial amount of studio time unsold. There are literally thousands of recording studios that have only 50 percent of saleable time actually booked. This means these studios have rooms that are just sitting, waiting for a client. I see this as a positive climate for artists and producers because this creates an opportunity for musicians and artists to make deals with studio owners. Smart studio owners should be willing to take advantage of their own misfortune.

In order to overcome the slow climate of studio bookings, more studio owners are getting creative with the use of their studios and the arrangements they are willing to make with artists and producers.

If you have a project to record but cannot afford the expense of studio time, you may want to strike a deal with a recording studio to use their facility. Here is one way such a deal could work. The artist or production company gets to use the recording studio for no money up front except for hard costs like tape and rentals. The artist or production company guarantees the recording studio two or three points on the project. These points could go toward paying back the studio owner for the investment of their facility and would continue until the studio has recouped two times what the agreed studio rate charge should be for your project.

As you can see, the studio owner would, in this case, make double the amount of money on the studio charges as he would make on a conventional booking. There is no downside for either party because the studio owner is selling time that would otherwise go to waste and the artist is giving up a little extra to get what he can't afford to pay for in cash. The hourly rate for the studio should be no more than ten percent above their discount price. Be sure to have an attorney draw up the papers. This kind of agreement can be done in a two page letter of intent and should cost no more than a couple of hundred dollars. The beauty in this kind of deal is that you are not limited to using one studio. Use whatever studio is willing to make a deal with you as long as it can get the job done. Studios range in price from $50 per hour to $250 per hour. In this climate, you should be able to make deals with studios for about $75 per hour. Most studios can be booked by the half day or by the day.

MUSICIANS

When financing your own project, you will most likely be responsible for the cost of musicians, if for no other reason than they are probably struggling as you are to make ends meet. If there is a core rhythm section that you will employ for the entire recording then it might be worth hiring them for a flat fee. Although it may sound foreign, bartering might come in handy at any time you need goods and services to achieve a goal.

BARTERING

Bartering is when two people trade goods and/or services instead of compensating one another with money. It is a solid concept and works well in most cases. Other nations have been using the barter system for centuries and with great success.

Here is an example of how bartering can work for musicians and artists. You're a drummer, you need guitar work performed on one or more of your recordings. Make a deal with a guitarist wherein you will play on the same number of his sessions as he does for you for no cash. Instead, as a trade, he receives a credit for your time and talent. Later down the line, when he needs a drummer for one of his recordings, he can call you and cash in on the time and talent that you owe him. It doesn't have to be one of his sessions. It could be someone else's session. Someone who needs a drummer's services and is able to pay cash. In this case, the guitarist could recommend you and at the end of the session you would give him the pay you received as compensation for playing on your session.

The concept is this: if you were hungry and had only a stove and you met another person who was also hungry but had only wheat and water, would it not be wise to come together and offer each other what the other needed in order for the two of you to enjoy delicious bread? I think you get the picture. It is crucial to keep an accurate record of your activities, dates, times and rates so that everyone involved can receive fair and timely compensation.

ENGINEERS

Engineers, like musicians, can be paid by the hour, day, session, or flat fee. Engineers, also like musicians, do their work largely out of the love they have for their craft. Most engineers I know have a thirst for knowledge and jump at any chance to learn something new about their field. Engineers earn from $25 to $100 per hour. If you are going to record an entire album, it would be best if you were able to use the same engineer on the entire project. Keep in mind that some engineers are best for recording and others best suited for mixing. In both cases ask for references and a tape of their work. Hiring the right engineer is important to the project because he will affect the outcome dramatically. Some engineers work best in one type of music and others prefer to work in a different style.

Find out the style of music the engineer is accustomed to working on before hiring him. If the engineer is going to work on the entire project with you, then it is reasonable to ask him to work for points. Of course, the engineer will require some upfront cash. Two points on a project along with a discounted rate should entice an engineer to take a job. The upfront money should be deducted from any royalties due the engineer as a result of record sales. After the upfront moneys have been paid back, the engineer should begin receiving royalties.

MASTERING

All music recordings require mastering to ensure the absolute highest audio quality of the end product the consumer will buy. In mastering, compression and equalization is used to gain better dynamics and overall perception of the music. The result of mastering is the best sound quality achieved so the music will sound impressive both on the radio and on home stereo systems. Mastering studios are basically a scaled-down version of a high tech recording studio, and like recording studios require an engineer to operate them. Unlike recording engineers, mastering engineers usually work one mastering studio. In fact, it is the mastering engineer's abilities that develop the reputation of mastering studios. Read the credits on your favorite albums and check the name of the mastering engineer and mastering studio. Try to have the sound quality as close to what you want your end product to sound like, and that will cut down the amount of time it will take to master your project. Mastering studio costs range from $150 per hour up to $300 per hour and usually include the engineer's fee.

Manufacturing

CASSETTES

This is also an expense that there is no way around. The going rate for cassette manufacturing ranges from 55 cents to 97 cents per 60-minute cassette for an order of 1000 or more. The difference in price depends upon whether you want high or normal bias cassettes. Normal bias cassettes will have a lesser sound quality and are not the industry standard for recorded music, but are totally acceptable for spoken word applications such as books and instructional recordings. High bias cassettes are more expensive but take much more level than normal bias cassettes. High bias cassettes will have less tape hiss than normal bias cassettes.

Keep in mind that the larger the quantity of cassettes ordered, the lesser the price per cassette. The pricing structures usually run in increments of at least 500. Before you can get to the next level down in price per cassette your order has to increase by at least 500. Artwork can be as expensive or inexpensive as you want it to be. My suggestion is to find a good photographer or artist at a university or college who understands what you need and employ him or her. Such artists are usually hungry for the work and willing to please at below market prices.

CD MANUFACTURING

The cost to manufacture CDs is a little different from that of cassettes, simply because the steps needed to reach a final product in CD manufacturing are a little more involved than those required for cassettes. In all cases of CD manufacturing there will be a glass master produced, which is what the final product is cut from. The one-time charge is most likely to be in the $300 range and will be waived on first time orders of one thousand or more, and is non-existent on reorders. There is a setup fee of approximately $100, which is also a one-time charge. Packaging costs about 40 cents per CD. This includes jewel cases, inserts, trays and shrink wrap. The smallest order taken by most independent CD manufacturers is 500 units. In this range, the price per CD is going to be quite a bit higher than if you were to order in larger quantities. Turnaround time, the time which elapses between when the order is taken and when it is filled and ready for the customer—is three to four weeks on rush orders and five to six weeks on regular schedules. Your first order is the most expensive because of the one-time charges of setup, glass mastering, and color separations. The cost of your first run of 500 CDs can run as much as $3.63 per CD, but on re-orders the cost can be as low as $1.90 each. In cases of large quantities when more than 2,000 units are produced, your average cost will go down to about $1.00 per unit. The information here is based upon the median price range for all stages of manufacturing. There are some places that will be cheaper and some, more expensive. Remember, your mama told you, "You Better Shop Around."

Speaking of shopping around, one of the best places in the country to get your CDs and cassettes manufactured is Tape Specialty. They specialize in making you feel special. They pay close attention to your product and know how to get the job done. They can be reached at (818) 786-6111. Tell Nancy I said hello. Another top of the line CD manufacturer is Future Media located in Valencia, California. They can be reached at (805) 294-5575. Tell Steve I said, "What's cooking?"

PROMOTIONAL, MARKETING, CD & CASSETTE ARTWORK

Promotional and marketing artwork will include posters, post-cards, flats, hats, T-shirts, bags, cassette inserts, CD inserts, etc. These items can be costly and it would be wise to shop around for a printer and supplier that can provide these items at a reasonable price. For instance, most cassettes and compact disks require inserts that contain information about that project. In some cases it will be to your advantage to have a printer supply these items instead of the cassette or CD manufacturer. I was recently made aware of a printer who offered extremely competitive prices on these items. For those of you who would like to get your paper items manufactured at a price that you can afford call Copy Page at (310) 453-3600. You won't be sorry. Make sure you have your art-work ready and follow the guidelines that your printer will provide.

PROMOTING YOUR PRODUCT

Once you have a finished recording and are manufacturing your product, it is then time to get down to the process of promoting, marketing and selling. Developing relationships with club DJs who can promote and play your works on the local club scene is an avenue of exposure to add to your promotional campaign. Organizing parties and participating in any local events that will give you the opportunity to expose and sell your music to the general public will only help your cause.

I know these suggestions sound like small potatoes, and they probably are, compared to the larger scope of things, but the point is that this is exactly what the larger record companies do to increase awareness of a new act in order to promote sales. You are closer to the front line than the average record company and this could work to your advantage. There is a lot of product to choose from in record stores and chances of someone happening upon your record are slim. That is why it will be important for you to publicize and promote your product as much as possible.

I believe records are sold at picnics, parties, in cars, at truck stops, and anywhere a person is likely to hear new music. Word of mouth is probably the biggest seller of records. Record stores are just where you go to pick up records. Sale of a piece of music happens in the mind of the prospective buyer, not in the record store. Notwithstanding the above, you should try to get your product into record stores, in case your record receives airplay and listeners want to purchase it.

INDEPENDENT RECORD PROMOTION

The most effective way of promoting your product is to have your record play on the radio. In order for you to do that you will need to hire an independent promotion specialist to solicit and gain airplay for your music. Independent promoters are persons who use influence and relationships they have with radio programmers to secure airplay for records they are hired to work on. Radio programmers are the persons hired to decide what music will be played on the station they work for. Every radio station has one.

Independent record promoters are usually hired on a record by record basis, but a number of the more powerful ones have retainer relationships with the larger record companies. Independent promotion is expensive, costing $50,000 for a national independent promotional campaign for R&B material. The stakes are higher for pop music, therefore the numbers go up dramatically. There are also more pop stations, which also helps drive up the cost of independent pop promotion. Two hundred and fifty thousand dollars is not an unrealistic figure for national pop promotion.

While these prices may be out of your range, negotiating a deal for independent promotion in just your local area may prove affordable by comparison. This is assuming independent promoters will accept assignments from local bands. My guess is that where there is a demand there will be a market. Gaining access to independent record promoters could prove challenging in itself. One way of finding them is to call local radio stations and inquire about who the independent promoters are that frequent your area. Most stations should be happy to give you a few names. Understand that record promoters are simply a go-between for your independent label and radio programmers. Independent promoters usually have pre-established relationships with radio stations. They can make the difference between a hit or not. Independent promotion has a quirky reputation, but is a necessity any way you look at the picture.

COLLEGE RADIO

College radio stations are increasing in popularity and are becoming more important in the scheme of promoting new music. They are easier to deal with and generally love to receive new music.

RADIO STATION LISTS

The *Yellow Pages of Rock* directory with its travel companion, *Junior* and fax guide, *Spot,* is a three-volume set of reference material vital to the broadcast/music industry. The *Yellow Pages* master volume begins with several formats of the most significant radio properties across North America. Consisting of main office addresses and phone numbers for all the "front-line" department personnel on the national level at major and independent record labels, distributors, music retailers, Press & P.R., cross-references of artists listed alphabetically with their managers, including well-established music video broadcast programmers and a lot more. You can place an order by simply calling the Album Network at (818) 955-4000.

TEST MARKETING

Test marketing your music at small events can give you a good indication of how the general public will respond to your project. When test marketing, be very careful to test fairly and resist the temptation of letting on that the project being tested is a creation of yours. I've been to parties and social events where music was being played and have inquired about what the DJ was playing because I found it interesting. Most people when they hear music for the first time and like it will inquire as to who the artist is.

Setting up your own custom distribution concept is not out of the question. Why not have your record available to purchase at parties, basketball games, family reunions, club meetings, bowling alleys and other places where people gather?

The first rule of sales is to know your customers. So don't go to a hip hop party trying to force the DJ to play your latest grunge rock creation. I would recommend the same kind of judgment be used in soliciting your songs to local radio. The bottom line is if you have a good product, make people aware of your product, and make the product available and easily acquired, you will have sales.

Generating sales even on a small scale can get the attention of the big boys. Once you have a sales base, you can negotiate a better deal for yourself with another independent record label or even a major. I am hoping some of you will stick to selling your records through your own outlets.

MARKETING & ADVERTISING YOUR PRODUCT

Marketing and advertising work hand in hand to drive the sales of a product. The marketing aspect includes obtaining the right photography for your product and positioning the product in the marketplace with the perception that you want the public to have about it. It also includes setting up displays and signing autographs in record stores.

Identifying the right vehicle for advertising is also a function of marketing. Taking out an advertisement in *Popular Mechanics Magazine* for your product will not get you sales. Identifying the proper demographics for a particular product is probably the most important step in the marketing of your product. "Know your customers" is the slogan of choice in marketing seminars and classes across the country.

Find other albums and music that have similar qualities as yours and pay attention as to where these products are advertised. Pay close attention to the types of advertisements and when they are run. Listening to the tones and moods of television and radio commercials will give you a perspective and insight into marketing and advertising. Developing relationships with local marketing firms is an easy way of learning the ropes. The cost of marketing a record is arbitrary and depends solely on how much money you have to spend and the importance of the project to you.

Distribution

DISTRIBUTORS

After manufacturing, your product will need to be delivered to wholesalers and retailers in order for the general public to purchase it. This is called distribution. Distributors deliver product to wholesalers, who in turn sell the product to retailers. Retailers, of course, sell the product to the consumer. This is the most common way to sell merchandise, unless the merchandise is being sold through mail order or by some other means.

Record labels have cassettes and CDs manufactured and then distributors pick the product up from the factory and distribute that product to either wholesalers, one-stops, or record stores. The cost of distribution ranges from 15 percent to 35 percent of sales. The more product to be distributed, the less the cost of distribution. You will have to decide whether you want to have your product distributed by independent distribution or major distribution.

All the major labels have their own distribution network. Distribution done by major labels is called major distribution. One of the main differences between a major label and an independent label is that the majors have their own distribution. Independent labels rely upon either independent distributors or are distributed by a major record label. Major labels have more money to spend on advertising and marketing and this can be of value to you if your product is being distributed though their network.

The downside to working with major distributors is that they will want a larger percentage of sales than an independent distributor. Major distributors also have a short attention span in terms of how long they will keep a record in their distribution chain if the record is not selling. Three months is the time period a record has to prove itself for a major label. If it does not perform well within that time it's pretty much dead in the water.

Independent distributors have no affiliation with major record labels. They have fewer artists to distribute and are more likely to stick with a record for a longer period of time.

Independent distribution has been gaining quite a reputation as a viable choice, and has proven it can be competitive in contributing to the success of a record. "The Most Beautiful Girl in The World" distributed by Bellmark Distributors is the most successful record the Artist Formerly Named Prince has released in a long time. Bellmark is an independent distributor. Yet, all the Artist Formerly Named Prince's prior releases were with Warner Brother Records, a major record label and distributor.

The downside is that some independent distributors have a reputation of not paying. Again, ask around and make sure to ask whatever distributor you are considering for references. As a last resort you can distribute your record yourself. Just load up the station wagon and make your rounds to the record stores.

As I stated before, most artists record on inflated budgets. In most cases, that's because they need the excess budget to live on, because with the current practices they will never be in a royalty earning position. That's why it makes so much sense to start your own record label, if at all possible.

MARKETING YOUR PRODUCT VIA ON-LINE SERVICES

The newest and most exciting way to promote and sell your product is through on-line services such as America Online, CompuServe, Prodigy, Microsoft Network Service and The Internet. On-line services are accessed using a computer, modem and telephone lines, and basically allows the user to connect to other computers and computer networks. Once the user is connected they may download, upload or simply access the information that is contained on the computers they are connected to. According to Leslie Helm of the Los Angeles Times, America Online boasts 3.7 million members, while CompuServe has 2.2 million, Prodigy 1.4 million, and the newly formed Microsoft Network Service has 525,000 members. Each of these services charges a monthly fee, and organizes all of the information by categories. They have proven to be an indispensable source of information regarding the record and entertainment industries. To learn more about online services ask a friend that subscribes to an on-line service to give you a demonstration.

THE INTERNET AND THE WORLD WIDE WEB

The Internet is made up of many different computer networks spread over the entire planet. Of all the on-line services it has the most promise for those looking to market and sell their products via computers. There is no charge directly to the user but in order to navigate this vast resource effectively you should sign up with a local internet access company. Contact your local computer store for details about internet access in your area. In order to market and sell your products on the Internet you must have a commercial account and must also develop a web site, which is essentially your address and store front on the Internet. One of the best web site developers happens to be a friend of mine. His name is Darroll Gustamachio. If you are interested in his services you can e-mail him at vsd@interport.net. or write him at P. O. box 410 Planetarium Station, New York , NY. 10024-0410.

~ *Keeping Your Dream Alive* ~

How to Establish a Recording Budget

Understanding Record Royalties

What is an Audit?

Contracts and Explanatory Notes

The Future of the Record Industry

Keeping Your
Dream Alive

With every release of a new record or compact disc there emerges a chance for the artist whose work is contained on that record or CD to become a star. But as exciting and desirable as it is to become a bona fide star those who have attained it will tell you it is no easy task to maintain that level of success. For most, the hard work has just begun. How many artists have we seen come and go because of, ultimately, the lack of a contingency plan just in case they became a success. You see, many of us desire stardom but few of us are prepared for it when it comes. Therefore many of those who reach that level of success are unable to maintain it.

What constitutes star status is highly subjective. My definition of star status is when one becomes recognizable, is able to make a living playing music, and whose recording has sold at least 100,000 units. Now some of you may say that in order for someone to be deemed a star his recordings should have sold over a half million units, but that is not necessarily true. For example, if a jazz album sells one hundred thousand units in the United States that would be considered a great success by industry standards. Unfortunately, it would not be considered a great financial success for the artist.

Just ten years ago a gold record was considered a great success for any type of music, while today record companies aim for platinum or beyond as their mark of success. Whatever the level of success that is obtained, there are certain things an artist, producer, and songwriter must do to continue growing.

In all businesses there are certain duties that must be executed on a regular basis in order to run the business profitably. These duties include negotiating deals, taking inventory, budgeting, reconciling the bank accounts, and collecting monies that are owed to your company. I refer to these functions as Keeping Your Dream Alive. Remember, in the Introduction I compared songwriters, artists and producers to small companies and corporations. If my analogy is logical, and I submit that it is, then every songwriter, artist, and producer has the same duties that must be attended to on a regular basis as any other company or corporation.

This group of chapters will give you an inside scoop about the steps you must take in order to properly maintain your success and keep your dream alive. You too must take inventory, budget, negotiate new deals, reconcile the balance sheets and collect money owed to you. With the exception of establishing recording budgets, all of the functions explained in these chapters will require the expertise and help of members of your dream team. Negotiating contracts will require an attorney, while running audits will require an accountant and maybe an attorney. Establishing recording budgets can be handled by a competent project coordinator or yourself once you get the hang of it.

Although you will have the help of your attorney, accountant and project coordinator, remember that *you* are ultimately responsible for the success of each of these functions. Remember that *you* are the chairman of the board and the head of the creative department. So rally your troops and be creative. This section of the book contains the chapters "Establishing Recording Budgets," "Understanding Record Royalties," "What is an Audit?," "Contracts & Contract Explanatory Notes" and the final chapter "The Future Of the Record Industry."

HOW TO ESTABLISH A
RECORDING BUDGET

If you're like most creative people, including myself, you'd rather not have to deal with the business part of producing records. Instead, you would rather be in the studio producing what you hope will be this year's chart buster. But unless you have a team that can be trusted to handle the massive amounts of paperwork, union forms and other business associated with producing records, or an assistant sent from heaven, you are stuck with the drudgery of handling these chores yourself. Even if you are fortunate to have a project coordinator to handle the paperwork for you, you should participate in this process at least once or twice before you permanently delegate these duties to a project manager or coordinator.

Participation in establishing, recording and administering budgets will give the new artist and producer insight into what it costs to produce different kinds of records and what the expected and unexpected occurrences are during the recording process. For instance, you will come to know that the cost of recording a four piece rhythm section is totally different from the cost associated with recording a full symphony orchestra for a Broadway musical.

Learning the fundamentals of creating and administering recording budgets will also give you an education that will allow you to be inventive in your approach to creative budget solutions and challenges, such as how to bridge the gap between your most ambitious creative ideas and what you can realistically afford, given the agreed upon budget.

ROAD MAP

A recording budget is, in a sense, like a detailed road map. If planned properly you will arrive at your destination more quickly and with more enjoyment than if you just jump into your car and start driving. There is nothing more frustrating than having somewhere to go and driving along for hours not knowing how to get there. Even if you like driving, without advanced planning it will cost you more to get wherever you're going. Recordings and road trips have something else in common; once you go down the road a few times you can predict how long it will take and what your expenses will be when the journey is over.

Many producers and artists go into the studio without fully planning their projects, which is a disservice to everyone involved and to the project itself. With proper planning the overall project will yield better results in all areas. I highly recommend that a complete budget be planned and adhered to as closely as possible without sacrificing the integrity of the music. This will help to insure the financial success of your career as a producer and/or recording artist.

The most inspiring reason for an artist or producer to master the art of establishing recording budgets is evident when the producer or artist negotiates a deal with the record company that allows the producer or artist to receive an all-in recording fund. In that case, the producer or artist is usually given the entire recording budget in three payments. He is responsible for paying all recording costs and is allowed to keep whatever is not spent on recording the records.

The expenses associated with recording an album include payments for musicians, engineers, recording studios, programmers, cartage companies and all other personnel and third party vendors.

They also include paying union fees, materials costs such as 24-track tape, cassettes, DATs, and editing costs. Before each recording project begins the artist or producer should put together a forecast of what each of these expenses will be on a song-by-song basis. This is commonly referred to as establishing a recording budget. Establishing a recording budget allows the artist, producer and record company a clear view of what the anticipated expenses will be in each area of a recording project, and what the total cost of the project will be. These areas include pre-production, production, overdubs, mix preparation and track organization, mixing, editing and overlays, and mastering. The cost of each of these areas combined should equal the total cost of the project.

Every producer has his or her own method of recording, and therefore, his or her own way in which to break down the recording process. The above breakdown of categories is an example of how I approach record projects. Mix preparation, track organization, overlays and other segments of the recording process I have outlined may be unique to my recording method, but there may be other producers who use the same methodology but refer to these segments by a different name.

While you should feel free to establish your own methods so they apply to your recording and production methods, the elements contained in every recording budget generally remain the same. For instance, there will always be preproduction, production and mixing. In fact, establishing a recording budget is as much a part of the recording process as any of the other processes that are accomplished in the studio.

The first step in establishing a recording budget is to identify your method of recording. An example of this is shown in the diagram below of the production budget cover sheet. The top of this sheet is self explanatory in its requirements. Note that each segment of the process has an estimated cost and an actual cost. The estimated cost should be entered as you create your recording budget. The actual cost should be filled in after the project is finished. The purpose of having both the actual and estimated cost listed is so that the producer or artist can see the difference between the original calculations and what each item actually cost. This will allow the producer or artist to sharpen his budgeting skills, and therefore make more accurate budgetary projections in the future.

Each phase of the recording process is listed in the order in which it would normally occur during the recording process, starting at the top and progressing downward. On this project, preproduction is first and mastering is last. Notice the letter listed next to each phase of the recording process on the cover sheet. These letters correspond with the letters that are listed in the title heading of each individual detail budget form. This allows a quick reference so that the producer or artist can quickly identify the detail form they are viewing.

In addition to the budget cover sheet there are individual forms that correspond with each phase of the recording process listed on the cover sheet. These individual forms are called detail forms and list all expenses associated with that phase of the recording process.

Listed on the left side of each form are the personnel and functions. Listed along the top of each detail form are the costs associated with each person or function that is listed on the left side of the form.

USING THESE FORMS

As stated above, the budget cover sheet's main function is to summarize the entire project at a glance. Individual detail forms allow the producer or the artist to review in detail each item related to that specific phase of the recording process. This allows you to make educated decisions as to what is and is not affordable.

Let's start with Diagram (1) the pre-production detail form, since it is the first item on the production cover sheet list. The easiest way to understand this form, as well as the other detail forms, is to remember that the functions or persons that require compensation are listed on the left of the page and proceed from top to bottom.

The amount of time or compensation is listed at the top of the page and reads from left to right. Notice that some items on the left of the list have either numbers or dollar figures in either the units/hrs.,

COVER SHEET

Artist:
Phynalee Rych & Faymos

Production Company:
California Hit Records

Producer:
Michael Watts

Address:
1717 Bluewater
Los Angeles, CA 90299

Phone:
310-555-1212

Fax:
310-555-1213

Contact:
Michael

Prepared by:
Steven Evans

Record Label:
Fair Shake

A & R:
Noah Yorstuff

Address:
84853 Return Masters
Hollywood, CA 90993

Phone:
213-555-8882

Fax:
213-555-8884

Artist Phone:
818-555-9999

Manager:
818-555-1212

Diagram 1

Production Cover Sheet			
Function	**Sheet**	**Estimated Cost**	**Actual Cost**
Pre-Production	A	$655	
Production, Overdubs & Vocals	B		
Trk Organization & Mix Prep	C		
Mixing	D		
Post Production Remix & Editing	E		
Mastering	F		
Grand Total			

Diagram 2

Sheet (A)   **PRE PRODUCTION BUDGET**

	Name	Unit/Hr	$ Per	Total	Cartage	Date	Time
Studio:							
Rehearsal							
Demo	Hit	9	$15	$135			
Engineer:							
1st		9	$15	$135			
Assistant							
Singers:							
Lead	Next Deva	5	$0			5/26/94	3:00a
Background	Hit	2	$20	$40		5/26/94	10:00a
Musicians:							
Drums	Tom	2	$30	$60		5/25/94	5:30p
Guitar	Bob Steel	2	$30	$60		5/25/94	5:30p
Bass	Tim Cuy	2	$30	$60		5/25/94	5:30p
Synths	Jay Sykes	2	$30	$60		5/25/94	5:30p
Piano	Jay Sykes	2	$30	$60		5/25/94	5:30p
Program:							
Drums							
Keyboard							
Sound							
Travel:							
Gas							
Car							
Air Line							
Hotel							
Parking	Jim's	7	$5	$35			
Material:							
Dats							
2 inch							
Disks							
Subtotal:			**$655**				

Diagram 3

Sheet (B)   **PRODUCTION & OVERDUBS**

	Name	Units/Hrs	$ per	Total	Cartage	Date	Time
Studio:							
24 & 48trk							
Transfers							
Engineer:							
1st							
Assistant							
Singers:							
Lead							
Background							
Voc. Arr.							
Musicians:							
Drums							
Guitar							
Bass							
Synths							
Piano							
Rythym Arr.							
Eqmt. Rent:							
Materials:							
Dats							
Cassettes							
2 inch							
Disks							
Travel:							
Gas							
Car Rentals							
Air Travel							
Hotel							
Parking							
Subtotal:							

Diagram 4

Sheet (C)   MIX PREPARATION

	Name	Units/Hrs	$ per	Total	Cartage	Date	Time
Studio:							
24 & 48trk							
Transfers							
Engineer:							
1st							
Assistant							
Last Ovrdbs:							
Drum Repl.							
Keyboards							
Sampling							
Vocal flys							
Materials:							
Dats							
Cassettes							
2 inch							
Disks							
Travel:							
Gas							
Car Rentals							
Air Travel							
Hotel							
Parking							
Subtotal:							

Diagram 5

Sheet (D)   MIXING

	Name	Units/Hrs	$ per	Total	Cartage	Date	Time
Studio:							
24 & 48trk							
Transfers							
Engineer:							
Mix Engineer							
Assistant							
Gear Rental							
Machines							
Outboard							
Aux. Mix Board							
Hard Disk Rec.							
Materials:							
Dats							
Cassettes							
2 inch							
Disks							
1/2 in Tape							
1/4 in Tape							
Travel:							
Gas							
Car Rental							
Air Travel							
Hotel							
Parking							
Subtotal:							

Diagram 6

Sheet (E)   OVERLAYS & REMIXING

	Name	Units/Hrs	$ per	Total	Cartage	Date	Time
Studio:							
24 & 48trk							
Transfers							
Hard Disk Studio							
Engineer:							
1st							
Assistant							
Edit Engineer							
Singers:							
Lead							
Background							
Vocal Arr.							
Musicians:							
Drums							
Guitar							
Bass							
Synths							
Piano							
Remix Producer:							
Eqmt. Rent:							
Materials:							
Dats							
Cassettes							
2 inch							
Disks							
Travel:							
Gas							
Car Rental							
Air Travel							
Hotel							
Parking							
Subtotal:							

Diagram 7

Sheet (F)   **MASTERING**

	Name	Units/Hrs	$ per	Total	Cartage	Date	Time
Studio:							
Mastering Std							
Transfers							
Engineer:							
Mastering Eng.							
Materials:							
Dats							
Cassettes							
2 inch							
Disks							
1/2 in Tape							
1/4 in Tape							
Reference CD							
Reference Lqrs							
12 in							
Travel:							
Gas							
Car Rental							
Air Travel							
Hotel							
Parking							
Subtotal:							

per hour and total categories. Other items on the left of the page, like rehearsal studio and programmers, are left empty. Only put numbers in the columns that correspond to the personnel or functions you intend to use. Each function or personnel listing has a column that provides for the Name of the person who will be hired for the job. The Unit/Hours category lists the number of hours the producer artist anticipates needing for each person or for performing each function.

In the case of the Demo Studio there are a total of nine hours needed. There is also a Per Hour column, which should be used to list the cost per hour of the item for which it corresponds. For example the cost per hour for the demo studio is $15. Next to that column is the Total charge for that item. For purposes of keeping up with this demonstration, let's continue with the demo studio item. The number of hours or units needed is nine hours. The cost per hour is $15, the total cost of the demo studio will be 9 x $15 = $135. To the right of the total column you will see a column for dates. The purpose of this column is so that you can list the date that each function or person will be utilized.

After the names, units, $ per hour, totals and dates have been entered for each item, the Total column should be added up and that number should be listed in the Sub-Total column located in the left hand column at the bottom of the page. It is this sub-total number that should also appear on the Production Cover Sheet next to the item that it represents. In this case the sub-total is $655 and would be placed next to Pre-Production.

When you complete the input of information required on the detail forms and all sub-totals have been applied to the Production cover sheet, add the sub-total numbers together to achieve your Grand Total. By following these steps for each phase of the recording process you will have established your first budget.

Congratulations!

One thing to keep in mind is that as your reputation as a producer grows and the number of contacts in your phone book also grows, so will your ability to make deals with the personnel you need to complete a record. The advancement of technology already has and will continue to affect the bottom line of recording budgets in a positive way. In other words, it will bring down the cost of recording.

PRODUCER-OWNED & ARTIST-OWNED STUDIOS

I have owned a few recording studios and have always had a hard time convincing record companies that I should be compensated for time booked and used on a project recorded in my studios that I was also the producer on. Of course this is a ploy on the record company's part to get the project done for less money. I have never given into this and have always demanded that my studios be compensated for the time that was used on projects that I was also the producer on.

Although I do question some decisions made by record labels, I do not question their intelligence in general. They are highly sophisticated organizations and know full well that studios owned by producers are also in business to make money and make the producer's job easier. These producer-owned studios should be treated as any other third party expense related to a recording project. It would be wise to give the record company a break on the hourly rate that you charge for your home studio.

Reasonable hourly rates for home studio recording range from $75 to $135 per hour. The difference in price per hour should reflect the level and quality of equipment contained in your studio. If all you have is a beefed-up midi setup then an hourly rate of $35 per hour is not unreasonable.

RECORDING FUND (ALL-IN BUDGET)

Record companies employ two methods of distributing money to producers and artists for the purpose of financing recordings. One is called the all-in recording fund which occurs when a record company gives the producer, manager or artist the entire recording fund to administer. Payments to the producer, manager or artist are usually in increments of thirds — one-third paid up front, one-third paid after commencement of recording and at the request of the producer or artist, and the balance paid after final mixes are delivered to the record company and have met with final approval.

THE RECORDING BUDGET

The other method by which record companies handle recording budgets occurs when the producer gets a fee, and the record company pays the bills and third-party expenses. The advantage for the producer is less paper work. The disadvantage for the producer or artist is not getting to keep the unused portion of the budget should the project come in under budget. In this arrangement, the A&R administration department of the record company will book talent and do all necessary paperwork. The record company does not prefer one method over the other unless the artist or producer has a history of going over budget, and in that case, they will want to watch every penny.

In both cases — of the all-in recording fund and the record company administered recording budget — the exact budget amount is negotiated between the producer, artist or artist's representative and record company.

The goal for the artist and the manager should be to keep the budget as low as possible by minimizing excessive recording costs. The more it costs to make a record, the more records must be sold before the artist will be in a position with the record company to receive artist royalties. As mentioned above, artists should be aware of dual charges. This occurs when the same charges are made against the artist's account and against the producer's account.

A, B & C LEVEL ACTS

Every record label has a system by which it ranks artists. These ranks are called levels. The top rank is an A level. The middle rank is the B level and lowest rank is the C level. Each level has a policy that is set by the record company that defines what amount of funding the company will be willing to invest in certain key areas on that artist's behalf. Those areas include promotion, album budget, tour support and marketing. The A level performer gets the highest recording budgets, points, recording funds, and marketing budget. These artists also receive the heftiest financial support in all other areas.

The diagram below shows the difference in recording budgets for the different levels at major record labels.

Recording Budgets:

Level A $ 1,000,000 and up
Level B $ 450,000 up to $ 700,000
Level C $ 250,000 up to $ 500,000
New Act $ 100,000 up to $ 225,000
Rap $ 100,000 up to $ 175,000
Jazz $ 10,000   up to $ 60,000

THE WRITTEN BUDGET

Sometimes a major label will demand that producers submit written budgets. It is largely a formality, because before a record company contacts a producer, they know exactly what the negotiated budget is for that project. However, a request for a written budget should not be taken lightly. Remember, this is an opportunity for you to see a breakdown of proposed expenditures including vocal, pre-production and mixing.

If you are a new producer, you're probably inexperienced and eager to get your first job. Be careful in your eagerness to get the job not to bid too low, because if you bid too low and the record company accepts your bid, you will be stuck with trying to complete the project with inadequate funding. If you establish a written budget, you will be able to see what is realistic and what is not.

When submitting a recording budget to a label, factor in 10 to 15 percent in excess of what your true budget needs are, just in case you need to go over budget. Inevitably you end up needing every cent for unforeseen complications.

OVER BUDGET

Record companies define over budget as the cost of a project exceeding the amount that was negotiated in the artist's or producer's contract. I think of over budget as the point at which the cost of the project exceeds the amount of money that is normally dictated by the record company's policy according to the artist's stature and level at that label.

If there are multiple producers working on one project and one of the producers goes over budget, the record company should only charge that over budget to the individual producer who is responsible. If a project is being delivered under budget and an individual producer requires an increase in his or her budget the record company will be more likely to approve the additional funding for those individual songs.

Sometimes, for any number of reasons, a project will go over budget. At that point, the artist's representative or producer will have to approach the record company and request additional funding for the project. The record company has two choices: either grant additional funding or deny it.

A record company's behavior in an over budget situation largely depends on the stature of the artist, the stature of the producer and how emotionally tied to the project the record company is. If the artist's previous efforts have resulted in substantial sales, the record company will most likely approve additional funding for the project. In keeping with the same logic, if the artist's prior efforts have met with marginal or disappointing sales, the record company will be hesitant about granting additional financing for the project. If the artist is a new artist and the record company is excited about the prospect of this new artist it will probably issue additional dollars. If the artist's type and stature at the label falls into the lower category (C level) it will be difficult to get additional funding.

CONTINGENCIES

Sometimes a record company will grant additional funding but will deduct the over budget amount from future advances and recording funds due the artist. Record companies will also try to deduct over budget cost from producer fees and royalties. Be aware of the remedies for over budget situations in your artists' and producers' contracts.

If the artist or producer is in a strong position, they may be able to negotiate an over budget contingency into his or her contract with the record label. An over budget contingency clause states the conditions under which the record company will grant additional financing for cost overruns. Contingency clauses are increasingly rare in production and artist's contracts. Over budget contingency clauses usually grant 10 or 15 percent of the original budget as additional funding for the project should it go over budget.

If the record company requests changes or additions to the music, it is imperative to take time and think about how the changes will impact the budget and the estimated completion time of the project. For instance, if you have finished recording a song and you send the ruff mix to the label and they request that you re-record the drums, that would impact the budget and the completion time. If those changes would cause the project to go over budget then it should be discussed with the record company before you make the changes.

A good way to gain more insight into budgets is to get your hands on an existing budget and change the numbers to suit your situation. You can probably get one from the A&R administration department of a record company or from a project coordinator.

Now that I have waved more than a few red flags, I will tell you that doing a budget is not as hard as it sounds. As much as I don't like doing them, I feel compelled to pass along this important information to you, my new constituents. Don't thank me now, wait until those fat royalty checks start flowing, and send me a generous portion. Just kidding.

MATERIALS COST

Cassettes, two inch tape, DATs, computer disks, 1/2 inch tape, video tape, musical instrument purchases and other necessary items should be listed under Material Costs. You should list these for their actual cost, including taxes. Be advised that many recording studios mark up the cost of materials considerably. It would be wise to purchase them from a local music store. Try to anticipate the quantity of cassettes, tapes, DATs, and computer disks needed before starting each project.

TAPE

Some studios charge as much as $250 for a roll of 2 inch tape. The actual cost from a local music store is about $130. Studios will charge as little as $5 per cassette and as much as $20, so be aware before ordering three or four cassettes after each session, because it adds up and will impact your budget. Ask the studio manager for a materials price sheet. Once you have an idea of what materials you will need and the quantity of each item, add the totals together and list them under material cost.

TAPE DISCOUNT HOUSES

There are tape warehouses that sell tape stock at low prices compared to retail stores. You can find them listed in most music magazines like *Keyboard* and *Musician*. Call these price-saving warehouses and request their price sheets.

Tip: Take the savings you make on one of the items and give it to your favorite charity. It will make you feel good.

PERSONNEL & STUDIO TIME

With the multitude of new computers and gadgets, one is able to approach every phase of recording as a do-it-yourself process. Personally, I find this kind of recording boring and lonely. Moments spent with people are precious. Think of all the great jokes you can tell to your favorite guitarist while the engineer is firing up the hard disk. You'll have a better chance of producing a superior product if you include other people and their ideas.

Now that I have force fed you my philosophy on personnel, lets get down to the business of figuring out how we can pay these people.

You can either pay musicians, engineers and singers a flat rate, hourly rate or daily rate. The less desirable way to pay is union scale, although in all likelihood your first budgets will not allow you to pay singers and musicians union scale anyway. The most desirable way to pay musicians and other personnel is by flat rate. It is important that you let musicians know that your relationship with them is a two-way street and that you are willing to help them in the future also. Don't just say it. Mean it.

For every hour you use a musician you will need to budget an hour for studio time. If the session requires an engineer, you will also have to include his fee or rate in the budget. If a keyboardist is required for six hours, you must pay the studio and engineer for six hours.

OTHER RECORDING BUDGET ITEMS:

Cartage: Delivery of musicians' and engineer's gear to and from studios.

Postage: Stamps and express delivery of tapes and lyric sheets to musicians and record companies. Sending payments by mail.

Rentals: The rental of instruments and mixing gear for recording and mixing sessions.

Rehearsal studios: If you are rehearsing the band or artist.

Satellite uplink time: If you are doing multi-location synchronized recording.

Food cost: Buying food for the artist and other talent (if the budget allows).

Union Fees: Fees paid to local musicians union and AFTRA.

IF YOU ARE THE ARTIST

Be aware of the trends and going rates for different level producers. Try not to insist upon the best of everything in the recording process. If you insist upon the fanciest studios you will be paying far more than you need. Choose a studio that can get the job done.

A problem with artists and budgets is that their egos get in the way and unfortunately find their way into the budget. This ends up costing the artist in the long run. Limousines, five star hotels and swanky restaurants have their proper place and time, but more often than not lead to the artist's financial demise if not handled with caution.

Artists should make sure that any over-budget request by independent producers is first authorized by the artist or artist's manager before the record company executes them. In other words, you as an artist want to have a say about whether or not your project goes over budget. Otherwise, you can end up with astronomical charges against your account that you will be unaware of until royalty time.

UNDERSTANDING
RECORD ROYALTIES

Before you go on to read this chapter I thought it best to inform you of how important it is to take the time to fully understand its contents. If you're a new artist not yet signed to a record company it will give you insight into what you can expect when you receive your first contract. It will also dispel some of the myths about the recording industry, help you to understand how record royalties are calculated, and teach you how to project future royalty income based on the number of records sold.

If you've recorded one or more albums that have been released on a major or independent label, the myths about the industry are already starting to dispel and you are beginning to see things as they really occur. What this chapter will do for you is help you understand the amount of royalties you do or do not receive, negotiate better deals for yourself in the future, identify clauses in past and current recording agreements that did not or do not work in your favor, and teach you how to calculate future royalty income based upon future record sales.

RECORD ROYALTIES

Record royalties are the percentage of sales the artist and/or producer receives from a record company. Let me make that a little clearer. Record royalties are monies derived from the sales of records that are paid to the artist and/or producer by the record company. They are based upon the number of records that are sold, the retail price, and standard deductions every record company subtracts from the gross income derived from the sales of those records. These deductions include the recording budget (the cost of recording the project), packaging, returns and reserves, discounted military sales, video cost, tour support, and free goods. I will list and explain each of these deductions below. Read carefully.

RETURNS & RESERVES

Re-serve (ri-zûrv) 1) To keep back, as for future use or for special purpose. 2) To set or cause to set apart for a particular person or use. 3) To keep or secure for oneself. (American Heritage College Dictionary)

Reserves, as referred to in the recording industry, are a percentage of income that a record company holds and will not pay royalties on, just in case a portion of records that have been purchased are returned to the stores or wholesalers. If these records are not sold the record company will never pay royalties on them.

Record companies have agreements with most large wholesale chains and retail stores that allow the them to return records that have not sold to consumers within a certain period of time. Sometimes record companies will manufacture large quantities of compact discs and cassettes in anticipation of blockbuster sales. Unfortunately, all too often the record bombs and the result is a large number of returns. The greatest danger for a large number of returns occurs when a record company releases an album recorded by a superstar artist. The record company has reason to believe that project will sell a huge number of units and it therefore manufactures and ships a large number of records to wholesalers and stores. If the project is not a success, the record company can look forward to truckloads of returns.

DEFECTIVE PRODUCT

In some cases defective CDs and cassettes are returned to the stores, but because CD manufacturing is such a perfected process, the number of defective CDs likely to make it past quality control and into stores is very small. The same is true in cassette manufacturing. The percentage of cassettes returned due to faulty product is very small.

RESERVES

Reserves are the record companies' protection from having to pay artist and producer royalties on records that are returned and therefore have not generated income.

The usual amount of reserves that a record company will hold is from 30 to 50 percent. The length of time a record company will hold these reserves before they will pay the artist or producer royalties on that percentage of sales can be two years or more. If you are a superstar artist you may be able to negotiate that the record label only has the right to hold a maximum of 35 percent of the total sales as reserves. You may also be able to negotiate that the label has to liquidate those reserves in less than the standard two years. (For more information on reserves see the explanatory notes which accompany the recording agreement.)

In any event, you should certainly negotiate that reserves being liquidated over a period of time must be paid in equal payments. For example if a label is holding $10,000 in reserves, and the time comes where they are bound by your contract to liquidate those reserves, and the amount of time they have to liquidate those reserves is two years, they should pay the artist or producer in four equal payments of $2,500.

If you are a new artist the best you can hope for is to negotiate that the record label has the right to hold a reasonable amount of reserves. This will protect the artist or producer from having the record company hold back 95 to 100 percent as reserves, which would obviously be to the record company's advantage. The new artist might also be able to negotiate a limit on the amount of time a record company can hold reserves before they have to liquidate them and pay the artist and producer royalties on those sales.

The problem with reserves and returns is in the way record companies account for them on royalty statements. Most royalty statements do not clearly show the difference between plain old record royalties and reserves that are being liquidated.

Overall royalty statements are designed to give artists and producers a minimum amount of information regarding the sales of their records, the number manufactured, shipped, sold, returned, the percentage of reserves, and foreign verses domestic sales. Because of this they are almost impossible to decipher.

We have all heard stories about record companies that don't pay artists and producers what they should. With royalty statements being designed the way they are, it is hard to tell which labels are honest and which labels are purposely cheating the artist and producers. A higher standardized royalty statement containing detailed information that is easy to read and understand is certainly worth rallying for in the near future.

SOUNDSCAN

In the summer of 1991 Soundscan was introduced as a method of tracking the sales of records. Soundscan is a computerized system that looks at the bar code that is printed on all CDs, cassettes and record. That bar-code is essentially an identification number that represents that artist and that album. When you buy a CD or cassette it is passed over a bar-code machine just like in your local super market. The computer recognizes the bar-code number and also keeps a record of every record that is sold. Soundscan is 90 percent accurate. With the introduction of Soundscan the charts contained in *Billboard* are more accurate than they were before Soundscan existed. In addition, record companies are now able to instantly calculate how many records an artist has sold and where those sales occurred. This being the case, reserves should be a thing of the past, but record companies still insist on holding between 35% and 50% of artist and producer royalties as reserves for a period of two years or more.

BDS

BDS is another computer system that helps track the success of a record. BDS tracks the number of times a song is played on the radio. It does this via a computer comparison system. The way it works is record companies pay the BDS company a monthly fee for every record they want to track. They also pay an additional fee for each radio format that they wish to track, e.g. Pop, R&B, Country & Western, etc. Every time a new record is released the record company sends a copy of that record to BDS. BDS in turn makes an electronic picture of that record. They then have computers compare what is being played on the radio to each song that they have been paid to track. When the computer sees a match between what is being played on the radio and a song it has in its memory it makes a note. On a weekly basis record companies receive BDS reports that show how many times a song is played on every radio station. Again this keeps the charts accurate.

Before BDS, record companies routinely falsified records of how many times their recordings were being played on the radio. The reason they did this is because a record's chart position is determined by both record sales and radio play. If record companies could show that a song was being played more than it actually was the effect would be realized as a higher chart position for that record. Radio station programmers sometimes used these charts to help determine which records they should be playing. The higher a song's position on the charts, the more radio programmers would pay attention. The more radio play, the higher the chart position. The result of this kind of horseplay was turntable hits, songs that were played on the radio a lot but did not sell.

PACKAGING & PACKAGING DEDUCTIONS

Record companies routinely deduct a certain amount of money from the income derived from sales for the cost of packaging records and CDs. They deduct up to 25 percent of the price on CDs for packaging, up to 20 percent for packaging on cassettes, and up to 15 percent for packaging LPs. Artists and producers will not receive royalties on the money that is deducted for these costs. If the price of a CD is $15.00, 25 percent of that price would be $3.75, which would be the packaging deduction. In my opinion this deduction is excessive and unjustifiable. Don't take my word for it; contact any CD manufacturer and ask for a quote for packaging on compact discs, including tray, jewel case and shrink-wrapping.

A jewel case is the case in which every CD is contained. The tray is the platform on which the CD rests. The booklet of course is the two (or more) page pamphlet that contains the information about the artist and the project. I have found that the average price of a jewel case is 21 cents per unit. The price of the tray, pamphlets and shrink-wrapping combined is an additional 16 cents per unit.

These prices are for small orders of 2,000 units or less. Major record companies usually order many times more than that amount, which means the price of packaging drops because of sheer volume.

CDs

$15.00	Basic price of CDs
-3.75	25% Packaging deduction
$11.25	**After packaging**

CASSETTES

$11.00	Retail price of Cassettes
-2.20	20% Packaging deduction
$8.80	**After packaging**

CLOSER TO REAL PACKAGING COSTS

$15.00	Retail price of CDs
-.37	Packaging cost
$14.63	**What artist should be paid on after packaging**
$11.00	Retail price of Cassettes
-.31	20% Packaging deduction
$10.69	**After packaging**

FREE GOODS

Free goods are defined by record companies as CDs, cassettes, and records the company gives away to record stores. Naturally, the artist will not receive royalties on these records. The truth about free goods is that they were devised as a way for record companies to make money on sales of records and at the same time not have to pay artists, producers, and publishers. The average deductions for free goods are 15 percent for CDs and cassettes, and 23 percent for singles. What this means is that for every 85 CDs or cassettes sold to a record store, an additional 15 are received as free goods.

Here's how it works. Artist royalties are based on the retail selling price. Record companies make their money based on the wholesale price. No matter what the record company charges a wholesaler, artist royalties are still based on the suggested *retail* price of the product.

Record companies inflate the wholesale price of records by 15 percent and pass along to wholesalers 15 records free for every 85 records the wholesaler buys. The wholesaler is still paying the same price for the same number of records, but since record companies don't pay royalties on free goods the artist does not receive royalties on the 15 records the wholesaler is supposedly getting for free.

Furthermore, most artists confuse the 15 percent free goods issue with the free goods that record companies give to record stores, radio stations, and television stations. Obviously there is a distinction. The free goods that labels give to stores for promotion, product visibility, and in-store airplay represents a further deduction of 5 to 10 percent from artist, producer, and publishing royalties.

GOODS SOLD TO THE MILITARY

Record companies sell records to the military at a price that is approximately 25% less than the price they charge domestic wholesalers. Artist and producer royalty rates on records sold to the military are usually the same as they are for foreign royalties. This means that artists and producers are paid less for records that are sold to the military. A large number of these sales also occur on

American military bases that are located outside of the United States, and the resulting royalties are calculated as foreign royalties.

FOREIGN ROYALTIES

Records sold outside of the borders of the United States are considered foreign sales. Royalties paid to producers and artists on records sold outside of the country are considered foreign royalties. In general, artists and producers get paid less for records sold outside of the United States than they do for records sold in the United States.

EUROPE

In Europe an artist and producer can expect to receive a royalty rate that is 60 to 75 percent of the royalty rate received in the United States. This means that if your royalty rate in the United States is based on 10 percent, you can expect to receive a royalty of 6 to 7.5 percent, or 2/3 of your domestic rate on records sold in Europe.

CANADA

For records sold in Canada, artists and producers can expect to receive a royalty rate based on up to 85 percent of the rate for records sold in the United States. If your royalty rate in the United States is 10 percent you can expect to receive a royalty rate of up to 8.5 percent in Canada.

THE REST OF THE WORLD

For records sold outside of Europe, the United States, and Canada artists and producers can expect to receive a royalty rate as low as 50 percent of the rate they are paid for records sold in the United States. These territories are referred to as the rest of the world in recording agreements.

COMPACT DISCS vs. CASSETTES

It used to be that the main format that records were sold in was vinyl and cassettes. Then CD technology was developed, and vinyl records have all but disappeared. Cassettes account for a little over thirty percent of sales compared to CDs. The calculation that is used to compute royalties paid to artists and producers overall is based on the suggested retail price of cassettes. The Retail price of a cassette is approximately $9.98, while the wholesale price is approximately $5.50 per unit. The average retail price for a compact disk is $15.00, while the wholesale price is approximately $10.00 per unit. As you can see the retail and wholesale price of CDs is much higher than that of cassettes. At a glance you would think that an artist or producer should earn fifty percent more income from a CD than from a cassette sale. However, royalties paid to artists and producers for the sale of compact disks is based on a complicated formula, which results in artists' and producers' royalty rates for CDs being approximately 110% of the cassette rate. What this means in plain English is that record companies enjoy a larger profit percentage on CDs than they do on cassettes. That larger profit margin is possible because even though the retail price of CDs is considerably higher than that of cassettes, record companies pay royalties on CDs at a rate that is only slightly higher than what they pay on cassettes.

Initially the justification was that there were no CD manufacturing plants in the US, and record companies needed to have a higher profit margin in order to offset the additional costs of having to import the CDs and because at that time CD manufacturing costs were at a premium. However, there are currently many CD manufacturing plants in the United States and record companies are enjoying a decrease in the manufacturing cost. So what happens to that extra money that should be going to the artist and producer now? It's simple — it's in the record companies' bank accounts.

CATALOG SALES

After the initial sales of a record have subsided, a record company will usually make that record available on a limited basis as what is refereed to as **catalog**. What this means is that the record company will reduce the price of that record as an incentive for consumers. Catalog items are usually priced at 65 to 80 percent of the suggested retail price of newly released records. Royalty rates on these records are usually based upon 75 percent of the royalty rate of that record when it was newly released. This is also referred to as a **midline** sales item. Such an item can no longer command a full retail price and the price has to be reduced in order for the item to continue to sell. There is a growing market for these records and the prices are increasing.

BUDGET ITEMS

When a record company feels the only way to sell off existing inventory of a record is to sell it at rock bottom prices, it refers to these records as budget items. The trick here is to negotiate how long after an initial release a record company must wait until they have the right to offer that record as a budget item. Royalties on budget items can be as low as 50 percent or even 0 percent of the base royalty rate. 0 percent means there will be no royalties paid on those items.

Psychologically there is nothing more embarrassing for artists than to walk into a record store and find their albums in the budget bin of that store for the low, low price of 99 cents

RECORD CLUB SALES

People who buy records from record clubs buy those records at a discounted price. Some record clubs require a one-time joining fee and others require the new member to commit to a buying a certain number of records within a certain period of time. That is one way they make their money. The other way they make money is from the records they sell to their customers.

Royalties paid on record club sales are calculated at one-half the net income the record company receives for licensing that record to a record club. Record clubs also receive an unusually high number of free goods, and unfortunately they do not yield royalties for artists or producers.

COMPILATION ALBUMS

Compilation albums are albums that contain the recordings of many different artists. You've seen the television commercials for "Disco Hits of The Seventies." What is being advertised is called a compilation album. Royalties paid on recordings contained on a compilation album are usually based on 50 percent of the net income the record company receives for licensing that song or songs from the company that releases the compilation album.

Royalties are also contingent upon how many songs are contained on that album. For ease of figuring let's say the album contained ten selections, and it contained one of your songs. You would get paid on one-tenth of the entire album. This method of calculation is called Pro-rata. It is a good idea to negotiate a limit on the number of songs and number of compilation albums your material can be used on over a specified period of time. In other words, you may not want to have ten of your songs appearing on ten different compilation albums in a given year.

DUETS

Duets is a term loosely used in the recording industry. Normally a duet is a performance of two persons on the same song. In the recording industry it is referred to as two or more artists on the same song. The easiest way to split the royalties from such a performance is to split them equally between each artist. If one of the duet partners is a group, that group's share of the artist royalties should be considered that of one artist.

CALCULATING RECORD ROYALTIES

Record companies know that there are thousands of new acts just dying for a chance at the big time. I'll paint the picture for you. An act has been training for years to develop its skills to the point where they can get the attention of someone who can help them get a record deal and finally that day comes. The act signs with a record label, records a project and embarks on an exciting promotional tour. It receives rave reviews and fans love the act everywhere it goes. They have finally made it. At least they think they have made it.

CALCULATING BASIC ARTISTS ROYALTIES

Have you ever wondered how an artist is paid? Here's a fairly accurate example. Remember artist's royalties are base on the retail selling price of cassettes, and CDs are based on a price just slightly high than that of cassettes. For ease of calculation and demonstration lets use the cassette royalty rate. Let's see how it works.

$9.98	Average retail price of cassettes
- 1.45	15% Packaging deduction
8.53	
- .99	10% of $9.98 deduction for free goods
$7.54	Amount artists royalties are really based on

$7.54	Amount artists royalties are really based on
x .12	Artist royalty rate
.90	Artist royalty per unit

Lets take this demonstration further and show what an artist will make if their record were to go gold (sells 500,000 units).

$ .90	Artist royalty per unit
x 500,000.00	Number of units sold
$450,000.00	Artist royalty before deductions

As you can see from the above number an artist stands to gain a substantial amount of income if their recording sales reach 500,000 units. But before the artist is paid, record companies will deduct certain expenses that greatly impact the amount of the actual artist royalties. Here is an example of standard deductions that record companies take from the artist royalties.

$450,00	Artist royalty before deductions
-$200,00	Recording cost
-$75,000	50% deduction for two videos
	(costing $75,000 each)
- $100,000	Tour support*
- $ 75,000	Independent promotion 50% of actual cost
- $ 10,000	Independent publicist 50% of actual cost
- $ 5,000	Retail marketing 50% of actual cost
-$ 15,000	Actual artist royalty if they are lucky

(*Artist must tour to help increase record sales. They must be able to pay band and road expenses. therefore they take a loan from record company)

The actual artist royalty does not reflect the 35% of total royalties due the artist that the record company will hold back as reserves. If we add in that number to the equation the picture changes dramatically.

$-15,000	Artist royalty after deductions
$-157,500	Reserves held by record company
$-172,500	Artist account with record company until reserves are liquidated.

THE SOPHOMORE ATTEMPT

As if the above mentioned numbers are not enough to discourage you, let's take a trip into the future when our act will begin to record their second album. The record company is telling the artists that everything looks good and that they are right on course and they feel good about the success of the first album. The executive is implying that they have laid down some solid ground work, and although the record company has not had the kind of sales they had hoped for on the first album, they are still behind the act and looking forward to building on the sales base they have already established. The artists agree because they are hypnotized by all the attention they are receiving from their public and the press.

Reality check time!

Take the outstanding negative balance from the first album, which is $172,500, which now appears on the act's account, and add to that a recording budget of $250,000 for the second album. The account will reflect a balance of -$422,500.

-$172,500	Artist negative balance from first album
-$250,000	Recording budget for second album
-$100,000	Two Videos for second album
-$100,000	Tour support
-$622,500	New unrecouped artist account before release of the second album.

By the time an act has recorded their sophomore attempt, they are beginning to wise up and realize they are not raking in the kinds of dollars they expected. Not only are they not having the kind of financial success they had anticipated, but in most cases, they find themselves in a financial crisis.

WHAT EVERY ARTIST SHOULD DO

There are certain exercises every artist and manager should go through before signing a recording contract. Every artist has the right to know how much money they are likely to make from record sales. Most artists and managers are so happy to have a contract they don't consider the reality of the situation. And that reality is that under the above circumstances most artists will never see a royalty check.

Any manager worth being involved with should get together with the artist and calculate how much money the artist will make at each level of sales. The wise manager will explain to the artist that nine out of every ten artists never have success. This heart-to-heart talk will educate the artist about what he is getting into before the contract is signed. Artists at this early point in their careers must understand that the manager will most likely have nothing to lose because they get paid as soon as you sign the recording contract.

Those of you who are artists and don't have managers should consult with an accountant for an hour or two. Ask the accountant to help you figure out how much you will make if your record sells the following number of units:

100,000 units
300,000 units
500,000 units
750,000 units
1,000,000 units

Ask the accountant to figure out how much a label would make ands how much your manager would realize.

The good news is, if your records reach sales of over 750,000 units, you will start to receive artist royalties, unless you have taken advances that will keep you in the un-recouped position.

The bad news is most artist's records do not reach sales of anywhere near 750,000 units and therefore 95 percent of all artists who have records released never receive a royalty check.

WHAT IS AN AUDIT?

Audit (ô dit) n. 1. An examination of records or financial accounts to check their accuracy. 2. An adjustment or correction of accounts. (The American Heritage College Dictionary)

If you are fortunate enough to have recorded an album as a producer or artist, and that album has sold well and all expenses that were associated with the recording of that album have been recouped, you should be receiving record or producer royalties. If the recording costs have not been paid back, then you will not receive record royalties until they are. Record royalties are paid to the artist and producer royalties to the producer. Both are paid by the record company. (For more information on record royalties see the "Record Royalties" chapter.) If you are receiving record or producer royalties, chances are there are some inaccuracies in your royalty statements (the outline of how you are to be paid that accompanies your royalty checks). These inaccuracies are almost always in favor of the record label, and therefore, result in the artist or producer not receiving the full amount of payment that they should. Unfortunately, royalty statements issued by record labels don't contain enough information to enable an artist or producer to easily detect these inaccuracies and for that reason they go largely unde-tected. Record companies keep detailed records of how much money they make and how much money they owe artists or pro-ducers. These records are what an accountant would need to review in order to determine if mistakes have been made that would result in the artist or producer receiving less royalties than they should. Some record companies have reputations for not paying royalties at all or paying them on a schedule that is later than what is stipulat-ed in the contract.

Although it is a well known fact that most record companies make mistakes in their accounting, most inexperienced artists and pro-ducers think that if they run an audit, the record company will view this as an antagonistic gesture. Sometimes it is antagonistic, but at all times it is business as usual.

It's the same as if you found that bank personnel were siphoning money from your bank account and storing it away for their per-sonal use. You would not hesitate to take the necessary legal action to rectify the situation, would you? After confirming with your accountant that in fact, you had been taken advantage of by the bank, you probably would not give much thought to whether or not they were upset with you about your findings. The same kind of thinking should be applied to money that might be owed to you by a record company, a publisher, or production company.

AN INTERESTING STORY

I have a friend who is a well known recording artist and has writ-ten and recorded quite a few hits. At some point in his career he decided he needed a break and because he was at the end of his contract with the label he decided not to negotiate a new deal. About two years before the release date of this book he decided to run an audit on the well known record company for which he recorded most of his hits. The result was that the record company had conveniently neglected to pay him a few hundred thousand dollars in royalties. As you can imagine, my friend wasted no time in demanding payment of those royalties to which he was rightful-ly entitled. The record company did agree that they owed some of those royalties but chose to interpret key clauses in the original contract in their favor. Thus, they claimed to owe the artist less than what the artist's audit reflected.

This was not an unusual position for the record company or the artist who had commissioned an audit. My friend at that time had two options: either sue the label or negotiate a compromise. He chose the latter and, ironically, ended up negotiating himself into a new recording contract with the label. One of the highlights of that contract was that he received a hefty advance from the label equal to the amount the record company owed him in unpaid royalties, and another advance that equaled the typical advance an artist of his stature would receive. I last saw my friend at a restaurant in Marina Del Rey, California and asked him when he was planning to record his next album. He replied with a wry smile that he was still on an extended vacation and had no idea when he would commence recording a new album. End of story. What had in fact happened was that the record company, rather than pay the artist outright the money that was rightfully his, elected to disguise the situation in order to save themselves the public embarrassment that could have resulted had that information found its way to the media.

ANOTHER TRUE AND FASCINATING STORY

I recently requested an audit of a record label with which I had enjoyed great success with quite a few artists, as a producer and songwriter. I contacted a well known audit accountant and asked him what the chances were that he would recover a substantial amount of unpaid royalties from the label. He replied there was a 95 percent chance that there would be a substantial windfall of royalties owed to me. Armed with the confidence of that information, I decided to have the him proceed with the audit.

A few weeks passed and my accountant called to say the record company would only allow him to audit two years, as was specified in my contract. He suggested that because I had such a positive relationship with the record company, I should call my contacts in the legal department and ask that they waive the two-year audit clause. I placed the call. During that conversation I could sense that my legal affairs contact at the record company was feeling a little uncomfortable with the position I had put him in. On one hand, he knew that if he refused to waive the two-year audit clause contained in my original contract, I would become suspicious and wonder what the record company had to hide. At the same time, he was concerned about preserving my relationship with the label. On the other hand, he was bound by his duty to his job to protect the record company.

He hemmed, he hawed, he yawned and he squirmed as he became even more uncomfortable. (I could tell that my years of knowing this executive were wearing on him.) I had already been with the label when he was hired and we had become friendly, so I gave him a break. He said he needed to think about it some more and would call me back. He called back in a few days, after obviously discussing my request with his superiors, and said they would prefer that I run a less detailed desk audit. I knew a desk audit would not yield the necessary details to allow my accountant to come to any conclusions in my favor. I also knew at that moment I had to stand firm or lose ground. I stood my ground and pressed for a full audit. He made it perfectly clear that while the company would not deny me a full audit, they would not be happy about it. I had won. My accountant would be allowed to run the full audit.

I cared for my friend and knew that my victory had been a defeat for him. I asked him why they did not want me to run a full audit. His answer was very amusing. He said that in the event the results of my audit showed that the record company owed me a considerable amount of money, that money would have to come out of an account that was used to pay the record company's employees bonuses. In other words, the "miscalculations" sometimes end up fattening the pockets of record company employees. My friend added that it was unfair to the current employees who were not working at the company at the time the miscalculations had occurred, because the new employees had nothing to do with the accounting mistakes of the past. But, they would suffer the penalty by receiving smaller bonuses. While I understood his position, I could not allow myself to feel sorry for them. I am currently in the midst of a full audit of that label.

MOST ARTISTS DON'T AUDIT

Record companies benefit financially because most artists don't audit. Most of the time when a record company is audited, discrepancies are found in favor of the artist, producer or publisher. I would suggest that every artist selling a million or more units should develop a relationship with an accountant that specializes in running audits. The most important thing to understand about auditing a record company is that if you don't audit them, you are almost sure to be giving away money that should be in *your* bank account.

TWO YEAR AUDIT CLAUSES

It is customary for record companies to insert provisions in their agreements with producers, artists and publishers that limit how far back an artist, producer or publisher will be allowed to audit. This provision usually comes in the form of a two year audit clause. In everyday English, this means you can only check the record company's books as far back as two years from the date of the commencement of the audit. This, of course, is always in the record company's favor because, if the bulk of your income was earned more than two years prior to running the audit, you're out of luck.

ACCOUNTANTS THAT SPECIALIZE IN AUDITS

Audit accountants based in New York and Los Angeles charge between $175 and $225 per hour. They, like lawyers, managers and business managers, should be interviewed for the job. The same list of questions that you would ask a manager or lawyer also apply when interviewing an audit accountant. She should have at least three to five years of experience dealing with record companies and publishers. The best case is when your auditor has worked in the royalty department of a record company or publisher. This experience gives her insight into the "creative" accounting methods of these companies.

THE ACCOUNTANT'S COMPENSATION

There are a number of ways in which an audit accountant can be paid. They include flat rates, contingency payment plans, percentage of what is recovered, retainer and some combination of all of the above. Again, the same negotiations one would have with an attorney should occur when hiring an audit accountant. There are no written rules. The object is to get the auditor to do the best job for the most reasonable amount of compensation. The best arrangement for an artist, producer or publisher who can't afford to retain an accountant is the contingency plan. I will list how each plan works below.

CONTINGENCY PAYMENTS

Audits can be expensive, with the cost ranging anywhere from $5,000 to $30,000. So, before you run out in to the streets shouting, "They owe me money!", take the time to consult with your audit specialists. Accountants who specialize in audits get paid in a number of ways. A contingency plan is most effective, as the auditor gets paid a percentage of the money she finds. This way you pay no out-of-pocket cash. The usual percentage provided in a contingency plan is twenty (20%).

FLAT RATES

Some situations may call for a flat fee. This will be the case when the accountant is not sure that the contingency plan would fairly compensate her for the amount of time and effort required to do a good job. This, like any other flat fee, can be negotiated.

PERCENTAGES AND CONTINGENCIES

There are also times when a combination of contingency and percentages is appropriate. I guess you could call this the middle ground. This combination plan usually occurs when the accountant feels there is a real chance she will find substantial miscalculations but also wants a guarantee of a minimum fee for her work.

Desk Audits And Full Audits

THE DESK AUDIT

The less detailed desk audit is almost always preferred by the record company because it provides minimum information. A desk audit is generally less costly and less disruptive to the record company's accounting and legal departments than a full audit. A desk audit really should be thought of as a preliminary audit, because an accountant will be able to figure out if you are being paid on the proper royalty rates. In some situations, a desk audit will lead to a full audit if gross miscalculations are found in the royalty rates.

THE FULL AUDIT

A full audit takes more time than a desk audit because it entails more research into the record company's books. An experienced accountant knows what to look for in the record company's books. She will know the accounting habits of each of the companies. She will recognize inconsistencies in royalty rates and be able to tell how much of a discrepancy exists.

There are some practices that are almost standard in record companies that take money away from the artist. In most cases, if an audit is performed and reveals discrepancies in the amount of royalties that were paid and royalties that should have been paid to an artist, producer or publisher, the record company will dispute the validity of the findings and will want to negotiate the amount of the discrepancy. The record company will attempt to justify the need for further negotiations around the amount of unpaid royalties by its interpretation of the original recording agreement. Most recording contracts contain loopholes that can work for either the record company or the artist, producer or publishers. The record company will cite these loopholes and naturally interpret them in its favor. For all practical purposes you will be in yet another negotiating stance.

Foreign sales, free goods, paid at source, foreign tax benefits, miscalculated royalty rates, performance thresholds, statutory rates, goods sold to the military — these are all areas that are vulnerable to miscalculations of royalties that should be paid.

Artists beware!

CONTRACTS
&
CONTRACT EXPLANATORY
NOTES

This chapter contains three contracts. They include a Co-publishing Agreement, which could serve as an agreement between a writer and a publisher. There is a Production Contract, which would serve as an agreement between a production company and an artist. And finally, there is a Recording Agreement, which would be entered into by a record company and an artist. In addition, each contract has explanatory notes that are written in plain English, and can be found on the pages following each contract.

The main function of this chapter is to give the reader a chance to become familiar with these types of agreements, and therefore, enhance his ability to understand the issues that make up such an agreement. You will notice that all three contracts have some things in common: a preamble, a place for signatures, and terms. As your career progresses you will most likely negotiate and enter into a number of these agreements with various companies, and will notice that most contracts are very similar in form.

EXPLANATORY NOTES

We have done our best to make the explanatory notes to each contract as easy to understand as possible. However, let us offer a word of caution to first time readers of these type of documents: Some of these concepts will seem foreign to you and may be difficult to grasp upon first reading. Don't be intimidated. It's similar to riding a bike for the first few times. You ride a few feet and you fall off, but you don't get hurt. The next time you ride you will be able to ride a little farther before your ride is interrupted with another fall. You get the point. The more you practice riding the more confidence you will have in your ability to ride, and soon you'll be as proficient a rider as you want to be.

Following each agreement contained in this chapter is a brief explanation of the most important issues contained in these documents. Gary and I decided that it would be most useful to include provisions which would normally be obtained as a result of negotiation, as opposed to what you might expect to receive as a first draft. Of course, the final contract you may actually receive will vary depending upon your leverage in a given situation, and the policies of the company with whom you are negotiating at the time. Actual dollar figures and royalty rates have been purposely omitted from the contracts because it is impossible to determine what a given deal will be worth. However, we will give you some idea of the range of those figures in the explanatory notes that follow each contract. For your easy reference, each note has the same paragraph number as the clause in the contract to which it pertains.

IMPORTANT NOTE

The information contained in this book and in its audio version is based on the experiences of the authors and may not apply in all situations. The authors and publishers assume no responsibility for any action taken based on the information contained in this book. Further, **any use of the contracts or other material provided here should only be done after consulting an expert music industry attorney.**

Sample of a
Co-Publishing Agreement
&
Co-Publishing
Explanatory Notes

Co-Publishing Agreement

Agreement made this __this day of _____, 199_, between
_____ doing business as _____ Music
(BMI/ASCAP), _____, ("you", below), and
_____ ("Publisher" below).

1. PARTIES.

1.01. You are sometimes called the "Artist" below. All references below to "you and the Artist", and the like, will be understood to refer to you alone.

2. DEFINITIONS

2.01. "Person" - Any natural person, legal entity, or other organized group of persons or entities. (All pronouns, whether personal or impersonal, which refer to Persons include natural persons and other Persons.)

2.02. "Affiliate" - Any Person which you or the Artist own or control, or in which you or the Artist hold any interest. You warrant and represent that Schedule 1 contains a complete list of all Affiliates and a description of the relationship which constitutes each Affiliation.

2.03. "Term" - of this agreement - the period prescribed in paragraph 3.01, as it may be extended under paragraph 3.02, or the period prescribed in paragraph 3.03, as it may be extended under paragraph 3.04, as the case may be.

2.04. "Territory" - the universe.

2.05. "Defined Compositions" - the following:

2.05.(a) "Old Defined Compositions" - That portion of all musical compositions now owned, controlled or administered by you, the Artist, or any Affiliate, in whole or in part.

2.05.(b) "New Defined Compositions" - That portion of all musical compositions wholly or partly written by you, the Artist, or any Affiliate during the Term of this agreement.

2.05.(c) "Acquired Defined Compositions" - That portion of all musical compositions (other than New Defined Compositions) in which you, the Artist, or any Affiliate acquire any ownership, control or administration interest during the Term.

2.06. "Qualifying Side", "Album", "Qualifying Album".

2.06.(a) "Qualifying Side" - (1) A newly recorded recording, not less than two and one-quarter (2-1/4) minutes in playing time, of the Artist's performance of a New or Old Defined Composition. Repetitions of a composition on the same Record (including recordings of more than one arrangement or version of it) will be considered, collectively, one Qualifying Side.

2.06.(a.2) A recording is not a Qualifying Side, if:

2.06.(a.2.i) Anyone (other than Publisher or another record company under contract for the Artist's exclusive recording services if such contract grants a mechanical license to the record company on terms no less favorable to the Artist than the terms contained in a standard controlled composition mechanical license clause) has been granted a license to use the composition on phonorecords in the United States at royalty rates or on any other terms more favorable the licensee than those applicable to compulsory licenses under the U.S. Copyright law; or

2.06.(a.2.ii) the composition is an arrangement or adaptation of a composition in the public domain.

2.06.(a.3.i) "Outside Interest", in this section 2.06(a)(3), means an interest owned by anyone else (i.e., anyone except Publisher and you) in the income earned from the exploitation of a Defined Composition.

2.06.(a.3.ii)   If anyone owns an Outside Interest in a Defined

Composition, a recording of it which would otherwise be a Qualifying Side will be treated under subparagraph 2.06(c) as a fractional portion of Qualifying Side, calculated on the basis of the same proportionate relationship as that between the interest owned jointly by Publisher and you and the aggregate of the Outside Interests. (For example: If Outside Interests amount in the aggregate to a one-third ownership interest in the composition, a recording of it which would otherwise be a Qualifying Side will constitute two-thirds of a Qualifying Side for the purposes of subparagraph 2.06.(c).)

2.06.(a.3.iii) If any Outside Interests apply in differing quantitative amounts to particular rights in a composition, the highest aggregate of the Outside Interests in any such right will be treated as the amount of the Outside Interest in that composition for the purposes of subparagraph 2.06(c). (For example: If a composition is subject to a one-half Outside Interest in respect of the right of reproduction in motion pictures and a one-third Outside Interest otherwise, a recording of it which would otherwise be a Qualifying Side will constitute one-half of a Qualifying Side under subparagraph 2.06.(c).)

2.06.(b) "Album" - one or more twelve-inch 33 1/3 rpm records, or the equivalent, at least thirty-five (35) minutes long in playing time, sold in a single package. ("Album" also means the recordings constituting a particular Album release, when appropriate in context.)

2.06.(c) "Qualifying Album" - an Album containing whichever of the following is more:

2.06.(c.1) Eight (8) Qualifying Sides, or

2.06.(c.2) Qualifying Sides constituting, in number (i.e., rather than in playing time), recordings of at least eighty percent (80%) of the total number of compositions recorded in the Album.

2.07. "Licensees" - includes, without limitation, wholly or partly owned subsidiaries, divisions or affiliates of Publisher, and Subpublishers.

2.08. "Subpublisher" - A Person authorized by Publisher, directly or indirectly, to administer and act as a publisher of one or more Defined Compositions on a general basis and grant rights in them to users or other Subpublishers, in a particular territory. Persons who administer particular rights only and do not assume general responsibility for exploiting the composition(s) concerned, such as performance and mechanical right licensing organizations, are not Subpublishers.

2.09. "Writers' Share" of public performance income - A portion of non-dramatic public performance income, expressly designated as a writers' share by the licensing organization which administers the performing rights concerned and paid directly by it to the Writers.

2.10. "Records" and "Phonograph Records" - Reproductions of sound alone or sound coupled with visual images, in all forms known now or in the future, manufactured or distributed primarily for home use, school use, juke box use, or use in means of transportation.

2.11. "Delivery" - when used with respect to a Defined Composition, means:

2.11.(a) The actual receipt by Publisher at its offices of a 1/4 inch tape or digital audio tape (DAT) recording and lyric sheet of the composition concerned, executed assignments of copyright and authorizations in the form of the annexed Exhibits, and copies of all data and records relating to the copyrights in the composition and the interests of any co-writers, co-owners and other Persons interested in them, including without limitation all agreements with other writers, copyright registration certificates (if any), mechanical licenses, notices of use, correspondence, and demonstration records; and

2.11.(b) compliance with the requirements of paragraphs 5.02 and 10.02 related to delivery.

2.12. "Advance" - a prepayment of royalties. Publisher may recoup Advances from royalties to be paid to you or on your behalf pursuant to this or any other agreement regarding music publishing rights.

2.13.(a) "Gross Income" -

2.13.(a.1) Uses in the United States: all monies earned and actually received by Publisher in the United States, or credited to Publisher's account against a prior advance actually received by Publisher in the United States, as compensation for uses of Defined Compositions in the United States.

2.13.(a.2) Uses outside the United States: all Income at Source. "Income at Source" - The full amount of compensation for uses of Defined Compositions outside the United States received by Publisher or by the first Subpublisher who receives it from the user or from any other Person who is not a Subpublisher (i.e., from a licensing and collection agency or other Person who receives such compensation from users and remits it to Publisher or to a Subpublisher). Income at Source includes all monies retained or charged by Subpublishers, but does not include any monies retained or charged by licensing or collection agencies or by other Persons who are not Subpublishers.

2.13.(b) "Net Income" - Gross Income, less all taxes, amounts deductible by Publisher under this agreement, including but not limited to costs in connection with copyright registration, arranging costs, costs of preparation and distribution of demonstration records and lead sheets, costs of collecting income, fees of trustees or collecting agents for the licensing of compositions, all expenses (including reasonable legal fees and expenses) incurred by Publisher in connection with any claim or suit brought by or against Publisher concerning Defined Compositions (other than those fully reimbursed under Article 10), and all other out-of-pocket direct expenses incurred by Publisher in connection with Defined Compositions and their exploitation. Expenses for salaries, rent and overhead will not be deducted.

2.14. "Cover Recording" - any recording of a composition used on Phonograph Records, other than recordings of the Artist's featured performances.

2.15. "Write" - when used with respect to musical compositions, means to write lyrics, compose music, arrange or adapt any composition, or do any other act of authorship or make any other creative contribution, alone or in collaboration.

2.16. "Commercial Release"; "Major Release"

2.16.(a) "Commercial Release" of Phonograph Records distribution by a record company throughout the United States on a top-line label of that company. The initial release or shipment date for Phonograph Record units established by the record company concerned will be treated as the date of initial Commercial Release for the purposes of this agreement.

2.16.(b) "Major Release" - Commercial Release by a major record company. (The major record companies are now Publisher, the WEA group, BMG, Capitol/EMI, MCA, Polygram, Geffen, Virgin, Giant, Charisma, SBK, A&M, Arista, Interscope, Morgan Creek, Chrysalis, Island and Zomba; provided, however, that if prior to entering into a recording agreement with a record company other than those listed above you inform Publisher in writing of the name of the record company, Publisher will notify you within ten (10) business days if in its good faith determination such record company will also be considered a major record company for purposes of this agreement.)

3. TERM

3.01.(a) The term of this agreement (the "Songwriter Term") will begin on the date of this agreement.

3.01.(b) The first contract period of the Songwriter Term will end on whichever of the following dates occurs later:

3.01.(b.1) The date thirty (30) days after you complete fulfillment of your Delivery Commitment (defined below) for that contract period in accordance with Article 3A; or

3.01.(b.2) The date one (1) year after the commencement of the Songwriter Term.

3.02. You grant Publisher three (3) separate options to extend the Songwriter Term for additional contract periods ("Songwriter Option Periods") on the same terms and conditions. Publisher may exercise each of those options by sending you a notice not later than the end of the contract period which is then in effect (the "Current Songwriter Contract Period"). If Publisher exercises such an option, the Songwriter Option Period concerned will begin upon the expiration of the Current Songwriter Contract Period.

3.03. Notwithstanding the foregoing in paragraphs 3.01 and 3.02 above, if you become a party to a recording agreement with a major U.S. record label (either directly or indirectly through an entity furnishing your exclusive recording services) during any contract period of the Songwriter Term (the "Recording Agreement"), then:

3.03.(a) The "Album Term" will commence and the Songwriter Term will terminate as of the effective date of the Recording Agreement.

3.03.(b) The first contract period of the Album Term will end thirty (30) days after whichever of the following dates is later:

3.03.(b.1) The date of initial Major Release of the first Qualifying Album released in a Major Release during that contract period or your notice to Publisher of that release date, whichever is later; or

3.03.(b.2) The fulfillment of all the following conditions: (i) The delivery of the next Qualifying Album recorded for Major Release to the record company entitled to release it Commercially (i.e. the Qualifying Album recorded after recording of the Qualifying Album referred to in section (1) above); (ii) your delivery to Publisher of that company's written confirmation of its acceptance of that Album for Commercial Release (or, in all events, your notice to Publisher of its actual Major Release); and (iii) your delivery to Publisher of a tape copy of that Album.

3.04.(a) You grant Publisher three (3) separate options (each, an "Album Term Option") to extend the Album Term for additional contract periods ("Album Option Periods") on the same terms and conditions. Publisher may exercise each of those options by sending you a notice not later than the end of the contract period which is then in effect (the "Current Album Contract Period").   If Publisher exercises such an option, the Album Option Period concerned will begin upon the expiration of the Current Album Contract Period.

3.04.(b) If Publisher does not exercise an option under subparagraph 3.04(a), the Defined Compositions in the Album referred to in section 3.03(b)(2) in connection with the contract period concerned (for example, the second Qualifying Album if Publisher does not exercise its option to extend the Term for the first Option Period) will not be subject to this agreement.   All other Defined Compositions will remain fully subject to this agreement in all events.

3.05. When the word "Term" is used herein below, it shall mean, collectively, the Songwriter Term and the Album Term, unless otherwise specified herein.

3.06.(a)   With respect to all Compositions which have been Commercially Exploited by Publisher ("Commercially Exploited" shall mean for purposes of this agreement, (1) Compositions which have generated Net Income in any way; (2) Compositions which have been licensed for exploitation and such licensing has generated Net Income; (3) Compositions which have been licensed for exploitation and Gross Income is in the "pipeline" on account of such licensing;   and (4) Compositions for which a Cover Recording has been obtained, during the Unexploited Song Retention Period (defined below), Publisher will retain the rights acquired by it under this agreement during the period beginning at the same time as the Term, and continuing perpetually for the life of the copyright, subject to the reversion of rights specified in subparagraph 3.06(b) below.

3.06.(b)   With respect to any Compositions not Commercially Exploited during the Unexploited Song Retention Period ("Unexploited Compositions"), Publisher will retain the rights acquired by it pursuant to paragraphs 4.01 and 4.02 of this agreement during the period beginning at the same time as the Term, and continuing until the date that is the later of two (2) years after the end of the Term and then continuing further until the next April 30th or October 31st, whichever is earlier, or the date when your royalty account under this agreement is in a fully recouped position (i.e., there are no outstanding Advances or other amounts recoupable from your royalties), according to your semi-annual royalty accounting statement ("Unexploited Song Retention Period"). Publisher will sign any and all assignments of copyright or other documents relating to Unexploited Compositions as you shall reasonably request in connection with the foregoing, and Publisher hereby appoints you as its attorney-in-fact for the sole purpose of executing such documents in the event Publisher fails to so execute within ten (10) business days after your written request.

3A. DELIVERY COMMITMENT

3A.01.(a) During each contract period of the Songwriter Term you will Write and Deliver to Publisher at least _____ (__) New Defined Compositions meeting the requirements prescribed in paragraph 3A.02 below (the "Delivery Commitment").

3A.01.(b) At least _____ (_) of the compositions Written in fulfillment of your Delivery Commitment will be Delivered within the first _____ (_) months of the contract period concerned (the "initial Delivery"). The balance of your Delivery Commitment for that Period will be fulfilled within six months after the initial Delivery or one year after the commencement of that contract period, whichever ends earlier.

3A.02.(a) No composition will apply in fulfillment of your Delivery Commitment unless it is accepted as satisfactory to Publisher in its good faith judgment for commercial exploitation. Each composition will be deemed accepted unless Publisher notifies you otherwise within forty-five (45) days after the completion of its Delivery. Any unsatisfactory composition will remain fully subject to Publisher's rights under this agreement. If any composition not accepted as satisfactory generates Net Income during the Term it will apply in reduction of your Delivery Commitment for the first contract period in which such income is earned, at your request.

3A.02.(b) Subject to the following sentence, no composition will apply in fulfillment of your Delivery Commitment unless it is entirely new, original, and copyrightable. Without limiting the generality of the preceding sentence: (1) No composition derived in any way from any other composition wholly or partly Written by the Writer will apply; and (2) No composition derived from a composition in the public domain will apply, unless ASCAP or BMI accords full credit for performances of it, equivalent to the credit accorded for performances of entirely new and original works; in which case the composition will apply in fulfillment of your Delivery Commitment as a portion of a composition, such apportionment to be based on the same ratio as used by ASCAP or BMI in determining the performance credit.

3A.02.(c)   No composition will apply in fulfillment of your Delivery Commitment if anyone has been granted a license to use it on phonorecords in the United States at royalty rates or on any other terms more favorable to the licensee than those applicable to compulsory licenses under the U.S. Copyright Law; provided, however, that if any such composition is licensed at a mechanical royalty rate less than the prevailing statutory mechanical royalty rate, it will be treated under paragraph 3A.01 as a fractional portion of a composition calculated on the basis of the same proportionate relationship as that between the mechanical royalty rate payable under the applicable "Controlled Composition" clause and the statutory mechanical royalty rate.

3A.03.(a)   If anyone else (i.e., anyone except Publisher and you) owns an interest in the income earned from the exploitation of a composition which is otherwise applicable in reduction of your Delivery Commitment ("Outside Interest", below), it will be treated under paragraphs 3A.01 and 6.03(b) as a fractional portion of a composition, calculated on the basis of the same proportionate relationship as that between the interest owned jointly by Publisher and you and the aggregate of the Outside Interests. (For example: If Outside Interests amount in the aggregate to a one-third ownership interest in the composition, it will constitute two-thirds of a composition for the purposes of paragraphs 3A.01 and 6.03(b).)

3A.03.(b) If any Outside Interests apply in differing quantitative amounts to particular rights in a composition, the highest aggregate of the Outside Interests in any such right will be treated as the amount of the Outside Interest in that composition for the purposes of paragraph 3A.01. (For example: If a composition described in section 3A.O2(b)(1) is subject to a one-half Outside Interest in respect of the right of reproduction in motion pictures and a one-third Outside Interest otherwise, it will be treated as one-half of a composition under paragraph 3A.01.)

4. RIGHTS GRANTED

4.01. <u>Assignment of Joint Interest</u> You assign to Publisher an undivided fifty percent (50%) share of your interest in all Defined Compositions, the copyrights in them and all renewals and extensions of those copyrights, all claims and causes of action related to any Defined Compositions accrued or accruing at any time, and all other rights in Defined Compositions, throughout the Territory and perpetually. All references to Compositions in this paragraph include their titles, words and music, all arrangements, adaptations and versions of them, and all other works derived from them. You will execute and deliver to Publisher such instruments of transfer and other documents regarding the rights of Publisher in Defined Compositions as Publisher may reasonably request to carry out the purposes of this agreement (including, without limitation, instruments in the form of Exhibits A, B, and C) and Publisher may sign such documents in your name or the name of the Artist and make appropriate disposition of them.

4.02. <u>Administration.</u> Publisher and its Licensees will have the exclusive rights, throughout the Territory and perpetually, to:

4.02.(a)   Exploit and authorize others to exploit Defined Compositions by any method and in any medium known now or in the future, including, without limitation, exploitation by broadcast and other public performances, the manufacture, distribution and sale of Phonograph Records, and use in motion pictures and other audiovisual works.

4.02.(b)   Administer and grant rights and licenses in Defined Compositions and under copyrights in them.

4.02.(c)   Publish and sell printed editions of Defined Compositions.

4.02.(d)   Collect all monies now payable or becoming payable with respect to Defined Compositions, including all performance royalties payable by the American Society of Composers, Authors and Publishers (ASCAP), Broadcast Music Inc. (BMI), or any other performing rights licensing organization, but excluding any Writers' Share of public performance income.   If a public performance is not licensed by a licensing organization but is licensed directly by Publisher, all income Publisher receives under it will be deemed Gross Income.

4.02.(e)   Make derivative works based on any Defined Compositions, and arrange, adapt, and change any Defined Compositions in any manner.

4.02.(f) Administer the Defined Compositions and the copyrights in them, act as the publisher of them, and exercise all rights in them as fully as if Publisher was the sole owner of the Defined Compositions and those copyrights.

4.02.(g) Notwithstanding the foregoing in this paragraph 4.02, it is hereby agreed and understood that Publisher's exercise of its rights hereunder shall be subject to the following conditions:

4.02.(g.1) Publisher shall not license synchronization rights for any Defined Composition in connection with a television and/or radio commercial without your prior consent.

4.02.(g.2) In the event that Artist intends to record any Defined Composition hereunder as a musical artist, Artist shall notify Publisher in writing of such intent upon delivery of said Composition to Publisher hereunder. Publisher shall put a "hold" (as that term is commonly understood in the music publishing industry) on such Composition and shall not grant a "first use" mechanical license for same to any other person or entity during the next six (6) months without Artist's prior written consent. If prior to the expiration of such six (6) month "hold" period, Artist decides that he will not record such Composition, Artist shall promptly notify Publisher thereof and the aforesaid mechanical licensing restriction will be deemed lifted.

4.02.(g.3) Publisher shall not make or authorize any fundamental changes to the words, music and/or title of any Composition here-under (except authorizing foreign translations) without Artist's prior written consent; provided, however, that any changes to the words and/or music of any Composition in a third party musical arrangement resulting from any change not authorized in a mechanical license granted by Publisher voluntarily in the ordi-nary course of business or involuntarily as a result of the compul-sory mechanical license provisions of the U.S. Copyright Act shall not be deemed to be a violation of this provision.

4.02.(g.4) Publisher will not, without your prior consent (which consent will be deemed given if you have not notified Publisher of your objection within ten (10) business days after Publisher has notified you of the proposed use), authorize the use in the United States of Defined Compositions in "X" or "NC-17" rated motion pictures. Publisher may refrain from exploiting or exercising rights in Covered Compositions in its sole discretion.

4.03. <u>Power of Attorney.</u>   You and the Artist hereby irrevocably appoint Publisher your attorney in fact, for the term of each copyright in a Defined Composition and each renewal and exten-sion of such a copyright, to secure and renew the copyrights in the Defined Compositions for Publisher's benefit and yours (as the respective interests of the parties may appear), to prosecute and compromise any claims or actions with respect to Defined

Compositions (including but not limited to claims or actions against infringers of any rights in them), and to execute, in your name and the name of the Artist or any Affiliate, any documents and instruments Publisher deems advisable for those purposes or to evidence Publisher's rights in Defined Compositions or other rights under this agreement.   That power is coupled with Publisher's interest in the Defined Compositions.   Publisher will have the right to apply for registration of claims to copyright in its name or otherwise at it deems appropriate.   Publisher will give you ten (10) days' notice before signing any document in your name.   Publisher may dispense with that waiting period when necessary, in Publisher's judgment, to protect or enforce its rights, but Publisher will notify you in each instance when it has done so.   Publisher will not be required to notify you before signing short form assignments of rights granted in this agreement for recordation in the Copyright Office.

4.05.   <u>Names and Likenesses.</u> Publisher and any Licensee of Publisher each shall have the right and may grant to others the right to reproduce, print, publish, or disseminate in any medium your name, the names, portraits, pictures and likenesses of the Artist and any other Writers of Defined Compositions   (including, without limitation, all professional, group, and other assumed or fictitious names used by them), and biographical material concerning them, as news or information, for the purposes of trade, or for advertising purposes (but not in connection with merchandise other than copies, phonorecords, and other reproductions of Defined Compositions).

4.05.1. Within sixty (60) business days after the execution hereof, you will supply Publisher with six (6) approved pictures of Artist and biographical material concerning Artist to be used by Publisher under paragraph 4.05 above. Your failure to comply with the preceding sentence shall not constitute a breach of this agreement.   In the event that Publisher disapproves of the approved pictures or biographical material supplied by you, Publisher will make available to you for your approval pictures (including portraits and likenesses) and biographical material concerning Artist to be used under paragraph 4.05 above.   Your approval will not be unreasonably withheld, and will be deemed given if you have been deemed to have approved the use of such pictures or biographical material under the terms of the Recording Agreement, and in all other instances such approval will be deemed given unless your notice of disapproval (including the reason) has been received by Publisher within five (5) days after the material has been made available to you. In the event that you timely disapprove of any pictures or biographical material, you will, within five (5) days of the date of your disapproval notice, supply to Publisher approved pictures and biographical material. In the event that the pictures or biographical material supplied by you, pursuant to the preceding sentence, are not satisfactory to Publisher or in the event that you do not supply the pictures or biographical material to Publisher pursuant to this paragraph 4.05.1, Publisher shall thereafter have the right to select and use such pictures and biographical material as it shall determine, in its sole discretion, and you shall have no approval rights in respect thereof. You may from time to time supply Publisher with more recent approved pictures or biographical material than in Publisher's possession at that time. If you do so, the procedures set forth in this paragraph shall apply. No inadvertent failure by Publisher to comply with this paragraph will constitute a breach of this agreement.

4.06. <u>Option to Purchase.</u> If you determine at any time to accept a bona fide offer to purchase all or any part of your interest in the Defined Compositions or any of them ("Third Party Offer"), you will first offer in writing to sell such interest to Publisher on the same terms (the "Second Offer"). The Second Offer will specify all of the terms of the Third Party Offer and the identity of the offeror. If Publisher does not accept the Second Offer within forty-five (45) days after its receipt you will have the right to accept the Third Party Offer, provided the sale to the third party is consummated within sixty-five (65) days after Publisher's receipt of the Second Offer, and on the same terms contained in the Second Offer. If that sale is not so consummated, Publisher's right of preemption under this paragraph will be reinstated automatically and you will not sell any part of your interest in any Defined Composition(s) without offering that interest to Publisher as provided in this paragraph. Publisher shall not be required, as a condition of accepting any

Second Offer, to agree to any terms or conditions which cannot be fulfilled by Publisher as readily as by any other Person.

5. DELIVERY: RELATED MATTERS

5.01.(a) <u>New Defined Compositions</u>.   You will Deliver each New Defined Composition to Publisher within ten (10) days after its completion.

5.01.(b) <u>Acquired Defined Composition</u> You will Deliver each Acquired Defined Composition to Publisher within ten (10) days after its acquisition.

5.02.(a) At the time of Delivery you will notify Publisher whether anyone else owns any interest in the Composition concerned, and whether or not there are in existence any adaptations or other versions of it, any other derivative works based on it, or any other work which it is derived from or based on; if so, you will furnish Publisher with such additional information regarding those matters as it may request.

5.02.(b) If any Defined Composition (or right in a Defined Composition) is jointly owned in unequal shares you will deliver to Publisher, simultaneously with the Delivery of the Composition concerned and the agreement required under paragraph 10.02, a declaration in the form of Exhibit D executed by each co-owner. If that declaration is not furnished Publisher will be entitled to rely conclusively on your advice regarding the extent of each co-ownership interest. Paragraph 10.07 will apply to any claim which is inconsistent with that declaration or advice.

5.03. You will notify Publisher promptly of the formation or acquisition of any Affiliate after the date of this agreement, and will promptly deliver to Publisher a counterpart of this agreement executed by that Affiliate in a manner satisfactory to Publisher. The execution and delivery of that counterpart will not relieve you of your obligations under this agreement.

6. ADVANCES: MINIMUM ANNUAL COMPENSATION

6.01. All monies paid by Publisher to or on behalf of you or the Artist during the Term of this agreement, other than royalties paid pursuant to Article 7, will constitute Advances.

6.02.(a) In connection with the commencement of the Songwriter Term, Publisher will pay you an Advance of $_____ payable as follows:

6.02.(a.1) $_____ promptly following execution of this agreement; and

6.02.(a.2) $_____ upon the latter of (i) the date six (6) months after the commencement of the Songwriter Term, or (ii) fulfillment of one-half (1/2) of your Delivery Commitment.

6.02.(b) If Publisher elects to exercise its first option under paragraph 3.02 above to extend the Songwriter Term, Publisher will pay you an Advance of $_____ in connection with exercising such option. If Publisher elects to exercise its second option to extend the Songwriter Term, Publisher will pay you an Advance of $_____ in connection with exercising such option. If Publisher elects to exercise its third option to extend the Songwriter Term, Publisher will pay you an Advance of $_____ in connection with exercising such option. Each Advance paid under this subparagraph 6.02(b) shall be payable as follows:

6.02.(b.1) one-half (1/2) of such Advance upon exercise of each applicable option; and
6.02.(b.2) the remaining one-half (1/2) of such Advance upon the date that is the later of (i) six (6) months after the exercise of such option, or (ii) fulfillment of one-half (1/2) of your applicable Delivery Commitment. In the event Publisher pays you the Album Term Advance (as defined in the following paragraph) prior to the payment of the remaining portion of any Advance under sections 6.02(a)(2) or 6.02(b)(2) above, Publisher will pay you the remaining portion of the Advance due under sections 6.02(a)(2) or 6.02(b)(2) concurrently with payment of the Album Term Advance.

6.03.(a) Promptly after execution of the Recording Agreement and commencement of the Album Term, Publisher will pay you an Advance of $_____ (the "Album Term Advance").

6.03.(b) In connection with each Qualifying Album recorded during the Album Term, Publisher will pay you an Advance in the applicable amount indicated below. (Such Albums are referred to in this paragraph 6.03 as "Advance-bearing Albums".)

6.03.(b.1) The amount of the Advance in connection with the first Advance-bearing Album will be $_____. This Advance will be paid promptly after the initial Major Release of such Advance-bearing Album.

6.03.(b.2) The amount of the Advance in connection with each Advance-bearing Album other than the first will be two-thirds (2/3) of whichever of the following amounts is less (subject to section 6.03(b)(3) below):

6.03.(b.2.i) The amount of the royalties credited to your account in respect of mechanical income earned in the United States under subparagraph 7.01(b) ("Mechanical Royalties") in connection with the Defined Compositions in the Advance-bearing Album whose initial Major Release has occurred most recently before the date of initial Major Release of the Album concerned, as shown by the last semi-annual royalty accounting statement rendered to you by Publisher before such latter date, and all mechanical "pipeline" monies; or

6.03.(b.2.ii)   the average of the amounts of such Mechanical Royalties and pipeline monies in connection with the Defined Compositions in the two Advance-bearing Albums whose initial Major Releases have occurred most recently before the initial Major Release of the Album concerned.

Publisher's estimate of so-called "pipeline" royalties in connection with those Defined Compositions (anticipated Mechanical Royalties earned in connection with Phonograph Records distributed in the United States but not yet payable to Publisher) will be treated as received for the purpose of calculating that Advance, provided you furnish Publisher with a current statement of net unit sales from the record company concerned.

6.03.(b.3) No Advance under section 6.03(b)(2) will be less than the applicable minimum or more than the applicable maximum specified below:

		Minimum	Maximum
6.03.(b.3.i)	Second Album:	$_____	$_____
6.03.(b.3.ii)	Third Album:	$_____	$_____
6.03.(b.3.iii)	Fourth Album:	$_____	$_____

6.03.(b.4) If your royalty account is not in a fully recouped position, including a credit for pipeline monies, (i.e., there are no outstanding Advances or other amounts recoupable from your royalty account) at the time of payment of the Album Advance in connection with the Second Album, such Advance will be reduced by the amount of such unrecouped balance, but in no event to less than $_____

6.03.(c) Each Advance payable under section 6.03(b) shall be payable as follows:

6.03.(c.1) Upon Publisher's exercise of each Album Term Option, Publisher will pay you one half (1/2) of the Advance payable in connection with the Advance-bearing Album recorded during the Album Option Period concerned; and

6.03.(c.2) The balance of such Advance payable promptly after the initial Major Release of such Album.

6.03.(d) If any Album which would otherwise be an Advance-bearing Album contains fewer than the number of Qualifying Sides required to constitute a Qualified Album under subparagraph 2.06(c), an Advance will be payable on that Album in the amount which would otherwise be payable on it under this Article 6, reduced in the proportion which the number of Qualifying Sides on it bears to the number of Qualifying Sides prescribed in subparagraph 2.06(c). (For example, if the Album concerned contains seven Qualifying Sides and the number of Qualifying Sides prescribed in subparagraph 2.06(c) is eight (8), the amount of the Advance payable on it under this paragraph 6.03 will be eighty-seven-and-one-half percent (87.5%) of the amount which would be payable on it if it constituted a Qualifying (and Advance-bearing) Album.

6.03.(e) If any Advance under paragraph 6.03 has been wholly or partly prepaid (under paragraph 6.02 or otherwise) and the Qualifying Album to which it is attributable has not been released in a Major Release within one (1) year after the prepayment, you will refund the prepayment to Publisher promptly upon its request.

6.03.(f) If any Composition delivered during the Songwriter Term is subsequently embodied on an Advance-bearing Album other than the first Qualifying Album (hereinafter referred to as a "Songwriter Recorded Composition"), then for purposes of reduction of the Advance otherwise due, a monetary value shall be assigned to each such Songwriter Recorded Composition as follows: the Advance made pursuant to paragraph 6.02 for the applicable contract period of the Songwriter Term in which such Songwriter Recorded Composition was originally delivered hereunder shall be multiplied by a fraction, the numerator of which shall be one (1), and the denominator of which shall be the total number of Composition(s) (including such Songwriter Recorded Compositions) delivered during the period of the Songwriter Term. The resulting amount shall be the "Monetary Value" for each such Songwriter Recorded Composition. Provided, however, that such reduction shall only occur in the event, and to the extent, that such Songwriter Recorded Compositions reduce the number of Compositions delivered during the applicable Songwriter Period below twelve (12). Without limitation of the foregoing and by way of example only, in the event that (A) twelve (12) Compositions were delivered, pursuant to paragraph 3A.01 herein, during the Initial Songwriter Period and (B) one (1) of those Compositions was subsequently embodied on an Album Commercially Released during any Album contract period other than the first Album contract period as "Songwriter Recorded Composition", then the Advance Payment specified in subparagraph 6.03(b) would be reduced by the sum of _____ Dollars ($_____) calculated as follows:

Compositions delivered during x $_____(Advance Initial Songwriter Period (12) paid in connection with the Initial Songwriter Period) = Monetary Value of each Songwriter Recorded Composition ($_____).

6.03.(g.1.i) In the event that during the Term hereof any Defined Composition is among the first twenty (20) songs in the principal weekly chart of best-selling "Adult Contemporary" songs in the United States published in BILLBOARD (i.e., the chart titled "Hot Adult Contemporary" during July 1991 or the chart corresponding most closely to those charts if they are re-titled or discontinued) and if you notify Publisher of that listing within ninety (90) days after the date of the issue of BILLBOARD in which it first appears, then Publisher will pay you an additional Advance of _____ Dollars ($_____) (the "Chart Advance") for each such Defined Composition.

6.03.(g.1.ii) Notwithstanding anything to the contrary contained in subsection 6.03(g)(1)(i) above, the Chart Advance shall only be payable once for each Defined Composition achieving the requisite chart position or certification, and each such Chart Advance shall be reduced proportionately if yours and Publisher's combined joint interest in any such Defined Composition is less than one hundred percent (100%) [e.g., if yours and Publisher's combined joint interest in the applicable Defined Composition equals fifty percent (50%), then the Chart Advance payable for such Defined Composition shall be $_____.

6.03.(g.2) In the event that during the Term hereof any Qualifying Album is certified "Gold" by the Recording Industry Association of America, then Publisher will pay you an additional Advance of $_____ for each such Defined Composition. In the event that such Defined Composition is certified "Platinum" by the Recording Industry Association of America, then Publisher will pay you an additional Advance of Five Thousand dollars ($_____) for each such Defined Composition.

6.03.(h) Publisher will also pay you an additional Advance (the "Equipment Advance") equal to fifty percent (50%) of the price paid by you for home studio equipment (the "Equipment") following your submission to Publisher of receipts or purchase orders of Equipment, provided, however, that such Advance shall in no event exceed $_____ (i.e., if the total price of Equipment was $_____). Prior to purchasing Equipment, you will submit to Publisher a list of Equipment that you propose to purchase and give Publisher a reasonable time to approve or disapprove such list. Publisher will not pay any Advance under this subparagraph 6.03(h) unless it approves the Equipment prior to your purchase thereof.

6.04. The aggregate amount of the compensation paid to you under this agreement will not be less than $9,000 for the first Fiscal Year, $12,000 for the second fiscal year, and $15,000 for each fiscal year thereafter.. "Fiscal Year" means the annual period beginning on the date of commencement of the term of this agreement, and each subsequent annual period during the term. If you have not received compensation of at least $6,000 under this agreement for a Fiscal Year, Publisher will pay you the amount of the deficiency before the end of that Fiscal Year; at least forty (40) days before the end of each Fiscal Year you will notify Publisher if each of you has not received such compensation and of the amount of the deficiency. Each such payment will constitute an Advance and will be applied in reduction of all monies payable to you under this agreement. Publisher may not withhold or require you to repay any such payment under any other provision of this agreement. If the term of this agreement ends before the last day of a Fiscal Year, the sums referred to in this paragraph will be reduced proportionately. You acknowledge that this paragraph is included to avoid compromise of Publisher's rights (including its entitlement to injunctive relief) by reason of a finding of applicability of California law, but does not constitute a concession by Publisher that California law is actually applicable.

6.05. If you do not enter into a Recording Agreement prior to the expiration of the first Songwriter Term and Publisher does not exercise its option to enter into the first Songwriter Option Period, you may purchase all of Publisher's interest in the Defined Compositions previously acquired by Publisher under this agreement by notifying Publisher in writing of your intent to make such purchase and delivering to Publisher a payment in the amount of all Advances then previously paid to you by Publisher under this agreement (including, but not limited to, the full amount of the Equipment Advance); provided, however, that the foregoing shall not apply to any Defined Composition used on a Cover Recording.

6.06. If Publisher gives you its written prior approval for the production of demonstration recordings ("Demos") of any compositions which are applied in fulfillment of your Delivery Commitment, Publisher will promptly reimburse you for your actual costs incurred in the production of those Demos, but not more than $___ in connection with any composition. Publisher will own those Demos and all rights in them, under copyright and otherwise, throughout the Territory and perpetually; provided, however, that Publisher will not commercially exploit those Demos without your prior written consent. Publisher will not be required to make any payments to you under this paragraph until you have furnished Publisher with documentation, reasonably satisfactory to it, substantiating the costs concerned and documenting those rights.

7. ROYALTIES.

7.01. Publisher will pay you the following royalties:

7.01.(a) Public Performance Income.

7.01.(a.1) Fifty percent (50%) of Net Income derived from the public performance of Defined Compositions, except as provided in section (2) below; and

7.01.(a.2) Seventy-five percent (75%) of Net Income derived from any direct public performance licenses referred to in the last sentence of subparagraph 4.02(d). (If any part of the income derived from any such license is paid directly to you and retained by you (not paid over to Publisher first under paragraph 7.02), the share payable to you under this section (2) will be reduced commensurately. For example: If half of such income is paid directly to you and retained by you, the 75% share prescribed in the first sentence of this section will be reduced to fifty percent (50%.)

7.01.(b) Mechanical Income.

7.01.(b.1) Seventy-five percent (75%) of Net Income attributable to the use of Defined Compositions on Phonograph Records, other than Records of Cover Recordings; and

7.01.(b.2) Sixty percent (60%) of such Net Income derived from Cover Recordings.

7.01.(c) Other Income. Seventy-five percent (75%) of Net Income derived from any other exploitation of Defined Compositions, including, without limitation, print use and synchronization in audiovisual works.

7.02. If you or the Artist receive any direct or indirect payments with respect to any Defined Composition (other than Writers' Shares of public performance income) you or the Artist will report and pay them over to Publisher immediately for accounting and distribution under paragraph 7.01. This paragraph applies, without limitation, to any such monies received by you or the Artist in connection with motion picture score Writing.

8. ROYALTY ACCOUNTINGS.

8.01. Publisher will compute your royalties as of each April 30th and October 31st for the prior six (6) months. (Publisher may change those accounting periods without notice, but not to more than six months each.) On the next September 30th or March 31st (or if Publisher changes the accounting periods, on the date ninety

(90) days following the period concerned) Publisher will send you a statement covering those royalties and will pay you any net royalties which are due after deducting unrecouped Advances. Publisher will not be required to send you a royalty payment for any period in which the royalties payable to you, on a cumulative basis, are $50 or less. Publisher will not maintain royalty reserves against anticipated credits, except with respect to income derived from print uses. If Publisher makes any overpayment to you, you will reimburse Publisher for it; to the extent not immediately reimbursed, Publisher may also deduct it from any payments due or becoming due to you.

8.02. Uses of Defined Compositions outside the United States are called "foreign uses" below. Publisher will compute royalties for any foreign uses in the same national currency in which Publisher's Licensee pays Publisher for that use, and Publisher will credit those royalties at the same rate of exchange at which the Licensee pays Publisher. For purposes of accounting to you, Publisher will treat any foreign use as a use occurring during the same six-month period in which Publisher either receives its Licensee's accounting and payment for it or receives a credit to its account for it against a prior advance actually received by Publisher. If any Publisher Licensee deducts any taxes from its payments to Publisher, Publisher may deduct a proportionate amount of those taxes from your royalties. If any law, any government ruling, or any other restriction affects the amount of the payments which a Publisher Licensee can remit to Publisher, Publisher may deduct from your royalties an amount proportionate to the reduction in the Licensee's remittances to Publisher. If Publisher cannot collect payment for any foreign use in the United States in U.S. Dollars it will not be required to account to you for it.

8.03. Publisher will maintain books and records which report uses of Defined Compositions for which royalties are payable to you. You may, at your own expense, examine those books and records, as provided in this paragraph only. You may make those examinations only for the purpose of verifying the accuracy of the statements sent to you under paragraph 8.01. You may make such an examination for a particular statement only once, and only within two years after the date when Publisher sends you that statement. (Publisher will be deemed conclusively to have sent you each statement on the date prescribed in paragraph 8.01 unless you notify Publisher otherwise, with respect to any statement, within thirty (30) days after that date.) You may make those examinations only during Publisher's usual business hours, and at the place where it keeps the books and records to be examined. If you wish to make an examination you will be required to notify Publisher at least 30 days before the date when you plan to begin it.   Publisher may postpone the commencement of your examination by notice given to you not later than five (5) days before the commencement date specified in your notice; if it does so, the running of the time within which the examination may be made will be suspended during the postponement.   If your examination has not been completed within one month from the time you begin it, Publisher may require you to terminate it on seven (7) days' notice to you at any time; Publisher will not be required to permit you to continue the examination after the end of that seven-day period. You will not be entitled to examine any records that do not specifically report uses of Defined Compositions for which royalties are payable to you. You may appoint a certified public accountant to make such an examination for you, but not if he or his firm has begun an examination of Publisher's books and records for any Person except you, unless the examination has been concluded and any applicable audit issues have been resolved.

8.03.1.   Notwithstanding the last sentence of paragraph 8.03, if Publisher notifies you that the representative designated by you to conduct an examination of Publisher's books and records under paragraph 8.03 is engaged in an examination on behalf of another Person ("Other Examination"), you may nevertheless have your examination conducted by your designee, and the running of the time within which such examination may be made shall be suspended until your designee has completed the Other Examination, subject to the following conditions:

8.03.1.(a) You shall notify Publisher of your election to that effect within 15 days after the date of Publisher's said notice to you;

8.03.1.(b) Your designee shall proceed in a reasonably continuous and expeditious manner to complete the Other Examination and render the final report thereon to the client and Publisher; and

8.03.1.(c) Your examination shall not be commenced by your designee before the delivery to Publisher of the final report on the Other Examination, shall be commenced within thirty (30) days thereafter, and shall be conducted in a reasonably continuous manner.

(The preceding provisions of this paragraph 8.03.1 will not apply if Publisher elects to waive the provisions of the last sentence of paragraph 8.03 which require that your representative shall not be engaged in any Other Examination.)

8.04. If you have any objections to a royalty statement, you will give Publisher specific notice of that objection and your reasons for it within two years after the date when Publisher sends you that statement.   (Publisher will be deemed conclusively to have sent you each statement on the date prescribed in paragraph 8.01 unless you notify Publisher otherwise, with respect to any statement, within thirty (30) days after that date.)   Each royalty statement will become conclusively binding on you at the end of that two-year period, and you will have no further right to make any other objections to it. You will have no right to sue Publisher in connection with any royalty accounting, or to sue Publisher for royalties derived from exploitation of Defined Compositions during the period a royalty accounting covers, unless you commence the suit within that two-year period. If you commence suit on any controversy or claim concerning royalty accountings rendered to you under this agreement, the scope of the proceeding will be limited to determination of the amount of the royalties due for the accounting periods concerned, and the court will have no authority to consider any other issues or award any relief except recovery of any royalties found owing. Your recovery of any such royalties will be the sole remedy available to you or the Artist by reason of any claim related to Publisher's royalty accountings.   Without limiting the generality of the preceding sentence, neither you nor the Artist will have any right to seek termination of this agreement or avoid the performance of your obligations under it by reason of any such claim. The preceding three sentences will not apply to any item in a royalty accounting if you establish that the item was fraudulently misstated.

9. RECORDING AGREEMENT - END OF TERM

9.01. In this Article 9:

9.01.(a) "recording agreement" means

9.01.(a.1) the Recording Agreement referred to in paragraph 3.03, and any successor Recording Agreement, and

9.01.(a.2) Any other agreement with a record company actually engaged in the business of producing master recordings and distributing and marketing Phonograph Records in the United States and internationally, providing for the rendition of the Artist's recording services, or for the production of recordings of the Artist's performances for the purpose of making Phonograph Records, on an exclusive basis.

9.01.(b) the "term" of a recording agreement means the period during which the Artist is obligated to render recording services or make recordings of the Artist's performances, and any additional period of exclusivity. The term of a recording agreement will not be deemed to have ended if it is extended, renewed, reinstated, or otherwise continued without interruption.

9.02. Upon the end of the term of the Recording Agreement for any reason:

9.02.(a) You will notify Publisher promptly;

9.02.(b) Publisher will have the option to terminate the Term of this agreement by notice to you at any time after the end of the term of the Recording Agreement, subject to section 9.02(c)(2) below; and

9.02.(c) If you enter into another recording agreement:

9.02.(c.1) You will promptly notify Publisher of its execution and furnish Publisher with a fully executed copy of it (with monetary amounts redacted if you so desire);

9.02.(c.2) Publisher's termination option under subparagraph 9.02(b) will expire sixty (60) days after its receipt of that notice and executed copy of that agreement; and

9.02.(c.3) if Publisher's termination option under subparagraph 9.02(b) expires under section 9.02(c)(2) following the execution of another recording agreement, Publisher's rights under this paragraph 9.02 will be revived and apply separately upon the end of the term of that recording agreement and upon the end of the term of each recording agreement entered into subsequently until the Term of this agreement has ended.

9.03. If Publisher has not exercised its termination option under subparagraph 9.02(b) following the end of the term of any recording agreement (the "last recording agreement", below) and you have not entered into a subsequent recording agreement within twelve (12) months after the termination of the last recording agreement and you have reimbursed Publisher the amount of any Advances paid to you in connection with an Album which was not released in a Major Release during the Album Term, the Term of this agreement will terminate and all parties will be deemed to have fulfilled all of their obligations under this agreement except those obligations which survive the end of the Term (such as indemnification obligations, Publisher's continuing administration rights under Article 4 and Publisher's accounting obligations).

10. ADDITIONAL WARRANTIES AND REPRESENTA-TIONS; RESTRICTIONS, WAIVERS, INDEMNITIES.

10.01. You warrant and represent:

10.01.(a) You have the right and power to enter into and fully perform this agreement.

10.01.(b.1)   All of the Old Defined Compositions are listed in Schedule 2. All of the Old Defined Compositions and all copyrights and other rights in them are your sole property, no Old Defined Composition is derived from or based on any other work, and no Person other than you or the Artist owns any rights in any derivative work based on any Old Defined Composition, except as specifically stated in Schedule 2.

10.01.(b.2)   Each New and Acquired Defined Composition and all copyrights and other rights in it will be your sole property at the time of its creation or acquisition, free from any restrictions and any claims by any other Person, except as expressly permitted in paragraph 10.02.

10.01.(c)   Publisher shall not be required to make any payments of any nature in connection with the acquisition, exercise, or exploitation of rights under this agreement, except as expressly provided in this agreement.   Without limiting the generality of the preceding sentence.

10.01.(c.1)   You shall be solely responsible for any payments due to the Artist, other Writers, and any other Person in connection with Publisher's exploitation of Defined Compositions or its exercise of its rights in them; and

10.01.(c.2)   Neither you nor the Artist has encumbered or will encumber any moneys payable by ASCAP, BMI, or any other Person with respect to uses of Defined Compositions.   Without limiting the generality of the preceding sentence, no advances or other payments made by ASCAP, BMI or any other Person will be chargeable against or recoupable from income derived or to be derived from any use of Defined Compositions, and no Person except you or the Artist is entitled to receive any portion of such income at the date of this agreement.

10.01.(d)   You are an affiliate in good standing of BMI pursuant to an affiliation agreement dated

10.01.(e) No Materials, as defined below, or any use of them, will violate any law or infringe upon or violate the rights of any Person. "Materials," in this Article, means: (1) all Defined Compositions, (2) each name used by the Artist, individually or as a group, in connection with Defined Compositions, and (3) all other musical, dramatic, artistic and literary materials, ideas, and other intellectual properties, created or selected by you or the Artist and contained in or used in Defined Compositions or in connection with them.

10.01.(f) All of the information in the attached Schedules is accurate and complete.

10.01.(g) You are not aware of any claim which is inconsistent with any of your warranties or representations in this agreement.

10.02.(a) During the term of this agreement neither you nor the Artist will: (1) Write or agree to Write any musical compositions other than those which are subject to Publisher's rights under this agreement; (2) enter into any other agreement which would be inconsistent with your obligations under this agreement; or (3) collaborate in Writing musical compositions with anyone else, subject to subparagraph (b) below.

10.02.(b) If the Artist Writes in collaboration with other Writers you will obtain from each collaborator in advance and deliver to Publisher a written agreement, expressly for Publisher's benefit, providing that each such composition will be subject to all of Publisher's rights under this agreement, except that the 50% ownership interest granted to Publisher in paragraph 4.01 will apply to the Artist's interest only, not to the interest of the collaborator.

10.03. Neither you, the Artist, nor any other Person with power to do so will grant any record company (other than Publisher or another record company under contract for the Artist's exclusive recording services if such contract grants a mechanical license to the record company on terms no less favorable to the Artist than the terms contained in a standard controlled composition mechanical license clause) or other Person any license or permission with respect to any Defined Composition, including, without limitation, any mechanical license for use on Phonograph Records (whether or not the proposed license provides for royalties at rates lower than the statutory compulsory license rate, or varies otherwise from the compulsory license provisions of the copyright law). You warrant and represent that you have disclosed to Publisher in writing any such licenses granted before the execution of this agreement.

10.04. You acknowledge that monetary damages would not adequately compensate Publisher for a breach of your obligations under this Article, and Publisher will be entitled to injunctive relief to enforce its provisions.

10.05. You waive and relinquish any right in the nature of termination or reversion of rights in the Compositions which you may have under copyright law or otherwise, to the extent to which you may effectively do so.

10.06.(a)   You will at all times indemnify and hold harmless Publisher and any Licensee of Publisher from and against any and all claims, damages, liabilities, costs and expenses, including legal expenses and reasonable counsel fees, arising out of any breach or alleged breach of any warranty or representation made by you in this agreement, provided the claim concerned has been settled or has resulted in a judgment against Publisher or its Licensees. If any claim involving such subject matter has not been resolved, or has been resolved by a judgment or other disposition which is not adverse to Publisher or its Licensees, you will reimburse Publisher for fifty percent (50%) of the expenses actually incurred by Publisher and its Licensees in connection with that claim. Pending the resolution of any such claim Publisher will not withhold moneys which would otherwise be payable to you under this agreement in an amount exceeding your potential liability to Publisher under this paragraph; provided, however, no moneys will be withheld longer than eighteen (18) months from the date of Publisher's written notice of such claim if suit is not commenced within such eighteen (18) month period.

10.06.(b) If Publisher pays more than $5,000 in settlement of any such claim, you will not be obligated to reimburse Publisher for the excess unless you have consented to the settlement, except as provided in the next sentence. If you do not consent to any settlement proposed by Publisher for an amount exceeding $5,000 you will nevertheless be required to reimburse Publisher for the full amount paid unless you make bonding arrangements, satisfactory to Publisher in its sole discretion, to assure Publisher of reimbursement for all damages, liabilities, costs and expenses (including legal expenses and counsel fees) which Publisher or its Licensees may incur as a result of that claim. Publisher will notify you of any action commenced on such a claim. You may participate in the defense of any such claim through counsel of your selection at your own expense, but Publisher will have the right at all times, in its sole discretion, to retain or resume control of the conduct of the defense.

11. AGREEMENTS, APPROVAL AND CONSENT

11.01. As to all matters to be determined by mutual agreement, or as to which any approval or consent is required, such agreement, approval or consent will not be unreasonably withheld.

11.02. Your agreement, approval or consent, or that of the Artist, wherever required, will be deemed to have been given unless you notify Publisher otherwise within ten (10) days following Publisher's written request for it.

12. NOTICES

12.01. Except as otherwise specifically provided herein, all notices under this agreement shall be in writing and shall be given by courier or other personal delivery or by registered or certified mail at the appropriate address below or at a substitute address designated by notice by the party concerned:

Notices shall be deemed given when mailed, except that a notice of change of address shall be effective only from the date of its receipt.

13. EVENTS OF DEFAULT: REMEDIES

13.01. If you fail to fulfill any of your material obligations under this agreement Publisher will have the following options:

13.01.(a)   To suspend Publisher's obligations to make payments under this agreement until you have cured the default, provided, however, that with respect to your Delivery Commitment under Article 3A, Publisher may not suspend its obligations to make payments to you unless you fail to cure the default within thirty (30) days after the last date specified in Article 3A for timely Delivery of the Compositions concerned; and

13.01.(b)   to terminate the term of this agreement at any time, whether or not you have commenced curing the default before such termination occurs, provided, however, that with respect to your Delivery Commitment under Article 3A, Publisher may not terminate the term of this agreement unless you fail to cure the default within thirty (30) days after the last date specified in Article 3A for timely Delivery of the Compositions concerned.

Publisher may exercise each of those options by notice to you. No exercise of an option under this paragraph will limit Publisher's rights to recover damages by reason of your default, its rights to exercise any other option under this agreement, or any of its other rights.

14. MISCELLANEOUS

14.01. This agreement contains the entire understanding of the parties relating to its subject matter. No change or termination of this agreement will be binding upon Publisher unless it is made by an instrument signed by an officer of Publisher. A waiver by any party of any provision of this agreement in any instance shall not be deemed to waive it for the future.   All rights and obligations under this agreement are cumulative and none of them will limit or exclude any other right or obligation of any party. The captions of the Articles in this agreement are included for convenience only and will not affect the interpretation of any provision.

14.02. Publisher may assign its rights under this agreement in whole or in part to any subsidiary, affiliated or controlling corporation, to any Person owning or acquiring a substantial portion of the stock or assets of Publisher, or to any partnership or other venture in which Publisher participates, and such rights may be assigned by any assignee. No such assignment shall relieve Publisher of any of its obligations. Publisher may also assign its rights to any of its Licensees if advisable in Publisher's sole discretion to implement the license granted.

14.03. Each option and election granted to Publisher in this agreement is separate and distinct, and the exercise of any such option or election will not operate as a waiver of any other option or election.

14.04. You shall not be entitled to recover damages or to terminate the term of this agreement by reason of any breach by Publisher of its material obligations, unless Publisher has failed to remedy such breach within a reasonable time following receipt of your notice of it.

14.05. This agreement has been entered into in the state of New York, and the validity, interpretation and legal effect of this agreement shall be governed by the laws of the state of New York applicable to contracts entered into and performed entirely within the state of New York. The New York courts (state and federal), only, will have jurisdiction of any controversies regarding this agreement; any action or other proceeding which involves such a controversy will be brought in those courts, in New York county, and not elsewhere. Any process in any such action or proceeding may, among other methods, be served upon you by delivering it or mailing it, by registered or certified mail, directed to the address first above written or such other address as you may designate pursuant to A12. Any such process may, among other methods, be served upon the artist or any other person who approves, ratified, or assents to this agreement to induce publisher to enter into it, by delivering the process or mailing it by registered or certified mail, directed to the address first above written or such other address as the artist or the other person concerned may designate in the manner prescribed in Article 12. Any such delivery or mail service shall be deemed to have the same force and effect as personal service within the state of New York.

14.06. You and the Artist will perform your obligations under this agreement as independent contractors. Nothing in this agreement will constitute you or the Artist as Publisher's agents or employees.

14.07. Monies to be paid to you under this agreement will not be assignable by you without Publisher's written consent, which Publisher may withhold in its unrestricted discretion.

14.08. This agreement shall not become effective until executed by all proposed parties.

My social security number is ___-__-____. Under the penalties of perjury, I certify that this information is true, correct, and complete.

SCHEDULE 1

(Reference - Paragraph 2.02)

AFFILIATES

<u>Name</u>   <u>Description of Affiliate Relationship</u>

SCHEDULE 2

Reference - Section 10.01(b.1)

Old Defined Compositions Title	Writer(s) and Percentage Ownership Interests	U.S. Copyright Registration No./Date

EXHIBIT A

(Reference - Paragraph 4.01)

ASSIGNMENT

The undersigned, _____ dba _____ Music (BMI/ASCAP) (the "Assignor"), for valuable consideration, hereby assigns to _____ (the "Assignee"), and its successors and assigns, perpetually and throughout the universe.

(1) An undivided fifty percent (50%) share of the Assignor's interests in the copyrights (including renewals, if applicable) and all other rights in the musical compositions listed in the attached Schedule; and

(2) The following exclusive rights in those compositions:

(2.i) to license and cause others to license the use of the compositions;

(2.ii) to administer and grant rights in the compositions and under the copyrights in them;

(2.iii) to publish and sell sheet music, folios, and other printed editions of the compositions;

(2.iv) to collect all monies payable with respect to the compositions, including monies earned but not paid before the effective date; and

(2.v) otherwise administer the compositions and the copyrights in them, and act as the publisher of them.

This Instrument is executed in accordance with, and is subject to the Agreement dated _____ __, 199_ between the Assignor and _____

Dated:

Assignor:

_____

Assignee:

_____

EXHIBIT B

(Reference - Paragraph 4.01)

To: ALL RECORD MANUFACTURERS
To: [ASCAP] [BMI] LICENSED TO REPRODUCE COMPOSI-
     TIONS DESCRIBED
To: HARRY FOX AGENCY BELOW IN PHONORECORDS
To: ALL OTHER PARTIES IN INTEREST

Effective, _____ __, 199_, I have granted to
_____ and its licensees and assigns the exclusive
right, throughout the world, in respect of compositions of which
the undersigned is the copyright proprietor, including those compositions listed on Schedule A annexed (the "Compositions"):

(i) to license and cause others to license the use of the Compositions;

(ii) to administer and grant rights in the Compositions and under
the copyrights in them;

(iii) to publish and sell sheet music, folios, and other printed editions of the Compositions;

(iv) to collect all monies payable with respect to the Compositions,
including monies earned but not paid before the effective date; and

(v) otherwise administer the Compositions and the copyrights in
them, and act as the publisher of them.

Dated:

EXHIBIT C

(Reference - Paragraph 4.01)

Date:

Publisher Relations Department
Broadcast Music, Inc.
40 West 57th Street
New York, New York 10019

Gentlemen:

This is to advise BMI that we have entered into an agreement with another BMI publisher for the administration of our catalog, and that BMI's records should be marked to reflect the agreement as follows:

1. Name of BMI publisher acting as our administrator: Publisher Songs Inc.

2. Effective date of agreement:

Immediately, including all royalties now payable or which hereafter become payable, regardless of when performances took place.

Check One Effective with performances on and after _____, __ 199_   (Must be as of the beginning of a calendar quarter, i.e., January 1, April 1, July 1 or October 1.)

3. Checks for all our BMI royalties, both domestic and foreign, should be made payable to the administrator and should be sent together with the statements and all other correspondence to the administrator at its address on BMI's records.

We understand that BMI cannot mark its records at this time so as to indicate the termination date of the administration agreement and that, therefore, the above information will continue to be reflected on BMI's records until such time as we or the administrator notifies BMI that the administration agreement is about to terminate.

Very truly yours,

_____

EXHIBIT D

(Reference - Paragraph 5.02)

Date:

TO WHOM IT MAY CONCERN:

We are the writers of the composition[s]:

[TITLE OR LIST]

Our respective ownership interests in [it] [them], and our shares of the royalties payable with respect to [it] [them], are stated below.

SIGNATURE/PRINTED NAME   % SHARE

Co-Publishing Agreement
Explanatory Notes

1. PREAMBLE

The most typical way that a songwriter sells rights to his or her songs is through what is a called a co-publishing and exclusive administration agreement. Co-publishing means that you and a publishing company will be sharing the copyrights to your song equally. Copyright is the legal term that identifies the owner of intellectual properties such as a musical compositions (songs), master recordings, and the rights that are granted them by law. Exclusive administration means that the publishing company will be solely responsible for deciding how your songs will be marketed and for collecting income that is derived from those songs. A co-publishing agreement will be entered into by the writer or writers and their individual publishing companies on the one hand, and the publishing company on the other hand. A writer should not confuse his personal publishing company with his co-publisher. The writer's personal publishing company is essentially the name that the writer uses to identify the company under which the writer's songs can be identified, along with the publishing interests of those songs. Before a writer starts using a name to represent his publishing company he should first check the availability of that name with local, state, and in some cases federal agencies. In addition, the writer needs to clear that name with either ASCAP or BMI. (See publishing chapter for explanation of ASCAP and BMI.) The reason for doing this is to avoid using a name that belongs to someone else, who could not only be paid your publishing royalties by mistake but could also sue you for infringing on their rights to the name of their publishing company.

2. DEFINITIONS

Since many of the definitions are self explanatory we will only explain those which require further elaboration.

2.02. Publishers want to ensure that they acquire rights to songs not only written by the writer, but any songs in which the writer or anyone affiliated with the writer may have an interest. For example: a writer may also be a publisher and therefore may have purchase rights to songs that he did not write. In that case the publisher with whom the writer was signing a publishing deal would obtain the publishing rights to those songs also. If a writer expects that he will engage in independent publishing activities, the writer should negotiate the exclusion of songs they do not write from their publishing agreement with the publisher with whom he is signing, or require that the publisher with whom they are entering into a publishing agreement pay an additional amount for the right to participate in the copyrights of the songs that the writer owns but did not write.

2.05. There are basically three types of compositions (songs) which can be subject to a co-publishing agreement: (1) songs previously written by the writer , (2) songs which are written during the term of the co-publishing agreement, and (3) songs which the writer did not write but for which he acquires the publishing interest.

2.06.   These definitions of what is a "Qualifying Side" and a "Qualifying Album" are relevant to the determination of whether a writer has satisfied his or her commitment under the publishing agreement. This will be explained more fully under the commitment section. [See section 3A in these explanatory notes.] However, a brief explanation of some of the terms used in this paragraph may be helpful. One of the basic ways that a song generates income is by being recorded on records. This income is calculated and based upon terms that are defined in copyright laws. One of these terms is what is called a mechanical license, which is discussed in the explanatory notes of the recording agreement and in the publishing chapter.

Another term is "compulsory" license, which refers to the unique provisions of U.S. copyright law which state that once a composition has been recorded, the owner of that composition (the publisher) cannot prevent other artists from recording different versions of the same song. However the record company that releases the new version of that song must pay the publisher of the original song mechanical royalties at the full statutory rate established by Congress. [A definition of the statutory rate is contained in the publishing chapter.] What these terms mean in the context of this agreement is that for the writer to receive full credit for the recording of his or her song, the publisher of that song must receive a mechanical license at the full statutory rate either through a compulsory license or mechanical license which is negotiated with the publisher. Sometimes a record company will not want to pay the full statutory rate on a song, the main reason being that it costs more to do so. In most cases they prefer to pay a rate that is based upon 3/4 of the full statutory rate. This is commonly referred to as a "three quarter rate". If a writer has a publishing deal and the publisher requires the writer to obtain the full statutory rate, which in most cases they do, and the writer has a song released that will only yield a 3/4 rate, that song will not count as a full song towards that writer's song commitment. Instead it will count for 3/4 of a song and that writer will have to deliver 1/4 of one full song to the publisher to make up the difference. Overall, most publishers will require writers to receive the full statutory rate on songs that are recorded and released. This is not always realistic, especially where the writer is the artist and will usually be required to grant his or her record company a license at 3/4 of the statutory rate. Therefore, the writer should attempt to negotiate that songs licensed at 3/4 or more of the statutory rate will count as a full composition towards the song commitment requirements under the publishing agreement. (Because of the complexity of this issue, ask your legal counsel about getting paid at the source for foreign royalties.) It is also unrealistic to expect that every song a songwriter writes will be written by him solely. For example some writers only write lyrics and others only write music, and may in fact collaborate in order to compose a complete song. What this means is that the writer who routinely collaborates should define compositions in the publishing agreement as songs which he writes at least 50 percent of. If not, every song they deliver to the publisher will only count as half a song, which would result in the writer having to fulfill twice the song commitment he thinks he is required to deliver.

2.09. Publishing income and rights are customarily divided into what is called the "publisher's share" and the "writer's share." Each of these shares represents 50 percent of the total income derived from a song. Since in a co-publishing agreement the writer is selling 50 percent of his publishing rights, the writer retains his right to the writer's share of his songs. However, the publisher will insist upon the right to use the writer's share of income, as well as the publisher's share, to recoup any advances that have been paid to the writer.

2.13.(a) This clause defines what income will be divided by the publishing company and the writer. The definition begins with gross income. An important component of this definition for the writer to negotiate is for all gross income to be calculated as "at source". Income at source means that once income is earned by songs outside of the United States, which is customarily collected by an foreign affiliate of the publisher, the publisher will not have the right to charge the writer any additional fees that might be paid to the sub-publisher. Otherwise the publishing company will be able to double dip against the writer's share of foreign income. If the writer is unable to negotiate for an at source definition, the writer should negotiate that the publisher limit the amount he can pay to their foreign affiliate as fees for administering the writers songs in those territories. These fees should not exceed 15 to 20 percent.

2.13.(b) The writer's co-publishing share of income is based on net income. Net income is broadly defined as gross income less the publisher's expense. The writer should negotiate to limit these expenses to reasonable, actual, out-of-pocket expenses incurred by the publisher which are directly related to the writer's songs.

2.16. In some co-publishing agreements the writer is required not only to deliver a certain number of songs, but to guarantee to the publisher that some of those songs will be recorded and released by an artist on a major record label. Since the writer cannot realistically guarantee that her songs will be recorded and released by an artist on a major label , the writer should resist agreeing to this type of provision. The reason is that if at the end of the writer's contract year the number of songs contained in the recorded and released provision of the publishing agreement has not been met, the writer will be put on suspension until those commitments have been filled. This means that during that suspension the writer will not be paid any advances, but will be required to give the publisher 50 percent of any songs written. In addition, the term of the original contract will be extended for as long as that suspension lasts. We know of situations where writers are put on suspension indefinitely and can never get out of the publishing deal. In any event, the number of songs a writer is required to record, release and deliver to a publisher should be kept to a minimum, preferably no more than two. Another way to negotiate this issue is to include independent record companies in the definition of what will constitute a release.

3. TERM

The term (overall length) of a co-publishing agreement can be structured in one of two ways. If the writer is not a recording artist, the term will be structured for an initial period of one year, with options for the publishing company to extend the term for three or four more individual years. However as discussed above, the overall length of the contract is subject to the fulfillment of the writer's delivery commitment.

If the writer is a recording artist, the term will be set up as an initial period of time covering the release of the artist's first album with options for the publishing company to extend the term to include up to three or four more albums. In some cases, as in this agreement, a combination of the two structures may be utilized. This covers a situation where a writer intends to be, but is not at the time of signing the co-publishing agreement, a recording artist. In that case, the agreement will commence as discussed in the above paragraph, with the possibility of conversion to a recording artist term, at such time, if ever, as the writer becomes a recording artist. [For a more detailed discussion on how options are exercises see clause 1 of the explanatory notes of the recording agreement.]

Any term which depends upon the writer's delivery of albums will be structured so that the publisher has the opportunity to hear each completed album and is allowed a certain period of time, usually 30 to 60 days, to decide whether to pick up the option to acquire rights to that album. Under most agreements, the publisher will obtain rights to all compositions written during the term of the agreement, whether embodied on albums by the artist, or any other artist, or otherwise exploited, as well as old songs and acquired songs. Publishers will insist upon obtaining these rights for the life of the copyright on the songs. Currently copyrights last for life of the author plus 50 years. Occasionally, a writer may negotiate a reversion of rights within a certain period of time, usually not less than 5 to 10 years after delivery of that song to that publisher, and usually only on the condition that the writer is in a fully recouped position with the publisher. Which means that all advances paid to the writer by the publisher have been paid back via income derived from that writers songs.

However, reversion of copyrights is usually only available for writers with strong bargaining power. A more realistic concession for a new writer is for the writer to get back his or her share of compositions which the publisher has been unable to commercially exploit during the term.

3A. DELIVERY COMMITMENT

Commitment as referred to in this paragraph means either the number of songs a writer agrees to deliver to a publisher as stated in their contract with the publisher, or the number of songs a writer will write that will be recorded and released by an artist on a major label.

3A.01. A typical songwriter term commitment will involve delivery of between 10 and 20 new songs per year. A common number is 12. In addition, most publishers will insist upon receiving the first half of the commitment within the first six months of the term to ensure a regular flow of material.

3A.02. The publisher will put restrictions upon what songs the writer presents to them which will count toward the writer's commitment. First, the material submitted must be satisfactory to the publisher. Most publishers exercise this provision in good faith. However, it is a good idea to provide that if a song generates income, it is deemed acceptable and therefore will count towards the writer's commitment. Another approach is to request that any song rejected by a publisher be returned to the writer. Unfortunately, this is a difficult concession to obtain.

3A.03. If the writer writes less than a full song, only the writer's share of that song will count towards the writer's commitment. If a writer knows in advance that they are solely a lyricist, melody writer or composer of music, the writer can structure their delivery commitment based upon authorship of 50 percent of a composition. Most publishers will increase the number of songs in the commitment if they agree to this request, but usually to not more than 20 songs.

4. RIGHTS GRANTED

4.01. In a co-publishing agreement, the writer is granting the publisher a full 50 percent interest in the publisher's share of his or her songs. Because the writer retains his or her full writer's share of income, this 50 percent grant actually translates to 25 percent of the total income earned from the writer's songs.

4.02. In addition to ownership of the copyright on the writer's songs, the publisher will require the exclusive right to administer the song. Administration means that the publisher will make all decisions concerning the compositions, including issuing licenses and collecting money generated by those songs. A writer should insist upon limits to these administration rights as he or she deems appropriate. An example of some common limitations are described in subparagraph (g) of this paragraph.

4.03/4.04. These paragraphs deal with additional rights being granted to the publisher, such as power of attorney. A power of attorney, in this case, gives the publisher the right to sign documents on behalf of the writer concerning the writer's songs. Before granting a power of attorney to a publisher, it is a good idea to insist that the publisher grant the writer the option to sign any such documents themselves before allowing the publisher to do so on his or her behalf.

4.05. For discussion of name and likeness issues please refer to paragraph 5A of the explanatory notes to the recording agreement.

4.06. As mentioned above, the writer will keep 50 percent of the copyright of the songs under a co-publishing agreement. If the writer decides to sell that 50 percent during the term of the co-publishing agreement, most publishers will insist upon the right to match any offer that the writer may receive to sell that interest. This could also include selling the writer's share of income. It should be noted that since the publisher retains administration rights to the entire song (even to those portions of the song which the writer owns), the value of those interests to another publisher is limited. This allows the original publisher the upper hand in any negotiation concerning disposition of these rights.

5. DELIVERY: RELATED MATTERS

This paragraph is self-explanatory.

6. ADVANCES: MINIMUM ANNUAL COMPENSATION

As in the recording agreement, the writer will negotiate for payment of advances during the term of the agreement. Under a songwriter term, the artist will typically be paid a portion of his or her advance upon execution of the agreement, and the balance either monthly, or at regular intervals throughout the initial term. In addition, most publishers require that the writer deliver songs on a consistent basis in order to continue to receive advances. For example, many publishers will require that the writer have delivered half of his song commitment for the year before he can receive the second half of that year's advances. In rare cases, the writer can negotiate for the entire advance to be paid up front. As with recording agreements, the range of these advances will vary depending upon the bargaining power of the writer. For a new writer with no songs previously exploited, the advance can be as low as $10,000 per year. For a writer with a track record, the advance can be as much as $150,000 per year or more. A typical advance for an unproven writer, signing with a major publisher would be $30,000 for the first year. As with the recording agreement, the amount of the annual advances should increase over the course of the deal. How these advances are paid has been discussed at the beginning of this paragraph.

If the writer's commitment with a publisher is based on that writer's delivery of albums featuring that writer as an artist, the advances will be paid upon the release of each of that artist's albums. If this is the case the writer should negotiate to receive a portion of the advance, usually one-half, upon the execution of the agreement with respect to the first album, and upon the exercise of the publisher's option with respect to subsequent albums. The remainder of those advances would be paid upon release of each of those albums. If a publisher agrees to pay a portion of an album advance before that album is released, it may insist on a right to require repayment in the event that the album is not released. Obviously it is important to negotiate for the removal of this type of provision, since the writer cannot control whether or not a label releases an album.

In the situation where the agreement is initially structured as a songwriter term, and the writer later becomes a recording artist, the writer may also negotiate for a one-time advance of $10,000 to $20,000, to be issued upon the execution of the recording agreement.

For all albums recorded by the writer after the first album, the writer should negotiate for advances to be based on an earnings formula with minimum and maximum advances. [For a full discussion of how earning formulas are structured, see paragraph 4.4 of explanatory notes for the recording agreement.] This formula will be based on U. S. mechanical royalties earned by the writer's records. The writer should request a broader definition of earnings, but is unlikely to receive it. It is also important to include a good faith estimate of "pipeline" earnings. Pipeline earnings are monies earned from the writer's songs, but not yet paid to the writer. One of the most important points to negotiate is that whatever minimum advances are negotiated be paid to the writer, regardless of whether the writer's account is in a recouped position. Many publishers will attempt to reduce the amount of advances by any unrecouped amount. For example; if the writer's minimum advance for the second year of their agreement is $40,000, but the writer's account is unrecouped by $30,000, without the provision just discussed the writer would only receive $10,000. If the writer is unable remove such a provision, the writer should negotiate for a guaranteed amount that the writer may depend upon receiving during each contract period of the agreement, even if that guaranteed amount is less than the full advance specified in the agreement. Using the same example if the writer had negotiated for a minimum guarantee of $20,000 for the second year of their agreement, the publisher would be required to pay that amount as opposed to $10,000. As discussed above, the amount of the advance will be reduced if the writer fails to deliver the minimum number of songs required in the agreement with the publisher.

Another somewhat complicated issue is where a songwriter term is converted to an album term and songs delivered during the songwriter term are subsequently included on the album. The publisher may request, as reflected in subparagraph (f) here, that the amount of the album advance should be reduced to reflect that portion of any advance previously paid for those songs as part of the songwriter commitment.

Finally, it is a good idea to negotiate additional payments in the event that songs written by the writer achieve a certain chart or sales status. Typical bonuses are anywhere from $5,000 to $20,000. Typical chart status would be top ten on the R&B charts and top twenty on the pop charts. Typical sales status would be gold or platinum albums, which are 500,000 and 1,000,000 respectively. For some writers it is also advantageous to request contributions from the publisher for the purchase of recording equipment, which the writer may use in the preparation of demonstration recordings for his or her material. This type of provision is reflected in subparagraph (h) here. Although the amount of such contribution will depend upon the bargaining power of the artist, a typical range is $5,000 to $20,000.

6.04. This is the same provision as paragraph 1.1/1.2/1.3 in the recording agreement relating to the preservation of rights to exclusive services. For discussion of this provision see paragraph 4.5 of the explanatory notes of the recording agreement.

6.05. Occasionally, a writer may be able to negotiate in advance for the right to re-purchase rights to his or her songs by repaying the publisher for the amount of any advances previously paid to the writer for those rights. This clause is an example of the terms that can be expected if the publisher will negotiate on this point.

6.06. An important feature of any co-publishing agreement is the publisher's agreement to finance the production of demonstration recordings (demos) of the writers songs. Although the amount a publisher will pay for those demos will depend upon the type of music and the publisher, a typical range is $350 to $750 per song. Although the publisher will own the demos, it is important for the writer to obtain consent before the publisher makes any commercial use of them. The writer should also attempt to negotiate that only 50 percent of these payments for demo cost will be recoupable against future earnings.

7. ROYALTIES

7.01. There are several types of income which musical compositions may generate. The first is income from the public performance of the compositions. This would include playing the songs on the radio, or in connection with television programs, and even the broader use of songs in public places, such as department stores. As mentioned above, the vast majority of this income is handled through one of the two major public performance rights societies, ASCAP or BMI. (See publishing chapter for more information on BMI and ASCAP) Given the complexity of attempting to track the public performance of a song, these societies have formulated royalty computation systems for tracking the number of public performances of songs, and the distribution of royalties derived from those performances to songwriters and publishers. I will not go into detail at this point as to how those royalties are computed. Both ASCAP and BMI will provide copies of their payment policies on request. See the chapter on publishing. In a co-publishing agreement, public performance income is split 50/50 between the co-publisher and the writer. The reason for a 50 percent, rather than a 75 percent share for the writer here, is that the writer will receive his or her writer's share directly from the performance rights society and not the publisher. This writer's share of public performance income is the only source of royalty income which is not collected by the publisher and subject to recoupment. Accordingly, the publisher will retain 50 percent of the publisher's share of public performance income. In rare circumstances, direct public performance licenses are obtained which are not handled by ASCAP or BMI. In that case, the writer would be entitled to 75 percent of the net income received by the publisher derived from those performances.

The second source of income is mechanical royalties, which have been discussed many times previously. [See publishing chapter.] 75 percent of this income goes to the writer. The only exception to this is in the case of the so-called "cover recording", or a synchronization license obtained by the publisher, for which a publisher will usually insist upon a larger percentage, often 40 percent. A cover recording is a new recording of a song that has been previously recorded and released by another artist. A synchronization license is a license granted to a motion picture producer to record a song to be used in a motion picture. This could include uses of the song to be used in a motion picture. This could include uses of the song on television as well.

Finally, there is usually a catch-all for other types of income, which will also be split 75/25. In this agreement. 75 percent of the income derived from the sale of printed music is being paid to the writer under the category of "other income". In many cases separate royalties will be specified for print uses. [See publishing chapter for details.]

8. ACCOUNTINGS

These provisions are essentially the same as in the recording agreement. A few important distinctions should be noted. First, as opposed to a recording agreement, there is no reason for a publisher to withhold reserves, except in the case of sales of printed uses of songs by the publisher. Another important point of clarification is that the publisher, as the administrator of the songs, will collect 100% of all income generated by those songs and will credit the writer's account with his or her applicable percentage of that income, and will retain the remainder. This means that royalties will not be paid to the writer until the amount of the payments credited to his or her account exceeds the amount of advances and other recoupable charges under the agreement. On very rare occasions, a writer may negotiate for some portion of his or her writer's share of royalties to be exempt from recoupment. It is also possible on rare occasions to exempt the writer's share of income derived from synchronization licenses from recoupment. However, such concessions are reserved for writers with great bargaining power.

9. TERMINATION OF RECORDING AGREEMENT

In the event that the co-publishing agreement requires the writer to record and release an album as part of the writer's commitment, it is essential for the writer to include a provision which deals with the consequences of the expiration of the writer's recording agreement before the writer has a chance to satisfy that commitment. The same concept applies if any part of a writer's commitment involves the release of songs by a major label. In the absence of such a provision, a writer may find himself in a state of limbo, where he is unable to satisfy his commitment to the publisher, but is not entitled to compensation because the writer is in breach of his commitment. The solution to this problem is to include an outside date in the agreement by which the agreement will terminate even if the writer has not met the commitments. This time period should not exceed two years from the date the writer is put on suspension. If the writer is a recording artist such provisions will typically provide that if the writer is able to secure a replacement recording agreement within a certain period of time, usually six to twelve months, the publisher will have the option to reinstate the agreement. On the other hand, if no replacement agreement is obtained within that time period, the co-publishing agreement will expire by its own terms.

10. <u>MISCELLANEOUS</u>

All of these provisions are discussed in the recording agreement. The schedules which are attached to the agreement itself basically are intended to define any compositions which are being included in the agreement and other information relating to the writer and his or her songs. The exhibits are short form documents which the publisher uses to notify relevant parties of the publisher's interests as defined in the agreement.

Sample of a
Production Agreement
&

Production Agreement
Explanatory Notes

PRODUCTION AGREEMENT

_____PRODUCTIONS
_____
_____
_____
_____

Dated as of _____, 199_

Artist
_____
_____
_____

Dear _____:

    This shall confirm the basic terms of agreement between you and us, and each of our respective publishing designees, as follows:

    1.   You have recorded or will record sound master recordings (the "demos") for us at studio(s) designated by us at our sole cost and expense of compositions (the "Demo Compositions") mutually chosen by us and you. We currently intend to present the completed demos to record companies for the purpose of obtaining distribution of records embodying your performances. For purposes of this Agreement, any such record company distributor shall be referred to hereinafter as a "Distributor", and any such agreement between us and a Distributor concerning the distribution of records embodying your performances shall be referred to hereinafter as a "Distribution Agreement".

2.   For good and valuable consideration, the receipt and sufficiency of which is hereby acknowledged, you hereby grant to us or our designee the exclusive option to acquire your exclusive services as a recording artist throughout the world on the terms set forth herein. Our option will commence as of the date hereof and must be exercised within __ months after the demos are completed (the "shopping period"). The foregoing option shall be deemed to have been automatically exercised if, during the shopping period, we have obtained a Distribution Agreement (or have an offer to enter into a Distribution Agreement and such Agreement is consummated within 3 months thereafter). If we do not exercise the foregoing option, from and after the date that option expires, the following shall apply: (a) we shall have no further rights to your services hereunder; (b) we will not commercially exploit the demos embodying your vocal performances without your consent, provided that we shall have the right to erase your vocals and use the instrumental tracks; (c) you may offer to purchase the demos, and we may, at our election, negotiate with you in good faith to arrive at a fair value therefor, provided that we shall be under no obligation to do so.

3.(a)   During the shopping period, you shall, at our request, record such number of demos, and perform such other services, such as, but not limited to, appearing at photo shoots, rehearsals, showcases and meetings, all as we may deem desirable to effectively shop for a Distribution Agreement. Promptly after the execution hereof, you may provide us with approved pictures of you and biographical material concerning you which you would like us to use. We shall have the right to reject said photographs and biographical material only on reasonable grounds. We will make available to you for your approval photographs and biographical material concerning you which we intend to use. Your approval of said materials shall not be unreasonably withheld and shall be deemed given unless your disapproval is accompanied by a reasonable reason therefore, and has been received by us within five (5) business days after such materials have been made available to you. All demos, photos, etc. shall be subject to the provisions of this Agreement. Only we, and our designees, shall have the right to shop the demos during the shopping period. You understand that we and/or our designees shall have the sole right during the shopping period to negotiate and enter into any Distribution Agreement on your behalf, provided that we shall consult with you regarding the principal terms thereof and shall provide you with executed copies thereof.

(b)   During the term of this Agreement, you will render your recording services entirely to us. Notwithstanding the foregoing we will consider any requests by you to perform as a so-called "sideman" or in audiovisual works, subject to the requirements of any Distributor.

4.   With regard to albums recorded under the Distribution Agreement (collectively, "Albums), we shall pay you the following non-returnable advances (collectively, "Advances"), each payable 50% on commencement of recording of the applicable Album, and 50% on delivery to and acceptance by us of the applicable Album:

(a)   For each of the first and second Albums,
_____ ($_____) Dollars.

(b)   For the third Album,
_____ ($_____) Dollars.

(c)   For the fourth Album,
_____ ($_____) Dollars.

(d)   For the fifth Album,
_____ ($_____) Dollars.

(e)   For all subsequent Albums,
_____ ($_____) Dollars.

For purposes of this Agreement, "Advances" shall mean all advances payable to you pursuant to this paragraph 4, as well as all costs incurred by us during the shopping period, including, without limitation, the cost of recording the demos (which costs incurred at our studios shall be charged at our normal rates), costs of publicity photos and other publicity materials, rehearsal and showcasing expenses, 50% of all reasonable attorney's fees incurred in connection with negotiating any Distribution Agreement on your behalf, and any other amounts paid to you or on your behalf with your consent or at your request.

5.   All Advances shall be fully recoupable from and chargeable against the following royalties payable to you hereunder in respect of Net Sales of Albums which are sold by the Distributor and not returned in the United States through Normal Retail Distribution Channels ("USNRC Net Sales") for which payment is actually received by us (as defined in the Distribution Agreement), less all applicable deductions, determined by multiplying the Suggested Retail List Price ("SRLP") of such Albums by the following applicable royalty rates:

(a)   For the first two Albums, a royalty
of _____ (_%) Percent.

(b)   For the third and fourth Albums, a royalty
of _____ (_%) percent.

(c)   For all subsequent Albums, a royalty
of _____ (_%) Percent.

(d)   The foregoing basic royalty rates shall be increased by one-half (1/2) of one (1%) percent for USNRC Net Sales of the applicable Album in excess of 500,000 units, and by another one-half (1/2) of one (1%) percent for USNRC Net Sales of that Album in excess of one million units.

(e)   Notwithstanding the foregoing, with respect to any Album, in no event shall we pay you less than an amount equal to 50% of our corresponding basic royalty rate under the Distribution Agreement for such Album (i.e., not including escalations). For example, if our basic rate is 13% (before escalations), your basic royalty rate shall be not less than 6.5%.

We shall be solely responsible to pay any producer royalties out of our share. Your royalties hereunder shall be pro-rated based on the ratio which the number of masters embodying your performances ("Masters") on the applicable record bears to the total number of master recordings on such record. With respect to all exploitations of Masters other than in the form of USNRC Net Sales of Albums by the Distributor, your royalty shall be calculated and adjusted (e.g. subject to the same proportionate deductions and reductions) in the same proportionate manner as our corresponding royalty is calculated and adjusted under the Distribution Agreement. No royalties shall be payable to you hereunder until all recording costs of the Masters and all other charges required to be recouped under the Distribution Agreement shall have been recouped. At such time as all such costs have been recouped, you shall receive your royalties, subject to recoupment of your Advances hereunder. We may, in our sole discretion, instruct the Distributor to account directly to you for all royalties owed to you hereunder. In the event that we do not elect to do so, we will account and pay your royalties to you within sixty (60) days after our receipt of the corresponding royalties from the Distributor, provided in no event shall accountings be rendered to you less frequently than on a semi-annual basis.

6.   If we, or our designee, enter into a Distribution Agreement hereunder, the following will automatically apply:

(a)   All of the terms and conditions of the Distribution Agreement applicable to you shall be binding upon you as if you were a direct party thereto, provided that in no way shall you be deemed to be a third party beneficiary of the Distribution Agreement or have any direct rights against the Distributor;

(b)   The term of this Agreement shall be co-terminus with the term of the Distribution Agreement and our right to exercise options to extend the term hereof shall be as set forth in the Distribution Agreement, it being understood that the Distributor's exercise of an option under the Distribution Agreement for recordings embodying your performances shall be deemed to be our exercise of the corresponding option for your services hereunder and thereunder, provided we so notify you in each case;

(c)   You agree to comply in a timely fashion with all recording and delivery schedules contained therein, and all other obligations and services required by you thereunder;

(d)   You shall execute so-called "inducement letters" in favor of that Distributor promptly after our request, as well as any other documents or more formal agreements which may be necessary to effectuate the intent of that Distribution Agreement, or this Agreement;

(e)   If so required by the Distributor, from the date of and during the term of the Distribution Agreement, we will guarantee that you shall receive not less than $9,000 per year, or such other amount as may be required in order to satisfy the provisions of California Civil Code section 3423 (5).

7.   Notwithstanding anything to the contrary contained herein, if the term of a Distribution Agreement expires or is terminated prior to the date such agreement would have ended had the Distributor exercised all of its options thereunder, we shall have a period of _ months from the date of such expiration or termination (such period being deemed a "shopping period" for purposes hereof) within which to secure a replacement Distribution Agreement. If we have not secured a replacement Distribution Agreement within that 6 month period, you shall have the right to terminate the term hereof at any time thereafter, unless we secure a replacement Distribution Agreement prior to such termination.

8.   You hereby grant to our publishing designee 50% of your share of the worldwide copyrights (including any extensions and renewals), as well as 100% of the exclusive worldwide administration rights to the Demo Compositions and any other musical compositions written by you, in whole or in part, from and after the date hereof which are recorded hereunder and released

under any Distribution Agreement (collectively, "Compositions"). Accordingly, our designee shall have the exclusive right to issue licenses and to receive all income generated by any such Compositions. Our designee shall pay to you that percentage of the so-called "writer's share" and that percentage of 50% of the so-called "publisher's share" of such income which equals the percentage of your creative contribution to a Composition, less any expenses or third party deductions related thereto, and less a 10% administration fee, if we or our publishing designee handles the administration of the Compositions ourselves, it being understood that if we license those administrative responsibilities to a third party, we shall not retain any fees in excess of those charged by said third party. You shall be entitled to receive your writer's share of public performance income from your own performing rights society. Without limiting the generality of the foregoing, you understand and agree that you shall be bound by the so-called "controlled compositions" provisions in any Distribution Agreement. We shall have the right to enter into a more formal co-publishing and exclusive administration agreement in the future embodying the foregoing terms, plus such other customary provisions as may be negotiated in good faith between us.

9. You hereby grant to us or our designee the worldwide right to exploit and reproduce your name (both professional and legal, and whether presently or hereafter used by you), images, likenesses and biographical material concerning you and any trade names used by you in connection with the sale and advertising of records made hereunder. Our use of photographs and biographies concerning you hereunder shall be subject to the approval procedures set forth in paragraph 3 above.

10. All references to "you" hereunder shall refer to the above named individual individually and collectively, if performing as part of a group, and/or to any entities furnishing the services of or owned or controlled by you. You shall not record, nor shall we require you to record as a member of any group without your and our mutual consent.

11.   You acknowledge that your services hereunder are of a unique nature, the loss by us of which would be difficult to value in terms of damages. Accordingly, you agree that in addition to any other rights available to us, we shall have the right to seek to enjoin a breach by you of your obligations hereunder. You shall not have the right to rescind or terminate this Agreement. Neither part, hereto shall be deemed to be in breach hereof unless until the non-breaching party shall have notified the other party of the alleged breach and such other party shall fail to remedy any such failure within 30 days. Without limiting the foregoing, if you fail to per-form any of your obligations hereunder, in addition to any other rights or remedies we may have, we shall have the right to either suspend the term hereof until you have remedied such failure, or terminate the term of this Agreement.

12.   We shall have the right to enter into a more formal exclusive recording artist agreement with you in the future embodying the relevant terms hereof, plus such other customary terms as may be embodied in the Distribution Agreement or nego-tiated in good faith between us. Until such time, if ever, as the more formal agreements referred to in this Agreement is/are entered into, this agreement shall constitute your and our full and final under-standing with respect to the subject matter hereof and shall be binding between us. In the event of any action, suit or proceeding by any party hereto against any other party hereto under this agreement, the prevailing party shall be entitled to recover its attor-neys' fees in addition to the cost of said action, suit or proceeding.

13.   As between you and us, shall own all of the results and proceeds of your services hereunder and under any Distribution Agreement. You represent that you have the right to enter into this Agreement and perform your obligations hereunder, and that all material prepared by you hereunder will be original and will not infringe upon anyone's rights. You agree to identify us and our licensees against any claims which are contrary to the fore-going.

14.   We may assign all or part of this Agreement to any entity affiliated with or owned or controlled by us or to any Distributor. We will notify you of any such assignment. You may not assign any of your obligations hereunder. All notices hereunder shall be in writing at the addresses first set forth above, or such other addresses as the parties may designate in writing.

15.   You have read and understand this agreement and by signing in the space provided below, agree to be bound by the provisions hereof.

Very truly yours,

_____ PRODUCTIONS

By:_____

AGREED TO AND ACCEPTED:

_____
Artist

Social Security No.:

MERCHANDISING PROVISIONS

You hereby grant to us or our designee the exclusive worldwide right during the term hereof, at our election, to exploit, reproduce and authorize others to exploit and reproduce your name (both professional and legal, and whether presently or hereafter used by you), images, likenesses and biographical material concerning you (subject to your approval in accordance with the approval procedures set forth herein) and any trade names used by you in connection with the manufacture, distribution, or sale of reproductions of your name, images and likenesses on products such as, but not limited to, T-shirts, posters, buttons and pins ("Merchandising Rights").

We shall credit your royalty account hereunder with the following royalties on the exploitation by us or our licensees of Merchandising Rights: _____ (__%) Percent of the flat-fee or royalty received by us (or credited to us in reduction of an advance previously paid to us) in the United States from the exploitation of Merchandising Rights, less all costs paid or incurred by us in connection with the exploitation of Merchandising Rights and the collection of those monies and less all taxes and adjustments, including, without limitation, any participation or other sums payable by us in connection with the exploitation by us or our licensees of Merchandising Rights. If we license our Merchandising Rights hereunder to a third party merchandising company, we will instruct said merchandising company to account for and pay you your share of royalties pursuant to this subparagraph 9(b) directly and to calculate those royalties in the same manner and subject to the same reserves, adjustments, etc. as our corresponding royalties are subject to under our licensing agreement with such third party merchandiser. If said merchandiser fails or refuses to so pay you, we shall account to you and pay you your share within 30 days of our receipt of the corresponding royalties from said merchandiser.

AUDIT PROVISIONS

You shall have the right upon reasonable advance written notice to us to inspect our books and records at our normal place of business during normal business hours, as the same may relate specifically to advances and royalties payable to you hereunder, provided that you shall: (i) only have the right to do so with respect to any royalty statement within 12 months of the date such statement was rendered, and only once with respect to any such statement, and (ii) not have the right to inspect and Distributor's books or records. Without limiting the foregoing, if we audit any Distributor's books and records and recovers additional sums for your recordings under any Distribution Agreement, we shall promptly pay you your share of such royalties after such recovery is received by or credited to us by such Distributor, after deduction of a proportionate share of the costs of such audit.

PRODUCTION AGREEMENT
EXPLANATORY NOTES

PREAMBLE

Although some production agreements are set up in traditional contract format this agreement is set up in the form of a letter. The format does not affect the validity of the agreement, which may be set up in a more traditional form like the recording and co-publishing agreements included in this book. The purpose of a production agreement is for a producer to secure rights to an artist, develop demos and shop that artist and their demos to record companies. If the production company is successful in securing a record deal for that artist, the production company will negotiate and enter into the recording agreement with that record company. The production company then becomes responsible for furnishing the services of the artist to the record company. Because the recording agreement is negotiated on the basis of the production agreement, many of the issues discussed with respect to the recording agreement will apply to a production agreement as well. For example, if the production agreement is with a group rather than with a single artist, group provisions will be included. (See the Group Provisions paragraph in the recording agreement explanatory notes. To avoid repetition, we will confine our discussion of the production agreement to the terms which are unique to it.

You will notice that the production agreement makes reference in the preamble to the respective publishing designees of the parties. This will only apply in situations where the production company is acquiring publishing rights to songs written by the artist. Because publishing is such a valuable asset, most production companies will want to negotiate for co-publishing rights to the artist's songs. On the other hand, a producer may feel that it is better to leave this asset undisturbed as an indication of good will toward the artist. This will depend upon the bargaining power of the parties, and the goals of the production company. However, artists should resist this kind of provision if at all possible. If the artist is unable to convince the production company to allow him 100% retention of publishing rights the artist should at least negotiate that the production company compensate him for whatever share of the publishing the production company demands. For fair market value dollar figures that might help you determine what you should be receiving as compensation for publishing rights to your songs see the chapter on publishing and paragraph 6 of the explanatory notes to the publishing agreement.

1. SERVICES

In most cases, one of the valuable services the production company can provide to a new artist is the ability to produce quality demos which can be presented to record companies. In some cases, demos will already exist, and the production company will merely perform the shopping function. The other valuable function that the production company offers is its contacts with record companies which the artist may not have.

2. TERM

A time period should be included in the production agreement within which the production company must record demos and/or secure a record deal. This time period in which the production company must complete demos on the artist should not exceed three months from the execution date of the agreement. The time period within which a record agreement must be obtained for that artist by the production company should not exceed six months to one year, from the completion date of the demos. What an artist is able to negotiate with a production company in these areas obviously depends upon the circumstances, such as whether the artist has experience and a track record in the industry, whether or not other companies are interested in the artist at that time, etc. This paragraph also deals with what the artist's rights should be in the event the production company is unable to obtain a recording agreement within the shopping period.

3. ARTIST'S OBLIGATIONS

This paragraph describes some of the activities which most production companies will engage in with the artist before approaching record companies. It also clarifies that the production company is being granted the sole right to negotiate and enter into the record deal on the artist's behalf. Depending upon the bargaining power of the artist, the artist may nevertheless insist upon involvement in the negotiation of the record deal. This may include the right to approve the terms of the recording agreement, although this may restrict the production company's ability to negotiate freely. If the artist is given the right to have input into the production company's negotiations with a record label the artist must demonstrate that he has a clear understanding of the key issues and is prepared to be reasonable in his demands. Otherwise the artist can blow the deal. As an alternative, the artist may negotiate for provisions in the production agreement that address key issues that must be in the recording agreement. By doing so the artist has indicated to the production company what he is willing to accept as a minimum before the production company starts to negotiate with a record label. It is common for a production agreement to provide that only a record agreement with a "major" record label, or a label affiliated with, or distributed by a major label, will be deemed acceptable to the artist.

4. ADVANCES / ROYALTIES

The financial arrangements between the artist and the production company can be established in a number of ways. The structure provided here is for the artist to receive a specific advance and royalty rate for each album. The amount of those advances and royalties will vary, depending upon the kind of deal the production company anticipates they will be able to negotiate with a record label, and the bargaining power of the artist and production company. Usually, in a production deal, the artist can expect to receive less of an artist advance than the artist would receive were they to be signed to a major record company directly. This is because the production company will take its share of advances and royalties out of the overall advances and royalties that a record company would otherwise pay to an artist if that artist were signed directly to that record company. Therefore the artist can expect to receive 25 percent to 50 percent of the advances and royalties mentioned in the explanatory notes to the record agreement.

Another popular structure is for the production company and the artist to agree to split any net profits derived from the recording agreement according to percentages negotiated between the artist and the production company in advance. The most common split of net profits between an artist and production company is an equal 50/50 split, although it is not inappropriate for an artist to request that the percentage be adjusted in his or her favor. For example, an artist may negotiate for the net profits to be split 60/40 in favor of the artist for the first two albums, 65/35 for the next two, and 70/30 for any albums recorded under the production agreement after that. The actual percentages will depend upon the bargaining power of the artist and production company, and the extent of the services to be performed by the production company. For example, if the production company is investing time and money to produce demos, and perhaps to even financially support the artist during the recording and shopping of the demos, a 50/50 split is probably reasonable. If on the other hand, all the production company is doing is using its contacts to obtain a record deal, a lower percentage of the net profits for the production company should be negotiated.

Obviously, the definition of "net profits" is crucial to both the artist and production company. The basic concept is that any advances paid to the production company by a record label, less recording costs and any royalties paid to the production company by the record company after recoupment of recording costs and other charges, would be considered "net profits." From those net profits, the production company may request that certain of its expenses be deducted off the top. Examples of these expenses are listed at the end of paragraph 4. Certain expenses, such as attorney's fees, should be negotiated by the artist. Another issue which needs to be addressed is who bears the responsibility for paying producers.

Under a percentage-based production deal, the producer royalties may either be deducted from the gross profits paid to the production company by a record label before net profits are split, or they may be deducted solely from the production company's share of net profits. This issue can be complicated if the production company itself is providing producer services. You will note that in this agreement the production company is assuming this responsibility. In effect, the production company has agreed to pay the artist a net advance and net royalty rate, which the artist will not be required to share with any producer. This structure works particularly well when the production company intends to produce most of or all of the songs contained on a project.

If the production company is producing part or all the of the album, and is deducting its producer's fees off the top, the artist should negotiate a fair market value for the producer's services in advance. Under no circumstances should the artist under a percentage based deal be required to bear sole responsibility for producer royalties. Another issue which the artist should negotiate in advance is a fair market value for the use of a production company's studio in determining how much a production company can charge for the use of that studio. This negotiation should address the recording of demos that are recorded prior to a record deal, and masters recorded after a record deal has been entered into. In other words, the artist and production company should agree in advance what rate the producer/production company will charge the project for services rendered at his or her studio. Depending upon the agreement, and the amount of the budget concerned, an artist should negotiate that the producer charge the project a discounted rate to use his studio.

Yet another possible financial structure where the production company is also the producer is for the producer to have a right to produce a minimum number of masters on the artist once a record deal is entered into. This is clearly the most advantageous for the artist. Under this scenario, the artist, not the producer, would be primarily responsible for negotiating the terms of the record agreement and would enter into it directly. Therefore, the production agreement would specify the financial terms payable to the producer for his or her producing services and the number of tracks guaranteed to that producer under the production agreement. The producer in that case should negotiate for a premium on his or her going rate as a reward for his or her assistance in obtaining the record deal for the artist. For example, if the producer normally receives a 3 point royalty, the producer should negotiate a 4 point royalty rate or higher, for masters produced by him or her as part of this type of production agreement. The producer should also negotiate to receive advances and royalties directly from the record company via a letter of direction from the artist to the record company. Further, the producer should be reimbursed off the top for any expenses that are incurred by the producer to record demos and shop for the record deal. It is also useful to include some provision in the production agreement in case the record company refuses to allow the producer to produce the number of tracks that are guaranteed them under the production agreement. One contractual solution is to provide that if the record company refuses to allow the producer to produce the number of tracks guaranteed in the production contract, the artist agrees to pay the producer 50 percent of his or her fee and royalties for any non-produced masters. This could apply equally in the event that the producer is unavailable to produce the number of committed masters because of other professional commitments.

In deciding whether to offer the artist a fixed advance and royalty or a percentage of net profits the production company should be realistic about the financial terms they are going to be able to negotiate for that artist with a record company. From the artist's perspective, the decision involves many of the same issues discussed in our explanatory notes for the recording agreement.

Since royalties and advances under any of the above scenarios will be based upon the royalties and advances paid by the record company, all royalties should be calculated by the same method of computation as are contained in the recording agreement. Both the artist and the production company may prefer that the record company pay them their respective shares of the royalties and advances separately if the record company will agree to do so. However, some production companies will prefer to handle all monies paid by the record company to ensure that they are paid properly. Finally, a provision may be added with respect to defining the audit rights of both the artist and the production company. Typically, the record company will only allow the party with whom it is contracting to audit its books and records. This means that an artist signed to a production company will not have the right to audit the record company. Accordingly, it is important for the artist to negotiate with the production company for the right to "piggyback" on any audit which the production company conducts against the record company. This means that the production company would be required to notify the artist of any audit it intends to conduct, and, subject to the record company's restrictions, allow the artist to participate in the audit, at his or her own expense. In any event, the artist should negotiate to be fully advised of the results of any audit and to be paid his or her share of any monies recovered after the deduction of his/ her share of expenses associated with the audit. An example of this type of provision is included at the end of this Agreement. If the artist is not paid directly by the record company, the artist should negotiate for separate audit rights against the company.

5. ADDITIONAL OBLIGATIONS

This paragraph summarizes the obligations of the artist after the recording agreement is entered into.

6. REPLACEMENT AGREEMENTS

This provision deals with the production company's right to obtain a replacement record deal in the event the original recording agreement ends prematurely. See paragraph 1.4 of the recording agreement explanatory notes.

7. PUBLISHING RIGHTS

If the production company intends to obtain co-publishing rights to songs written by the artist, this provision should be included. If the artist is forced to accept this provision, the artist should negotiate that the production company be entitled only to the publishing rights of compositions that are recorded and released under the record deal. Many production companies will insist upon obtaining rights to all compositions written by the artist during the term of the recording agreement. It is our opinion that a production company is not entitled to an artist's publishing simply because the production company is helping to secure a record deal. If the production company insists upon obtaining publishing rights from an artist the production company should be prepared to function as a real publisher. This means providing competent administration of the artist's songs, as well as paying the artist separate non-cross-collateralized advances. These advances should be reasonably comparable to what the artist could expect to receive if he were to sign a publishing deal directly with a third party publisher.

Whether or not the production company intends to demand publishing rights the production company must include a provision that the artist agrees to be bound by the controlled composition provisions contained in the recording agreement. As a practical matter, the artist will probably be required to make this agreement for the direct benefit of the record company under the artist inducement letter, but the production company should have this provision in its agreement with the artist as well. If publishing rights are obtained by the production company, it is best that these rights be formalized in the form of a real co-publishing and exclusive administration agreement like the one included in this book.

The production company and the artist may decide to enter into that formal co-publishing agreement at the same time as the production agreement is entered into. However, since production agreements are speculative as to the company's ability to get an artist signed, a production company may not want to go to the expense and time of preparing and negotiating a formal co-publishing agreement until a record deal is obtained.

8. NAME AND LIKENESS

This is essentially the same name and likeness provision as is discussed in the recording agreement explanatory notes. Some production companies will attempt to obtain merchandising rights, as well as publishing rights from an artist. We recommend that an artist resist any attempts on the production company's part to obtain rights to exploit merchandise containing the artist's name and likeness. Nevertheless, we have attached a typical merchandising provision for contracts which include such a provision. If a contract does include such a provision, the production company will probably ask for 50 percent of any merchandising revenue. The artist should negotiate this percentage down to between 15 percent and 25 percent. As with the publishing issues, the artist's share of these monies should not be cross-collateralized with any other advances. In rare circumstances an artist may request an advance for these rights as well.

9. MISCELLANEOUS

All of the issues addressed in the following paragraphs are discussed in the explanatory notes of the recording agreement. See paragraph 13.

One new provision contained in this paragraph is a provision that in the event there is lawsuit by either the artist or the production company against one another, the prevailing party in any lawsuit would be entitled to have his attorneys' fees paid by the other party.

One final note: If the production company is entering into an agreement with a minor — an individual under the legal age of 18 who has not been emancipated from his or her parents — the production company must obtain approval from the parents, and ultimately from a court, in order for the production agreement to be binding.

Sample of a
Recording Agreement
&

Recording Agreement
Explanatory Notes

Recording Agreement

AGREEMENT made as of the __th day of _____, 199_, by and between Artist ("you") and _____ Records, Inc. ("us").

For good and valuable consideration, receipt of which is hereby mutually acknowledged, the parties hereto agree as follows:

1. SERVICES/TERM.

1.1. During the term of this agreement (the "Term"), you will render to us your exclusive recording services on the terms and conditions contained herein. (You are sometimes called "the Artist" below; all references in this agreement to "you and the Artist", and the like, will be understood to refer to you alone.)

1.2. The Term will commence on the date hereof and will continue, unless extended as provided herein, for a first period (the "first Contract Period") ending ____ (_) months after the Delivery to us of the Recordings comprising the Recording Obligation (defined in Article 2 below) for the first Contract Period, but will not end earlier than one year after the date of its commencement.

1.3. We shall have ____ (_) separate and consecutive options to extend the Term for additional periods on the same terms and conditions as the first Contract Period, except as provided below ("Option Periods"). (The first Contract Period and the Option Periods are sometimes referred to herein as "Contract Periods".) Each Option Period will commence immediately upon the expiration of the then-current Contract Period. Each such option will be deemed to be automatically exercised by us unless we send you notice in writing to the contrary at any time before the expiration of the then-current Contract Period.

1.4. Reference is hereby made to the production and distribution agreement between us and Distribution Records, Inc. (the "Distribution Agreement"). Notwithstanding anything to the contrary contained or implied herein, in the event the Distribution

Agreement terminates or expires for any reason prior to our exercise of all of the foregoing options, the term of this agreement shall be automatically extended for a period of time reasonably necessary for us to secure a replacement distribution arrangement. Any such period of time not exceeding _____ (_) months shall be deemed to be reasonable. During that extension period, you will cooperate with us in our efforts to obtain a replacement distribution arrangement, and except for our obligation to account for and pay you royalties on previously released Recordings made hereunder, all of our other obligations shall be extended accordingly. We will notify you when we have obtained a replacement distribution arrangement, at which time, provided that such replacement distribution arrangement is with a so called "major" record company, or a label distributed by or affiliated with a major record company, or with a so-called major independent label with national independent distribution, the term of this agreement shall continue from the date of the commencement of the extension period, and all terms and conditions herein shall continue in full force and effect as if no such extension had occurred. From and after the effective date of the replacement distribution agreement, all references to Distributor hereunder shall be deemed to refer to the replacement distributor, and all references to the Distributor Agreement hereunder shall be deemed to refer to the replacement distribution agreement. In addition, you agree to execute any documents reasonably required by any replacement distributor, as well as any amendments to this agreement which may be necessary to conform the non-material provisions of this agreement to the requirements of such replacement distributor.

2. RECORDING OBLIGATION.

2.1. During each Contract Period you will record and Deliver to us Recordings sufficient to constitute one (1) Album (the "Recording Obligation").

2.2. You will Deliver the Recording Obligation for each Contract Period within the first _____ (_) months of that Contract Period.

2.3. No Composition previously recorded by you nor any medley, "live" Recording, Joint Recording or Multiple Record Album will be recorded as part of any Recording Obligation without our prior written consent. Recordings not made in full compliance with this agreement will not apply in fulfillment of the Recording Obligation.

2.4. You shall not deviate from the Delivery schedule specified in paragraph 2.2 above without our written consent; timely Delivery as provided therein shall be deemed a material obligation hereunder. Each Album delivered in fulfillment of a Recording Obligation shall consist entirely of Recordings made in the course of that Album recording project.

3. RECORDING PROCEDURE.

3.1. Not later than fifteen (15) business days before commencement of recording of each Recording Obligation, you shall submit to us for our approval, a written proposal specifying: (a) the material you plan to record, including the number of Compositions, the titles and publishers thereof and the names of the vocalists, musicians and individual producer(s) you plan to engage; (b) a proposed budget for all Recording Costs ; and (c) the date and time of each recording session and the name and address of the recording studio to be used. You shall not commence recording any Recordings hereunder until we have approved in writing all of the foregoing items. The recording of any part of the Recording Obligation may not be commenced earlier than three (3) months after our acceptance of all of the Recordings constituting the Recording Obligation for the preceding Contract Period. You shall notify us of all recording sessions and we shall have the right to have a representative present at all times.

3.2. You shall notify the appropriate Local of the American Federation of Musicians in advance of each recording session. All Recordings hereunder and performances embodied thereon shall be produced in accordance with the rules and regulations of the American Federation of Musicians, the American Federation of Television and Radio Artists and all other unions having jurisdiction.

3.2.(a) As and when required by us or Distributor, you shall allow our or Distributor's representatives to attend any or all recording sessions hereunder, at our or Distributor's non-recoupable expense.

3.3. You will timely furnish us with all information which we require in connection with the making of the Recordings and in order to comply with our union obligations, including session reports, and the dates and places of any prior sessions relating to each Recording, all Immigration and Naturalization Form I-9's, all W-4's and "Form Bs" covering each session, and all changes of title, music and lyrics of the Compositions recorded.

3.4. We may require you to cancel and/or terminate any recording session, even if previously approved hereunder and without limiting any of our other rights, if we reasonably anticipate that the amount of Recording Costs will exceed those specified in the approved budget by 10% or more, or that the Recordings being produced will not be satisfactory.

3.4.(a) You will not be required to perform together with any other royalty artist without your consent. We shall not be deemed to be unreasonable in rejecting any request for you to record with another royalty artist.

3.5.(a) The term "Delivery" or "Deliver" in this agreement means, with respect to each Album recorded pursuant to a Recording Obligation hereunder, our receipt of: (i) two (2) fully mixed, edited, sequenced and equalized digital stereo master tapes, commercially satisfactory to us for the manufacture and sale of Phonograph Records. Each such master tape shall contain the Compositions, timings and sequence approved by us for the particular analog or Audiophile Record version. One (1) master tape shall be properly configured for the purpose of cutting lacquer or equivalent masters for the manufacture of analog Phonograph Records and one (1) master tape shall be properly configured for the manufacture of Audiophile Records, with SMPTE time coded logs, quality control verification, and all other customarily required technical information and such master tapes shall be in a digital Sony 1630 format or such other digital format as is reasonably required by Distributor; and (ii) fully-proofed final reference discs; all original and duplicate Recordings of the material recorded including all out-takes and unused recordings; all necessary licenses, affirmations and appropriate permissions, including mechanical licenses, sideman clearances, and Producer Affirmations; and all "label copy" and other information needed by us to manufacture and market Phonograph Records from the Recordings.

3.5.(b) Our election to make a payment to you which was to have been made upon Delivery of Recordings or to release a Record derived from such Recordings shall not be deemed to be our acknowledgement that such Delivery was properly made, and we shall not be deemed to have waived either our right to require such complete and proper performance thereafter or our remedies for your failure to perform in accordance therewith.

3.6. You agree to deliver (or cause the individual producer of the Recordings to deliver) the Immigration and Naturalization Service certificates described in paragraph 3.8 below, Form Bs and W-4s to us within seventy-two (72) hours after each session hereunder so that we may timely make all required union payments, and you agree to deliver all other applicable invoices, receipts, vouchers and documents within one (1) week after your receipt thereof. If we incur late-payment penalties by reason of your failure to make timely delivery of any such materials, you will reimburse us for same upon demand and, without limiting its other rights and remedies, we may deduct an amount equal to all such penalties from monies otherwise payable to you under this agreement. We shall be responsible for late-payment penalties caused solely by our acts or omissions.

3.7. You will furnish the services of the individual producers of Recordings hereunder, and shall be solely responsible for engaging and paying them. If you request us to pay any producers on your behalf, the budget for the recording project concerned will be charged with a Recording Cost (as defined in Article 4.2 below) item in the amount that we are obligated to pay those producers in connection with that project or is allocated in the approved budget (but with respect to any Distributor staff producer, in no event less than _____ Dollars ($_____) per Side, or _____ Dollars ($_____) per Album if such producers produce an entire Album). (The preceding sentence will not apply unless you have consented to the engagement of the producer concerned and the terms of such engagement, or the assignment of the staff or contract producer concerned to the recording project).

3.8. In connection with each recording session conducted hereunder, you will comply with the following procedures required by United States Immigration Law:

3.8.(a) Before any individual renders services in connection with the recording of any Recording hereunder (including, without limitation, each background instrumentalist, background vocalist, producer and engineer):

3.8.(a.1) You will require each such individual to complete and sign the EMPLOYEE INFORMATION AND VERIFICATION ("employee section") of a U.S. Immigration and Naturalization Service ("INS") Employment Eligibility Certificate ("Form I-9"), unless you have already obtained (and retained) such certificate from that individual within the past three years;

3.8.(a.2) You will complete and sign the EMPLOYER REVIEW AND VERIFICATION ("employer section") of each such certificate; and

3.8.(a.3) You will attach copies of the documents establishing identity and employment eligibility that you examine in accordance with the instructions in the employer section.

3.8.(b) You will not permit any such Person who fails to complete the employee section (or to furnish you with the required documentation) to render any services in connection with Recordings made under this agreement.

3.8.(c) You will deliver the employee and employer certificates (with copies of the necessary documents attached) to us within seventy-two (72) hours after the conclusion of the session concerned.

3.8.(d) You will comply with any revised or additional verification and documentation procedures required by the INS in the future.

3.9. You will cause each individual producer who will render services in connection with any Recording made hereunder to execute a "Producer's Affirmation" in the form of Exhibit "A" hereto. You will cause each "sideman" rendering services in connection with any Recording made hereunder to execute a "Sideman's Affirmation" in the form of Exhibit "B" hereto. No Recording will be considered to be Delivered under this agreement until we have received the aforesaid documents.

4. RECOUPABLE COSTS.

4.1. We will pay all union scale payments required to be made to the Artist in connection with Recordings made hereunder, all costs of instrumental, vocal and other personnel specifically approved by us in connection with Recordings hereunder, and all other amounts required to be paid by us pursuant to any applicable law or any collective bargaining agreement between us and any union representing persons who render services in connection with such Recordings. Notwithstanding the foregoing, you agree that the Advances hereunder include the prepayment of session union scale as provided in the applicable union codes, and you agree to complete any documentation required by the applicable union to implement this sentence. (Union contracts will be filed and supplied to us and pension benefits will be paid on your behalf by us, which payments shall be an Advance.)

4.2. All amounts described in paragraph 4.1 above plus all other amounts representing direct expenses paid by us, or incurred in connection with the Recordings produced hereunder (including, without limitation, travel, rehearsal, and equipment rental and cartage expenses, costs incurred in connection with remixing and/or "sweetening," advances to individual producers, transportation costs, hotel and living expenses approved by us, all studio and engineering charges, costs of editing, remixing and mastering (including sequenced, equalized reference master disc and sequenced equalized coded digital master), in connection with our facilities and personnel or otherwise, and all costs necessary to prepare Recordings for release on digital media are herein sometimes called "Recording Costs" and shall constitute Advances. Notwithstanding any of the foregoing to the contrary, costs of metal parts other than lacquer, copper or equivalent masters will not be recoupable from your royalties or reimbursable by you. All packaging costs incurred in creating or producing Album covers, sleeves, and other packaging elements in excess of our then standard design, engraving or manufacturing costs shall be recoupable from all monies payable to you hereunder. Notwithstanding any of the foregoing to the contrary, in preparation for the initial release in the United States of each Album comprising part of your Recording Obligation, we will endeavor to consult with you regarding the proposed Album cover artwork if such artwork will exceed our than standard design, engraving or manufacturing costs. Such artwork will be made available to you at Distributor's offices. We will request that Distributor make any such changes in the artwork as you may reasonably request in order to eliminate any such excess costs, provided that Distributor shall not be required to make any changes which would delay the release of the Album or which Distributor would otherwise find objectionable. Fifty percent (50%) of costs incurred in connection with the production, acquisition or exploitation of motion pictures containing your performances (audiovisual or otherwise) will constitute Advances, and all direct expenses paid or incurred in connection with independent promotion of recordings of your performances (i.e., promotion by Persons other than our employees or those of the distributor of the Records concerned) will constitute Advances. Payments to the AFM Special Payments Fund and the Music Performance Trust Fund based upon record sales (so-called "per-record royalties"), shall not constitute Advances and shall be paid by us.

4.3. Any Recording Costs which are in excess of the budget approved by us will be your sole responsibility and will be promptly paid by you (or reimbursed by you if paid by us), provided that solely with respect to Recording Costs which exceed the budget approved by us by no more than 10%, such Excess recording costs will be paid by us, provided that any such costs will be deemed advances hereunder, and provided further that we have given our prior written approval for you to incur such excess recording costs in advance in each instance. To the extent you have not reimbursed us for such excess amount(s), we may deduct such amounts from any sums that may become payable to you hereunder. Recording Costs with respect to any Joint Recording will be apportioned in the same manner as your royalties under subparagraph 7.8(b) below. Proper Recording Costs shall be paid promptly by us after our receipt of an approved and appropriate voucher for each item thereof.

4.4.(a.1) With respect to the Master Recordings constituting your Recording Obligation for the Contract Period concerned, we will pay you the following Advances. Each Advance will be payable one-half (1/2) on commencement of recording of the Master Recordings concerned and the other one-half (1/2) within thirty (30) days after the Delivery to us of the Master Recordings constituting your Recording Obligation for the Contract Period concerned.

4.4.(a.2) The amount of the Advance for the Album Delivered in fulfillment of the Recording Obligation for the first Contract Period will be $_____. You hereby acknowledge receipt of the full amount of the foregoing Advance.

4.4.(a.3) The amount of the Advance for each Album, other than the first Contract Period, will be two-thirds (2/3) of whichever of the following amounts is less (subject to 4.4(a)(4) below):

4.4.(a.3.i) the amount of the royalties credited to Artist's account on Net Sales through Normal Retail Channels in the United States of the Album made under this agreement released most recently before Delivery of the Album concerned (the "Preceding Album"), but only for the nine month period subsequent to the date of initial release in the United States of the Preceding Album, as determined by us from our first monthly trial balance accounting statement for the nine month period concerned or, after deduction of reasonable reserves for returns and credits not to exceed __% of the aggregate number of units of the Album shipped to Distributor's customers; or

4.4.(a.3.ii) the average of the amounts of such royalties on the two such Albums released most recently before the Delivery of the Album concerned; less whichever of the following amounts is more (subject to 4.4(a)(4) below):

4.4.(a.3.iii) the amount of the Recording Costs for the Album recorded most recently hereunder in fulfillment of your Recording Obligation before the Delivery of the Album concerned; or

4.4.(a.3.iv) the average amount of the Recording Costs for the two (2) such Albums recorded hereunder in fulfillment of your Recording Obligation before the Delivery of the Album concerned (or, if only one Album has been recorded hereunder, the amount of the Recording Costs for that Album).

4.4.(a.4) The Advance for each Album Delivered in fulfillment of your Recording Obligation for each Contract Period, other than the first Contract Period, will be no more than the applicable maximum or less than the applicable minimum below:

	MINIMUM	MAXIMUM
4.4.(a.4.i) Album Delivered during the first Option Periods:	$_____	$_____
4.4.(a.4.ii) Album Delivered during the second Option Period:	$_____	$_____
4.4.(a.4.iii) Album Delivered during the third Option Period:	$_____	$_____
4.4.(a.4.iv) Album Delivered during the fourth Option Period:	$_____	$_____
4.4.(a.4.v) Album Delivered during the fifth Option Period:	$_____	$_____

4.4.(a.5.vi) Album Delivered during
the sixth Option Period: $_____ $_____

4.5. The aggregate amount of the compensation paid to you under this agreement will not be less than Nine Thousand Dollars ($9,000) for the first Fiscal Year, $12,000 for the second Fiscal Year, and $15,000 for each Fiscal Year thereafter. "Fiscal Year", in this paragraph, means the annual period beginning on the date of commencement of the term of this agreement, and each subsequent annual period during the continuance of that term beginning on the anniversary of that commencement date. If you have not received compensation of at least the applicable amounts set forth in this paragraph under this agreement for a Fiscal Year, we will pay you the amount of the deficiency before the end of that Fiscal Year; at least forty (40) days before the end of each Fiscal Year you will notify us if you have not received such minimum compensation for that year, and of the amount of the deficiency. Each such payment will constitute an Advance and will be applied in reduction of any and all monies subsequently becoming due to you under this agreement. We may not withhold or require you to repay any such payment under any other provision of this agreement. If the term of this agreement ends before the last day of a Fiscal Year, the applicable sum referred to in the first sentence of this paragraph will be reduced proportionately for the purpose of computing the payment to be made under this paragraph for that Fiscal Year. You acknowledge that this paragraph is included to avoid compromise of our rights (including our entitlement to injunctive relief) by reason of a finding of applicability of California law, but does not constitute a concession by us that California law is actually applicable.

4.6. Unless otherwise specified, all sums paid to you or on behalf of you or Artist during the Term, other than royalties paid pursuant to Articles 7 and 9, will constitute Advances.

5. RIGHTS.

5.1. Each Recording made hereunder or furnished to us by you or the Artist under this agreement or during the Term will be considered a "work made for hire" (as specified in the United States

Copyright Act) for us. If any Recording shall not constitute a "work made for hire" for any reason, then this agreement will automatically operate as an irrevocable assignment from you to us of all rights, including the sound recording copyrights, therein. All Recordings made or furnished to us by you or the Artist hereunder or during the Term from Inception of Recording and all matrices and Phonograph Records manufactured therefrom, together with all performances embodied therein will be our sole property of, and we shall have the exclusive right to copyright all such Recordings in its name as the owner and author thereof throughout the world for the full term of copyright, including any renewals and extensions thereof. You and the Artist will promptly execute and deliver to us such short form copyright assignments and all other documents regarding our rights in the Recordings, as we reasonably requests in order to implement the provisions of this agreement. Upon your failure or refusal to comply with such requests, we may sign such documents in your name or the name of the Artist and make appropriate disposition of them. We will give you five (5) days notice before signing any document in your name. We may dispense with that waiting period when necessary, in our judgement, to protect or enforce our rights, but we will notify you in each instance when we have done so. We will not be required to notify you before signing short form assignments of rights granted in this agreement for recordation in the Copyright Office.

5.2. Without limiting the generality of the foregoing, we and any Person authorized by us shall have the unlimited, exclusive and perpetual rights, throughout the world: (i) to manufacture Phonograph Records derived from Recordings in any form and by any method now or hereafter known; (ii) to sell, transfer, advertise, publicize or otherwise deal in the same under any trademarks, trade names and labels, or to refrain from such manufacture, sale and dealing; and (iii) to reproduce, adapt, and otherwise use such Recordings in any medium in any manner including but not limited to use in audiovisual works, without payment of any compensation to you or any other Person except the royalties, if any, which may be expressly prescribed for the use concerned under Articles 7 and 9.

5.3. Provided you are then in compliance with all of your material obligations hereunder:

5.3.(a) We will cause Distributor to release each Album constituting your Recording Obligation and Delivered by you hereunder in the United States within nine (9) months after your Delivery to us of the Album concerned. If Distributor fails to do so you may notify us, within five (5) days after the end of the nine-month period concerned that you intend to terminate the term of this agreement unless we cause Distributor to release the Album within sixty (60) days after Distributor's receipt of our notice to Distributor (the "cure period"). If Distributor fails to do so, you may terminate the term of this agreement within thirty (30) days after the end of the cure period (the "Termination Notice"), subject to the extension provisions of paragraph 1.4 above. On receipt by us of the Termination Notice, but subject to the extension provisions of paragraph 1.4 above, the term of this agreement will end as if it had expired by the passage of time and all parties will be deemed to have fulfilled all of their respective obligations under this agreement, except those obligations which survive the end of the term (e.g. warranties, re-recording restrictions and obligations to pay royalties). Distributor's failure to release any Album this subparagraph shall not constitute a breach of this agreement and your sole and exclusive remedy for failure by Distributor to release any Album shall be termination as setforth in this subparagraph. If you fail to give us either of the notices described in this subparagraph within the period specified, your right of termination hereunder will lapse. The running of each nine month, six-month and sixty day period specified above will be suspended (and the expiration of each of those periods postponed) for the period of any suspension of this agreement. If any such nine-month or sixty-day period would otherwise expire on a date between October 31st and January 15, its running will be suspended for the duration of the period between October 31st and January 15th and its expiration date will be postponed by the same amount of time. An Album will be deemed released for the purposes of this paragraph, when Distributor has announced its availability for sale in the United States. This paragraph will not apply to any Recording Obligation Album not Delivered within the time prescribed herein.

5.4. During the term, with respect to Phonograph Records manufactured for sale in the United States, we will not without your consent:

5.4.(a)   initially release any Album comprised of Recordings Delivered pursuant to any Recording Obligation under any label other than the "Distributor" label, or other "top-line" label then in use by Distributor, or the replacement distributor, if applicable, for Records by artists then under exclusive term contract to Distributor.

5.4.(b) License any Master Recording made under this agreement to a third party for use in any television commercial which either promotes the sale of alcohol or tobacco or endorses a political candidate or position.

This paragraph will not apply to any Album constituting a Recording Obligation not Delivered within the applicable time period.

5A. NAMES AND LIKENESSES.

5A.1. We and our licensees shall have the right and may grant to others the right to reproduce, print, publish, or disseminate in any medium your name, the names, portraits, pictures and likenesses of the Artist and producer(s), and all other persons who render services in connection with the Recordings (including, without limitation, all professional, group, and other assumed or fictitious names used by you or them), and biographical material concerning them, for purposes of advertising, promotion and trade in any manner or any medium. We and our licensees shall have the exclusive right and may grant to others the rights to reproduce the Artist's name, portraits, pictures and likenesses including, without limitation, all professional group, and other assumed or fictitious names used by you on merchandise of any kind, without payment of any compensation to you, the Artist or any other Person (except as provided in paragraph 5A.1(a), subject to the next sentence. With respect to merchandise other than Phonograph Records, the merchandising uses authorized by the preceding sentence shall be limited to merchandise containing adaptations or reproduction of Album cover artwork, graphic materials used for marketing or publicity and other materials owned or controlled by us or Distributor. During the Term, neither you nor the Artist will permit any Person to use the name (including, without limitation, all professional, group, and other assumed or fictitious names) or likeness of the Artist in connection with Phonograph Records, or in connection with blank recording tape or tape recording equipment.

5A.1.(a) If we receive any payments for any use of the Artist's name or picture in connection with merchandise other than Phonograph Records ("Merchandise Uses"), your royalty account will be credited with fifty percent (50%) of the net amount of those receipts, as computed after deduction of any direct expenses actually incurred by us in connection with Merchandise Uses. If any item of revenues or expenses is attributable to receipts from names or pictures of others, the amount of that item to be taken into account in computing net receipts under this paragraph will be determined by apportionment.

5A.2. You and the Artist will cooperate with us, as we reasonably request, in connection with preparing photographs and other materials and rendering other services to promote and publicize you and the Recordings, including appearing at photo sessions arranged by the Distributor for the purpose of creating Album artwork.

5A.3. We or Distributor will make available to you for your approval, any pictures of you or biographical material about you which we or Distributor propose to use for packaging, advertising or publicity. We will not use any such material which you disapprove in writing, provided you furnish substitute material, satisfactory to us in our sole discretion, in time for our use within our production and release schedules. This subparagraph will not apply to any material previously approved by you or used by us or Distributor. No inadvertent failure to comply with this subparagraph will constitute a breach of this agreement, and we will not be entitled to injunctive relief to restrain the continuing use of any material used in contravention of this paragraph.

6. INTENTIONALLY DELETED.

7. <u>ROYALTIES</u>.

7.1. As full consideration for all of the rights granted to us hereunder and provided you have fully complied with all of your material obligations hereunder, we will pay you, subject to all of the terms and conditions hereof, a royalty computed at the applicable percentage indicated below of the applicable Royalty Base Price with respect to the Net Sale of Records consisting entirely of Recordings (other than audiovisual Recordings) recorded hereunder and sold by us or our licensees through Normal Retail Channels in the United States ("UNRC Net Sales").   Such royalties shall be inclusive of all royalties payable to you and any other Persons engaged on your behalf or at your request on account of the sale of Records or other exploitation of the Recordings made hereunder:

7.1.(a)   <u>On Records sold for distribution in the Unites States</u>:

7.1.(a.1) On Albums:

7.1.(a.1.i) Albums Delivered during the first
Contract Period and the first Option Period: __%

7.1.(a.1.ii) Album Delivered during the second
Option Period: __%

7.1.(a.1.iii) Album Delivered during the third
Option Period: __%

7.1.(a.1.iv) Album Delivered during the fourth
Option Period: __%

7.1.(a.1.v) Album Delivered during the fifth
Option Period: __%

7.1.(a.1.vi) Album Delivered during the sixth
Option Period: __%

7.1.(a.2) On Singles: __%

7.1.(a.3)   The royalty rates pursuant to subsection 7.1(a) (1) will apply to the first five hundred (500,000) units of UNRC Net Sales in the United States ("USNRC Net Sales") of each Album consisting of Master Recordings made hereunder. The applicable royalty rates will be increased by one-half (1/2) of one percent (1%) on the next five hundred units of USNRC Net Sales of any such Album, and by another one-half (1/2) of one percent (1%) on USNRC Net Sales of any such Album in excess of 1 million (1,000,000) units.

7.1.(b) <u>On Records sold for distribution outside the United States</u>:

7.1.(b.1) ___% on Albums and ___% on Singles sold for distribution in Canada.

7.1.(b.2) ___% on Albums and ___% on Singles sold for distribution in Japan, The U.K., France, Germany, Italy, Spain, Belgium, the Netherlands and Luxembourg; and

7.1.(b.3) ___% on Albums and ___% on Singles sold for distribution elsewhere.

7.2. The royalty rate with respect to Net Sales of Phonograph Records sold through any record club or similar distribution plan owned or controlled by us or Distributor shall be one-half (1/2) of the royalty rate applicable to Records sold for distribution through Normal Retail Channels, but shall not exceed a rate of ____ percent (_%). No royalty shall be payable with respect to (i) Phonograph Records received by members of any record club in an introductory offer in connection with joining it or upon recommending that another join it or as a result of the purchase of a required number of Phonograph Records including, without limitation, records distributed as "bonus" or "free" Records, or (ii) Phonograph Records for which such record club is not paid.

7.2.1. Notwithstanding clause (i) of the last sentence of paragraph 7.2, at least 50% of all Phonograph Records distributed through any record club owned or controlled by us or Distributor during the term of this agreement will be deemed to have been sold. That computation will be made on an overall basis rather than at the end of each accounting period.

7.3. The royalty rate on any Record described in clause (a) or (b), of this sentence will be one-half (1/2) of the royalty rate that would apply if the Record concerned were sold through Normal Retail Channels: (a) any Phonograph Record sold through any Special Markets Plan owned or controlled by us; and (b) any Record sold outside the United States by us or its principal Licensee in the country concerned in conjunction with a television advertising campaign, during the calendar semi-annual period in which that campaign begins or either of the next two (2) such periods. The royalty increase provisions of subsection 7.1(a)(3) will not apply in computing royalties on any Records described in the preceding sentence.

7.4. We will pay you fifty percent (50%) of our net receipts in respect of: (i) Records sold through any record club or similar distribution plan not owned or controlled by us or our Licensees; or (ii) any Master Recording leased by us or our Licensees to others for their distribution of Phonograph Records in the United States, we will pay you fifty percent (50%) of our net receipts from our Licensee. ("Net receipts", in the preceding sentence, means receipts or credits as computed after deduction of all copyright, AFM and other direct out of pocket applicable third party payments.)   If another artist, a producer, or any other Person is entitled to royalties on sales of such Records, that payment will be divided among you in the same ratio as that among your respective basic royalty percentage rates. The royalty will be fifty percent (50%) of our Net Receipts with respect to: (a) any Record sold through a record club or similar distribution plan not owned or controlled by us; (b) any Record sold through a Special Markets Plan not owned or controlled by us or a similar sales plan; and (c) Recordings licensed or otherwise furnished by us or our principal licensees to others for inclusion on Phonograph Records.

7.5.(a) The royalty rate on any Midprice Record or any Record sold to Armed Forces Post Exchanges or to the United States or a state or local government will be two-thirds (2/3) of the otherwise applicable royalty rate. (The preceding sentence will not apply to a Midprice Record sold within one (1) year after the initial release of the Master Recordings concerned on Phonograph Records in the

United States.) The royalty rate on any Budget Record, any "picture disc" (i.e., a disc phonorecord with artwork reproduced on the surface of the Record itself) will be one-half (1/2) of the otherwise applicable royalty rate. (The preceding sentence will not apply to a Budget Record made hereunder sold within eighteen (18) months after the initial release of the Recordings concerned on Phonograph Records in the United States.) The royalty rate on any Record which is not an Album or Single (for example, a twelve-inch "dance single") will be one-half (1/2) of the otherwise applicable Album royalty rate set forth in paragraph 7.1 subject to subparagraphs 7.4(b) and (c) below.

7.5.(b) The royalty on Compact Discs will be a royalty computed at eighty-five percent (85%) of the rate which would otherwise apply under this agreement.

7.5.(c) The royalty on any Audiophile Record (other than Compact Discs) will be the amount determined under section (1) or (2) below, whichever is less:

7.5.(c.1) A royalty computed at eighty-five percent (85%) of the rate which would otherwise apply under this agreement; or

7.5.(c.2) The amount of money equal to the royalty applicable in the territory concerned to: (A) an analog-tape unit of the same Record release (i.e., an analog-tape released under the same title as the Audiophile Record concerned and containing a substantial amount of the same material); or (B) a top-line single analog-tape unit in the same marketing category (e.g., Album, Extended Play Record, etc.) marketed by Distributor (or its principal licensee in that territory), if no analog-tape version of the same Record release is in the active catalogue of Distributor (or that licensee); or (C) a top-line single analog-tape unit in the marketing category most comparable in content to the Audiophile Record concerned, if there is no tape Record marketing category which corresponds to the marketing category of that Audiophile Record.

7.5.(d) The royalty rate on a Multiple Record Set will be one-half of the applicable Album royalty rate prescribed in paragraph 7.1, if the

Royalty Base Price of that Set is the same as the Royalty Based Price applicable to the top-line single-disc Albums marketed by Distributor or its principal Licensee in the territory where the Set is sold at the beginning of the royalty accounting period concerned. If a different Royalty Base Price applies to a Multiple Record Set, the royalty rate prescribed in the preceding sentence will be adjusted in proportion to the variance in the preceding sentence will be adjusted in proportion to the variance in the Royalty Base Price (but will not be more than the applicable Album royalty rate prescribed in paragraph 7.1). For the purpose of those computations, "top-line" Albums will not include Audiophile Records other than Compact Discs. That adjustment of the royalty rate will be made using the following formula:

(X divided by Y) multiplied by Z - adjusted royalty rate.

(subject to the parenthetical limit in the second sentence of this subparagraph).

("X" represents the Royalty Base Price for the Multiple Record Set concerned; "Y" represents the Royalty Base Price for a top-line single-disc Album described in the first sentence of this subparagraph (c), multiplied by the number of disc Records in the Multiple Record Set concerned; and "Z" equals the otherwise applicable royalty rate.

7.5.(e) The royalty increase provisions of subsection 7.1(a)(3) will not apply in computing royalties on any Records described in this paragraph 7.5, other than Compact Discs.

7.6. We will pay you the following royalties in connection with its sales or other exploitation of Controlled Videos:

7.6.(a) With respect to uses of Controlled Videos in audiovisual Records:

7.6.(a.1) With respect to audiovisual Records comprised of Controlled Videos which are manufactured and distributed by any licensee of ours, or which are sold in any manner other than as set forth in (B) below: a royalty of fifty percent (50%) of our Video Net

Receipts.

7.6.(a.2) If Distributor manufactures and/or distributes any audio-visual Records containing Controlled Videos (e.g. videodiscs or videocassettes), we will pay you a royalty computed in accordance with this Article 7, but at the royalty rate of _____ percent (_%) of the applicable Royalty Base Price on Net Sales of audiovisual Records distributed through Normal Retail Channels in the United States. Such royalty shall be subject to adjustment in accordance with the other provisions of this Article 7 and shall be inclusive of all copyright, AFM and other applicable third party payments. The royalty increase provisions of subsection 7.1(a)(3) will not apply in computing royalties on any Records described in this paragraph.

7.6.(a.3) The term "Distributor" as used in this subparagraph 7.6 shall mean Distributor, and its parent and affiliated company(ies).

7.6.(b) With respect to uses of Controlled Videos other than in audiovisual Records, such as by means of theatrical distribution, on television (including free, pay, subscription, cable and CATV), we will pay you a royalty of fifty percent (50%) of our Video Net Receipts after deducting therefrom a distribution fee equal to twenty percent (20%) of our gross receipts derived from those uses. No royalties will be payable with respect to the exploitation of Controlled Videos by third parties for which we do not receive a fee for its use.

7.7.(a) Except as otherwise provided in subparagraph 7.7(b) below, no royalties shall be payable to you with respect to Phonograph Records: (a) distributed by us or our licensees, for promotional purposes, to disc jockeys, independent promotion persons, motion picture companies, radio and television stations, or as review copies to periodicals and other customary recipients of free, discounted or promotional Records for fifty percent (50%) or less of the Record's highest posted wholesale price in that configuration,; (b) deleted from Distributor's catalogue or the catalogue of its licensee in a particular territory or sold as overstock; (c) distributed as free, no-charge, or bonus Records (whether or not intended for resale); (d) given to our employees or the employees of

Distributor; (e) sold or licensed for use in connection with means of transportation; (f) for which we do not receive payment; or (g) on "sampler" Records intended for free distribution to purchasers of products and containing not more than two (2) Recordings hereunder. Records distributed as "free" or "no-charge" under subsection (c) shall include Records which are sold to distributors, sub-distributors or dealers at a discount from our or our distributor's (or their respective licensees'), as applicable, posted wholesale list price. For the purpose of determining the number of Records sold at a discount which are treated as "free" or "no-charge" under said subsection, the percentage discount shall be multiplied by the number of Records sold at such discount.

7.7.(b)   If top-line Albums distributed as "free" or "no charge" which are intended for resale Through Normal Retail Channels in the United States exceed 25% of the total number of Albums distributed under this agreement, we will pay you your normal royalty on the excess.

7.8.   The royalty rate with respect to any Joint Recording shall be computed by multiplying the royalty rate otherwise applicable thereto by a fraction, the numerator of which shall be one (1) and the denominator of which shall be the total number of royalty artists (including you) entitled to receive royalties with respect to their services on such Recording.

7.9.   The royalty rate with respect to any Phonograph Record embodying Recordings made hereunder together with other recordings will be computed by multiplying the royalty rate otherwise applicable by a fraction, the numerator of which is the number of Sides embodying Recordings made hereunder and the denominator of which is the total number of royalty bearing Sides contained on such Record. The royalty rate on any audiovisual Record containing a Controlled Video, together with other audiovisual material, will be apportioned based on the playing time of such Video in relation to the total playing time of such Record.

7.10.   With respect to Records sold at a discount to distributors, sub-distributors, dealers or others, the Royalty Base Price shall be reduced in the same proportion as the regular wholesale price of such records is reduced on such sales; provided, however, that when such reduction is equal to 50% or more, no royalty shall be payable.

7.11. The provisions of subsection 7.1(a)(3) will not apply in computing royalties pursuant to subparagraph 7.1(b), and paragraphs 7.2, 7.3, 7.4, 7.5, and 7.6.

8. ACCOUNTINGS.

8.1. We will render statements on October 31 and April 30 of each year of all royalties due and owing to you at the end of the semi-annual periods ending on the preceding June 30 and December 31, respectively. Such statements shall be accompanied by payment of royalties shown to be due and owing to you, if any, after deducting any and all unrecouped Advances and chargeable costs under this agreement and such amount, if any, which Distributor may be required to withhold pursuant to the U.S. Tax Regulations or any other applicable statute, regulation, treaty or law. In computing the number of Records sold, only Records for which we have been paid shall be deemed sold, and we shall have the right to deduct returns and credits of any nature and to withhold reasonable reserves therefor from payments otherwise due you. We will have the right to maintain reasonable reserves against anticipated returns, credits and defective Records. Reserves will not be established for any Album or Single during any semi-annual accounting period in excess of thirty-five percent (35%) of the aggregate number of units of that Album shipped for sale. Each such reserve will be liquidated equally over four (4) semi-annual accounting periods following the accounting period in which it is established. If we make any overpayment to you, you will reimburse us for such overpayment upon demand. In the alternative, we may deduct such overpayment from any sums which may become due to you. If we adopt a general policy to account at time periods different from those provided herein, we shall account to you at such different periods, but not less frequently than semi-annually. In rendering statements to you hereunder, we shall be entitled to rely conclusively on corresponding statements received by us from Distributor or any of our other licensees. If we, in our sole discretion, elect to audit the books and records of Distributor, and as a result thereof, obtain a recovery of additional royalties with respect to any Master Recordings made hereunder, we will pay you your share thereof, after deducting therefrom a proportionate share of the costs of such audit, which will be included with the next regular accounting rendered to you hereunder.

8.2. Royalties with respect to Records sold outside the United States will be computed in the same national currency in which we are paid or credited for such sales, and at the same rate of exchange at which we are paid or credited. Any such sale will be treated as a sale occurring during the same six-month period in which we receive our accounting and payment or are credited for that sale. If any licensee or distributor deducts any taxes from its payments to us, we may deduct a proportionate amount of those taxes from your royalties. If we cannot collect payment for a sale in a foreign country in the United States in U.S. dollars we will not be required to account to you for that sale unless we elect to accept payment or equivalent credit of royalties in such foreign country in the currency of such foreign country. In such event, we will deposit the amount due you in your name in a depository we select in such foreign country and will notify you thereof. Deposits in accordance with the preceding sentence will fulfill our royalty obligations to you with respect to such sales.

8.3. We will maintain books and records which report the sales of the Phonograph Records, and the calculation of Net Receipts derived from the exploitation of Controlled Videos, on which royalties are payable to you. You may, at your own expense, examine those books and records, as provided in this paragraph only. You may make those examinations only for the purpose of verifying the accuracy of the statements sent to you under paragraph 8.1. You may make such an examination for a particular statement only once, and only within two (2) years after the date when we send you that statement under paragraph 8.1. (We will be deemed conclusively to have sent you each statement on the date prescribed in paragraph 8.1 unless you notify us otherwise, with respect to any statement, within thirty (30) days after that date.) You may make those examinations only during our usual business hours, and at the place where we keep the books and records to be examined. If you wish to make an examination you will be required to notify us at least thirty (30) days before the date when you plan to begin it. We may postpone the commencement of your examination by notice given to you not later than five (5) business days before the commencement date specified in your notice; if we do so, the running of the time within which the examination may be made will be suspended during the postponement. If your examination has not been completed within one month from the time you begin it, we may require you to terminate it on seven (7) business days' notice to you at any time; we will not be required to permit you to continue the examination after the end of that seven-day period. You will not be entitled to examine any of Distributor's or our other licensees' records, any manufacturing records or any other records that do not specifically report sales or other distributions of Phonograph Records, or calculations of Net Receipts, on which royalties are payable to you. You may appoint a certified public accountant or other qualified individual to make such an examination for you, but not if he or his firm has begun an examination of our books and records for any Person except you unless the examination has been concluded and any applicable audit issues have been resolved.

8.4. If you have any objections to a royalty statement, you will give us specific notice of that objection and your reasons for it within two (2) years after the date when we send you that statement under paragraph 8.1. (We will be deemed conclusively to have sent you each statement on the date prescribed in paragraph 8.1 unless you notify us otherwise, with respect to any statement, within thirty (30) days after that date.) Each royalty statement will become conclusively binding on you at the end of that two-year period, and you will no longer have any right to make any other objections to it. You will not have the right to sue us in connection with any royalty accounting, or to sue us for royalties on Records sold or Net Receipts derived by us during the period a royalty accounting covers, unless you commence the suit within that two-year period. If you commence suit on any controversy or claim concerning royalty accountings rendered to you under this agreement, the scope of the proceeding will be limited to determination of the amount of the royalties due for the accounting periods concerned, and the court will have no authority to consider any other issues or award any relief except recovery of any royalties found owing. Your recovery of any such royalties will be the sole remedy available to you or the Artist by reason of any claim related to our royalty accountings. Without limiting the generality of the preceding sentence, neither you nor the Artist will have any right to seek termination of this agreement or avoid the performance of your obligations under it by reason of any such claim.

9. MUSICAL COMPOSITIONS.

9.1.(a.1) You hereby grant to us and to Distributor an irrevocable license to reproduce each Controlled Composition on Phonograph Records containing the Recordings, to manufacture such Records, and to distribute them in the United States and Canada.

9.1.(a.2) For such license we or Distributor will pay mechanical royalties on the basis of Net Sales of Phonograph Records, other than audiovisual Records, at the following rates:

9.1.(a.2.i) <u>On Records manufactured for distribution in the United States</u>: seventy-five percent (75%) of the minimum compulsory license rate under the United States copyright law (without regard to playing time) on the earlier of the following dates: (A) at the date of Delivery of the Album (or other recording) project concerned, or (B) the date by which the Recording concerned is required to be Delivered under Article 2.

9.1.(a.2.ii) <u>On Phonograph Records manufactured for distribution in Canada</u>: The rate equal to the minimum compulsory license rate applicable to the use of musical works on Phonograph Records under the copyright law of Canada on the date referred to in subsection 9.1(a.2.i) above, but not less than 2 cents per Composition, and not more than the rate which would be applicable to the Records concerned under subsection 9.1(a.2.i) above if they were sold for distribution in the United States ("U.S. Rate"). If no compulsory license rate is fixed by the copyright law of Canada, the rate applicable there will be the U.S. rate or the lowest rate prevailing in Canada on a general basis, whichever is less.

Mechanical Royalties shall not be payable with respect to Records otherwise not royalty bearing hereunder, with respect to nonmusical material or with respect to Compositions of one minute or less in duration. No Mechanical Royalties shall be payable in respect of Controlled Compositions which are in the public domain or are arrangements of Compositions in the public domain. The Mechanical Royalty on any Record described in paragraphs 7.2 through 7.5 will be three-fourths (3/4) of the amount fixed above.

9.1.(b.1) The total Mechanical Royalty for all Compositions on any Audiophile Record, including Controlled Compositions, shall be the amount set forth in section 9.1(a.2) multiplied by the number of Compositions on the Album concerned, in all events, not to exceed twelve (12) times the rate set forth in paragraph 9.1. Except as set forth in the preceding sentence, the total Mechanical Royalty for all Compositions on any Album other than an Audiophile Record Album, including Controlled Compositions, will be limited to ten (10) times the amount which would be payable on it under section 9.1(a.2) if it contained only one Controlled Composition. The total Mechanical Royalty on any Extended Play Record will be limited to five (5) times that amount. The total Mechanical Royalty on any Single will be limited to twice that amount. The total Mechanical Royalty on any Record which is not an Album or a Single will be limited to three (3) times that amount.

9.1.(b.2) The maximum Mechanical Royalty under this subparagraph (b)(2) on a Multiple Record Set will be the same amount prescribed in section 9.1(b.1), if the Royalty Base Price of that Set is the same as the Royalty Base Price applicable to the top-line single-disc Albums marketed by us or our principal Licensee in the territory concerned at the beginning of the royalty accounting period concerned. If a different Royalty Base Price applies to a Multiple Record Set, the maximum Mechanical Royalty will be adjusted in proportion to the variance in the Royalty Base Price (but will not be more than twice the maximum royalty prescribed in section 9.1. For the purpose of those computations, "top-line" Albums will not include Audiophile Records other than Compact Discs. That adjustment of the maximum Mechanical Royalty will be made using the following formula:

(X divided by Y) multiplied by Z = adjusted Mechanical Royalty.

(subject to the parenthetical limit in the second sentence of this section (2).)

("X" represents the Royalty Base Price for the Multiple Record Set concerned; "Y" represents the Royalty Base Price for a top-line single-disc Album described in the first sentence of this section (2); and "Z" equals the maximum Mechanical Royalty otherwise applicable under section 9.1(b)(1).)

9.1.(c) We or Distributor will compute Mechanical Royalties on Controlled Compositions in each calendar quarter (or other accounting periods as we or Distributor may in general adopt) in which there are sales or returns of Records upon which Mechanical Royalties are payable to you. We or Distributor will send a statement with accompanying payment, if any is due, on or about a date forty-five (45) days following the end of the applicable accounting period - May 15th, August 15th, November 15th, and February 15th. We will have the right to maintain reasonable reserves against anticipated returns, credits and defective Records. Mechanical Royalty reserves will not be established for any Album or Single during any quarterly accounting period in excess of thirty-five (35%) percent of the aggregate number of units of that Album shipped for sale. Mechanical Royalty reserves maintained by Distributor against anticipated returns and credits will be held for a period of two (2) years and will be liquidated equally over that two year period. If we make any overpayment of Mechanical Royalties with respect to Controlled Compositions (e.g., but, without limitation, by reason of an accounting error or by paying Mechanical Royalties on Records returned). You will reimburse us for it; we may also recoup it from any payments due or becoming due to you. If we pay any Mechanical Royalties on Records which are returned later, those royalties will be considered overpayments. If the total amount of Mechanical Royalties which we pay on any Record consisting of Master Recordings made under this agreement (including Mechanical Royalties for Compositions which are not Controlled Compositions) is higher than the limit fixed for that Record under subparagraph 9.1(b), that excess amount will be considered an overpayment also. Your right to audit our books and records with respect to Mechanical Royalties shall be as set forth in Article 8.

9.2. You also grant to us and our licensees an irrevocable license to synchronize and reproduce each Controlled Composition in Controlled Videos and other audiovisual works and to reproduce, distribute and perform them, to manufacture audiovisual Records and other copies from them and to exploit them by any method and in any form now or hereafter known throughout the world, without payment of any kind in connection with such uses.

9.3.(a) With respect to Compositions, other than Controlled Compositions, you will use your best efforts to obtain, licenses covering those Compositions for our benefit on the same terms as those which apply to Controlled Compositions under this Article 9.

9.3.(b) You will also cause licenses to be issued for our benefit and the benefit of our licensees to reproduce each Controlled Composition on Phonograph Records and to distribute those Records outside of the United States and Canada. Such licenses shall be granted on terms not less favorable to us or our licensees than those terms generally prevailing in the applicable country with respect to the use of musical compositions on Phonograph Records.

9.4. You warrant and represent that the "Schedule of Publishers" appended to this agreement is a complete list of the music publishers in which you or the Artist has a direct or indirect interest. You will notify us promptly of each additional music publisher in which you or the Artist acquire any such interest and of every other change required to keep the list currently accurate. No inadvertent failure to comply with this paragraph will constitute a breach of this agreement.

9.5. You agree to indemnify and hold us harmless from the payment of mechanical royalties in excess of the applicable amounts in the provisions of this Article 9. If we or Distributor pay any such excess, such payments shall be a direct debt from you to us, which, in addition to any other remedies available, we may recover from royalties or any other payments hereunder.

10. WARRANTIES.

10.1 You warrant and represent that:

10.1.(a) You have the right and power to enter into and fully perform this agreement.

10.1.(b) No Person or entity other than us has any right to use any existing Recordings of the Artist's performances for making, promoting, or marketing Phonograph Records.

10.1.(c) During the Term:

10.1.(c.1) No Person other than us will be authorized to use any existing Recordings of the Artist's performances for making, promoting or marketing Phonograph Records.

10.1.(c.2) Neither you nor the Artist will enter into any agreement or undertake any obligation which would violate the provisions hereof or interfere with the full and prompt performance of your obligations under this agreement, and you will fully and promptly perform your obligations to the Artist.

10.1.(c.3) Except as set forth in paragraph 10.2(b), the Artist will not perform or render any services, as a performing artist, a producer, or otherwise any or the purpose of making, promoting, or marketing Master Recordings or Phonograph Records for any Person except us.

10.1.(d) The Artist will not perform any material contained in a Recording for the purpose of making any Recording or Phonograph Record for any person or entity other than us until the later of the following dates: (i) two (2) years after the expiration of the Term; or (ii) five (5) years after the Delivery of such Recording to us hereunder. The Artist will not, without our prior written consent, perform or authorize the recording during or after the Term of such material for use in advertisements.

10.1.(e) The Recordings hereunder and performances embodied thereon shall be produced in accordance with the rules and regulations of the American Federation of Musicians, the American Federation of Television and Radio Artists and all other unions having jurisdiction. You are or will become and remain to the extent necessary to enable the performance of this agreement, a member in good standing of all labor unions or guilds, membership in which may be required for the performance of your services hereunder.

10.1.(f) None of the Recordings hereunder, nor the performances embodied thereon, nor any other Materials, as hereinafter defined, nor any use thereof by grantees, licensees or assigns, will violate any law or infringe upon the rights of any third party. "Materials" as used in this subparagraph means: (i) all Controlled Compositions, (ii) each name used by you in connection with the Recordings, and (iii) all other musical, dramatic, artistic and literary materials, ideas, and other intellectual properties, furnished or selected by you, the Artist or any producer and contained in or used in connection with any Recordings or their packaging, sale, distribution, advertising, publicizing or other exploitation.

10.1.(g) We shall not be required to make any payments of any nature for, or in connection with, the acquisition, exercise or exploitation of rights by us pursuant to this agreement, except as specifically provided in this agreement.

10.1.(h) No Person who will render or has rendered any services in connection with the making of the Recordings will grant or has granted to you the rights referred to in this agreement and will have or has the rights to so render such services and grant such rights. None of the persons whose performances are embodied in the Recordings or whose services are used in the making of such Recordings shall be bound by any agreement with any other Person that would prevent or restrict such performances or services (or to the extent otherwise bound, you will obtain all necessary clearances with respect thereto).

10.2.   If you or the Artist become aware of any unauthorized recording, manufacture, distribution, sale, or other activity by any third party in contravention of the terms of this agreement, you will immediately notify us thereof. You and the Artist will at all times cooperate with us in any action or proceeding we commence against such a third party.

10.2.(a)   Artist may perform as a background musician ("sideman") accompanying a featured artist on Recordings made for third parties, provided that: (i) Artist shall not record any Composition which Artist has recorded for us; (ii) Artist will not render a solo or "step-out" performance; (iii) such sideman engagement shall not interfere with the continuing prompt performance of Artist obligations to us; (iv) Artist's name may be used only in a "courtesy credit" to us and Distributor on the Album liners and packaging materials used for such Records in the same position, size, type style and the same in all other respects as the credits accorded to other sidemen. Except as set forth in section (iv) above, neither Artist's name, picture or other likeness may be used in connection with such Recordings or the packaging thereof, or in any advertising, publicity or any audiovisual works, without our prior written consent. Before Artist accepts any sideman engagement, Artist shall furnish us with a fully-executed document satisfactory to us signed by such third party, in which such party has agreed to the foregoing restrictions.

10.2.(b)   Artist may serve as a producer for the purpose of making Phonograph Records for others, provided: (A) Artist has then fulfilled all of Artist's material obligations under this agreement, and the engagement does not interfere with the continuing prompt performance of your obligations to us; (B) Artist will not produce Recordings of any material which Artist has then recorded for us, and will not agree to be restricted from recording the same material for us; (C) Artist will not accept the producing engagement unless the Person for whom the Recordings are being produced agrees in writing, for our and Distributor's benefit, that: (1) Artist's name may be used in credits on Record labels and the reverse sides of Record packages, comparable in size and prominence to the credits generally accorded to record producers, and (2) except as expressly provided in the preceding clause (C)(1) neither the Artist's name nor any picture, portrait, or likeness of the Artist will be used in connection with such Recordings, including, without limitation, on the front of any Record package or in any advertising, publicity or any other form of promotion or exploitation without our express written consent, not to be unreasonably withheld.

10.3. The Artist will not render any musical performance for the purpose of making any motion picture, television program or any other audiovisual work ("Picture") for any Person or entity other than us and no Person other than us will be authorized to reproduce, distribute, exhibit or otherwise exploit any Picture, without an express written agreement providing that: (i) the Picture will not be embodied on any Phonograph Record; (ii) the Picture will not contain more than two (2) Compositions performed by you, in whole or in part; and (iii) not more than one-half (1/2) of any version of such Picture shall contain your musical performances or those of any other recording artist. You shall cause each Person or entity which exhibits any Picture permitted pursuant to the provisions of this paragraph to include a courtesy credit to us and Distributor in such form as we approve in the end titles of the picture or in such other location in which credits customarily appear.

10.4. You shall at all times indemnify us and our licensees against any and all claims, damages, liabilities and expenses (including reasonable legal expenses) arising out of any breach or alleged breach of this agreement or of any warranty, representation, or covenant made by you herein. Pending the resolution of any such claim, we may withhold sums (in an interest bearing account) otherwise payable to you in amounts reasonably related to such claim. You shall be notified of any such claim and shall have the opportunity to participate in the defense thereof by an attorney of your choice and at your expense but Distributor shall at all times control the conduct of the defense. Unless you make bonding arrangements, satisfactory to us in our sole discretion, to assure us of reimbursement for all damages, liabilities, costs and expenses (including legal expenses and counsel fees) which we or our licensees may incur as a result of that claim. We will release such monies withheld under this paragraph if suit on the claim concerned is not commenced within one (1) year after such monies are first withheld. If suit is commenced after monies are so released, we may resume withholding monies under this paragraph.

11. FAILURE OF PERFORMANCE.

11.1.(a)   Provided you have fulfilled all of your obligations under this agreement, if we refuse without cause to allow you to fulfill your Recording Obligation for any Contract Period and if, not later than twenty (20) days after that failure takes place, you notify us of your desire to fulfill such Recording Obligation, and thereafter we fail to permit you to fulfill said Recording Obligation within sixty (60) days of our receipt of your notice, you shall have the option to terminate this agreement by notice to us within thirty (30) days after the expiration of such sixty-day period ("Termination Notice"). Upon receipt by us of your Termination Notice, this agreement shall terminate and all parties will be deemed to have fulfilled all of their obligations hereunder except those obligations which survive the end of the Term (e.g., warranties, re-recording restrictions and obligation to pay royalties); and we will pay to you, in full settlement of all of our obligations to you and as liquidated damages, an Advance in the amount equal to:

11.1.(a.1)   The applicable minimum Advance set forth in paragraph 4.4 for the Album then remaining unrecorded, of the Recording Obligation for the Contract Period in respect of which such termination occurs; less:

11.1.(a.2)   Any portion of the applicable minimum Advance previously paid for the Album then remaining unrecorded.

In the event you fail to give us either of the above notices within the prescribed periods, we shall have no obligation to you whatsoever for failing to allow you to fulfill such Recording Obligation, and this agreement shall continue in full force and effect.

11.2.   We shall be entitled to suspend the running of the then current Contract Period and all subsequent Contract Periods under this agreement, if we become materially hampered in the recording, manufacture, distribution or sale of Phonograph Records by reason of labor disputes, fire, natural disaster, shortage of materials, illness or incapacity or unavailability of you or producers, or other cause not reasonably within our control. In such event, the current Contract Period will be suspended for the duration of such contingency and the commencement of all subsequent Contract Periods postponed, and the Term extended by a number of days equal to the total of all such days of suspension plus an additional seven (7) days. If any suspension imposed under this paragraph 11.2 by reason of an event which affects no record company or distributor other than us continues for more than six (6) months, you may request by notice to us to end such suspension. If we do not do so within sixty (60) days after our receipt of your notice, this Agreement will terminate at the end of said sixty (60) day period, and all parties will be deemed to have fulfilled all of their obligations hereunder except those obligations which survive the end of the Term (e.g. warranties, re-recording restrictions and obligation to pay royalties).

11.3. If you do not fulfill any portion of your Recording Obligation within the time prescribed in Article 2, we will have, without prejudice to any other rights we may have, the following rights:

11.3.(a) to suspend our obligation to make payments to you under this agreement until you have cured the default;

11.3.(b) to terminate this agreement at any time, whether or not you have commenced curing the default before such termination occurs, except that the foregoing right of termination shall not apply if you cure the default within sixty (60) days after the time prescribed in this agreement for timely Delivery of the Album concerned; and

11.3.(c) to require you to repay to us the unrecouped amount of any Advance previously paid to you by us and not specifically attributable under Article 4 to an Album which has actually been fully Delivered.

We may exercise each of those rights by sending you the appropriate notice. No exercise of any of the aforesaid rights by us will constitute a waiver of any of our other rights, including but not limited to its rights to recover damages by reason of your default.

11.4. If your voice should be or become materially and permanently impaired or if you should otherwise become physically disabled to perform recording and/or personal appearances and/or if you should cease to pursue a career as an entertainer, Distributor may elect to terminate this agreement, by notice to you at any time during the period in which such contingency arose or continues and thereby be relieved of any liability for the executory provisions of this agreement.

12. DEFINITIONS.

12.1. "Advance": a prepayment of sums which may thereafter become payable. Advances shall be recouped by us from any and all royalties or other sums to be paid to or on behalf of you or any affiliated entity pursuant to this agreement or any other agreement. Mechanical Royalties will not be chargeable in recoupment of any Advances except those which are expressly recoupable from all monies payable under this agreement. "Any other agreement" in this paragraph, means any other agreement relating to the Artist as a recording artist or as a producer of recordings of the Artist's own performances.

12.2. "Album":

12.2.(a) with respect to Audiophile Records: one (1) or more Audiophile Records containing at least ten (10) Sides and of at least sixty (60) minutes duration in playing time, sold in a single package.

12.2.(b) with respect to Records other than Audiophile Records: one or more twelve-inch 33 1/3 rpm audiodisc Records (or the equivalent thereof in non-disc configurations) containing at least ten (10) Sides and of at least thirty-five (35) minutes duration in playing time, sold in a single package.

12.3. "Audiophile Records": Phonograph Records (other than audiovisual Records) marketed in a specially-priced catalogue series by reason of their superior sound quality or other distinctive technical characteristics. CDs, DATs and all other Records made for digital playback shall be Audiophile Records.

12.4. "Budget Record": a Record bearing a Retail Selling Price which is sixty-seven (67%) percent or less of the Retail Selling Price of a "top-line" Phonograph Record in the same configuration in the same territory.

12.5. "Compact Disc" ("CD"): a 120-mm diameter (or other size) disc Record primarily reproducing sound signals which are read and transmitted from such disc by means of laser.

12.6. "Composition": a single musical work, irrespective of length, including all spoken words and bridging passages and including a medley. If any Record includes Recordings of more than one (1) arrangement or version of any Composition, all such arrangements and versions will be deemed to be one (1) Composition.

12.7. "Container Charge":

12.7.(a) Records (other than as provided in (b) or (c) below): fifteen (15%) percent of the Retail Selling Price on single-fold disc Records, other than seven-inch Singles; and twenty (20%) percent of the Retail Selling Price on Records in non-disc configurations.

12.7.(b) Audiophile Records: twenty-five (25%) percent of the Retail Selling Price (where the royalty is determined as a percentage of the Royalty Base Price).

12.7.(c) Audiovisual Records: twenty (20%) percent of Distributor's published wholesale price.

12.7.1. "Controlled Video": An audiovisual work owned or controlled by us or Distributor Records, Inc. and containing one or more Master Recordings subject to this agreement.

12.8. "Delivery", when used with respect to Master Recordings - means the actual receipt by us of the Master Recordings concerned and all documents and other materials required to be furnished to us in connection with them. Without limiting the generality of the preceding sentence, no Master Recordings will be deemed Delivered until we have received all of the related documentation required under subparagraph 3.3, subject to the next sentence. Your failure to deliver applicable mechanical licenses (other than mechanical licenses covering any first use(s) of the Composition concerned) within the time prescribed in paragraph 2 will not itself constitute late Delivery, provided such licenses are delivered prior to the date of scheduled release of the Album project concerned.

12.8. "Digital Audio Tape ("DAT")": a digitally encoded audio tape Record intended for digital playback.

12.9. "Inception of Recording": the first recording of performances and/or other sounds with a view to the ultimate fixation of Recording. "Recordings from the Inception of Recording" include, without limitation, all rehearsal recordings, "outtakes", and other preliminary or alternate versions of sound recordings which are created during the production of Recordings made under this agreement.

12.10. "Joint Recording": a Recording embodying the Artist's performance together with the performance of another artist with respect to whom we are obligated to pay royalties.

12.10.1. "Licensees" - includes, without limitation, wholly or partly owned subsidiaries, affiliates and other divisions of ours and/or Distributor Records, Inc.

12.11. "Long Play Single": a 12-inch 33 1/3 rpm audiodisc Record embodying Recordings of not more than three (3) different Compositions.

12.12. "Midprice Record": a Record bearing a Retail Selling Price not more than eighty (80%) percent but not less than sixty-seven (67%) percent of the Retail Selling Price of a "top-line" Phonograph Record in the same configuration in the same territory.

12.13. "Multiple Record Album": an Album containing two (2) or more 12-inch 33 1/3 rpm audiodisc Records or the equivalent in a CD or non-disc configuration, packaged as a single unit. For purposes of the Recording Obligation hereunder and for computing the applicable Recording Fund or Advance, a Multiple Record Album accepted by us shall be deemed only one (1) Album.

12.14. "Net Receipts": gross receipts actually earned and received by us solely attributable to the Recordings hereunder from the distribution of Records, Recordings or other uses as set forth in paragraph 7.4, less all manufacturing and packaging costs, less all advertising expenses and less any costs or expenses which we are required to incur (such as, without limitation, production costs, copyright, AF of M and other union or guild payments) and costs of collection, if any.

12.15. "Net Sales": eighty-five percent (85%) of the total number of Records sold for which we have been paid or credited less returns, credits, and reserves against anticipated returns and credits. Returns will be apportioned between Records sold and free goods in the same ratio in which Distributor's customer account is credited.

12.16. "Normal Retail Channels": sales other than those described in paragraphs 7.2, 7.3, 7.4, 7.7, subparagraph 7.6(b) and section 7.6.(a.1).

12.17. "Controlled Composition": a musical composition wholly or partly written, owned or controlled by you, the Artist, an individual producer engaged by you, or any Person in which you, the Artist, or such individual producer has a direct or indirect interest.

12.18. "Person": any individual, corporation, partnership, association or other organized group of persons or legal successors or representatives of the foregoing.

12.19. "Recording": every recording of sound, whether or not coupled with a visual image, by any method and on any substance or material, whether now or hereafter known. Recordings include, without limitation, all rehearsal recordings, "outtakes", and other preliminary or alternate versions of sound recordings which are created during the production of Recordings made under this agreement.

12.20. "Records" and "Phonograph Records": all forms of reproduction, now or hereafter known, manufactured, distributed, and/or transmitted by means of electronic transmission primarily for personal use, home use, school use, juke box use, including those of sound alone and those coupled with or accompanied by visual images including but not limited to vinyl discs in all configurations, audio cassettes, digital audiotapes, compact discs, videodiscs, videocassettes, laser discs and reel-to-reel tapes.

12.21. "Retail Selling Price":

12.2.1.(a) With respect to sales other than Audiophile Records, Retail Selling Price shall mean:

12.2.1.(a.1) on Records sold for distribution in the United States, the retail price suggested by the manufacturer in the United States.

12.2.1.(a.2) on Records sold for distribution outside the United States, the retail price suggested either by the manufacturer in the country of manufacture or by the seller in the country of sale, whichever price Distributor's reporting licensee utilizes in computing record royalties payable to Distributor.

12.2.1.(a.3) Notwithstanding the foregoing:

12.2.1.(a.3.i) If no retail price for a particular Record is suggested or recommended by the manufacturer or seller in the relevant territory, then the Retail Selling Price shall be deemed to be such price or basis as may be established by Distributor or its licensees in conformity with the general practice in the phonograph record industry in such territory (for example, the price adopted by the local mechanical rights society for copyright royalty accounting purposes).

12.2.1.(a.3.ii) If, with respect to any sales, presently or at any future time, we use, or are paid on the basis of, a "base price to dealer" or other wholesale price instead of the Retail Selling Price, the royalty rates herein shall be adjusted so that the royalty amount in the currency of the particular territory for the particular Record would be the same as it would be had it been computed on a retail basis. Such royalty will be adjusted for all sales and for all configurations in accordance with the applicable provisions of this agreement.

12.2.1.(b)   With respect to sales of Audiophile Records, "Retail Selling Price" shall mean:

12.2.1.(b.1) In the United States: one hundred thirty percent (130%) of Distributor's lowest published wholesale price, in the category of sale concerned.   In the event such wholesale price changes during an accounting period, the applicable wholesale price for the entire accounting period shall be deemed to be the lowest average daily wholesale price during the period.

12.2.1.(b.2) In all other territories: The suggested retail list price or other price utilized by Distributor's licensee in computing monies to be paid to Distributor for the Record concerned.

12.22.   "Royalty Base Price":

12.22.(a) the Retail Selling Price for a particular Record at the commencement of the applicable accounting period, less all excise, sales and similar taxes and less the Container Charge.

12.22.(b) with respect to audiovisual Records, Distributor's published wholesale price as of the commencement of the applicable accounting period, less all excise, sales and similar taxes and less the Container Charge.

12.23. "Side": a Recording of a continuous performance of a particular arrangement or version of a Composition, not less than three (3) minutes in playing time. If any Album or group of Sides comprising any Recording Obligation includes Recordings of more than one arrangement or version of any Composition, all of those Recordings will be deemed to constitute one Side.

12.24. "Single": an audiodisc Record not more than seven (7) inches in diameter and containing not more than two (2) Sides, or the equivalent in a non-disc configuration.

12.25. "Special Markets Plan": any marketing plan for the distribution of Records through "key outlet marketing" (such as distribution through retail fulfillment centers in conjunction with radio, television or printed advertisements), or direct mail, mail order, or by any combination thereof or any similar method, but excluding record club distribution plans or similar distribution plans through direct transmission.

12.26. "Video Net Receipts": gross receipts actually earned and received by distributors directly from the exploitation of Videos in the manner prescribed in subparagraph 7.6.(b) or section 7.6.(a.1), as the case may be, less all copyright, AFM and other applicable third party payments, and costs of collection, if any.

13.   MISCELLANEOUS.

13.1. Neither party will be entitled to recover damages or to terminate this agreement by reason of any breach hereof by the other party, that might otherwise entitle you to recover damages or the right to terminate this agreement, unless the latter party has failed to substantially remedy such breach within a reasonable time following receipt of your notice thereof. For the purposes of this paragraph 13.1 and solely with respect to our obligation to make payments to you under this agreement, "reasonable time" shall be forty-five (45) days, it being understood however, that you shall not be entitled to recover damages or terminate the term of this agreement if the breach of our payment obligation cannot be remedied within thirty days, and we have commenced to remedy it within that time and proceeds with reasonable promptness. (The first sentence of this paragraph will not apply to any termination by us under paragraphs 11.3 or 11.4 or to any recovery to which we are entitled by reason of your failure to fulfill Artist's Recording Obligation or your Delivery Commitment).

13.2. This agreement contains the entire understanding of the parties. No change of this agreement will be binding upon us unless it is made by an instrument duly executed by us. No changes of this agreement will be binding on you unless it is made by an instrument signed by you.

13.3. We may assign our rights under this agreement in whole or in part to any subsidiary, affiliated or controlling corporation, to any person owning or acquiring a substantial portion of the stock or assets of us or Distributor, or to any partnership or other venture in which we or Distributor participates, and such rights may be assigned by any assignee.

13.4. This agreement will be governed and construed pursuant to the laws of the State of New York applicable to contracts entered into and performed entirely within the State of New York, and any disputes or controversies arising hereunder shall be subject to the jurisdiction of Courts of the State of New York or of the U.S. Federal District Court for the Southern District of New York. Any process in any action or proceeding arising under or relating to this agreement may, among other methods, be served upon you by delivering or mailing the same by registered or certified mail, directed to the address first written above or such other address as you designate by notice to us. Any such delivery or mail service shall be deemed to have the same force and effect as personal service within the State of New York.

13.5. Each election of rights or remedies granted to Distributor in this agreement is separate and distinct, and the exercise thereof shall not operate as a waiver of any other right or remedy. A waiver by either party of any provision of this agreement in any instance will not constitute a waiver of any other provision hereof or of such provision in the future. The headings of the paragraphs contained in this agreement are intended for convenience only and shall not be of any effect in construing the contents of this agreement.

13.6. The services of the Artist are unique and extraordinary, and the loss thereof cannot be adequately compensated in damages, and we will be entitled to injunctive relief to enforce the provisions of this agreement.

13.7. As to any matter for which your approval or consent or that of the Artist is required, such approval or consent will not be unreasonably withheld. Your agreement, approval or consent, or that of the Artist, whenever required, shall be deemed to have been given unless you notify us otherwise within seven (7) days following the date of our written request to you therefor.

13.8. We shall have the right at any time during the Term hereof, at our non-recoupable expense, to obtain insurance on the life of Artist, at our sole expense and cost, with us being the sole beneficiary thereof. The Artist will fully cooperate with Distributor in connection with the obtaining of such a policy, including, without limitation, Artist's submission to any required physical examination and completing any documents necessary or desirable in respect thereof. Neither you, Artist nor your or Artist's estate shall have any right to claim the benefit of any such policy obtained by us. If Artist fails the physical examination, such shall not be a breach of this agreement, but thereafter we shall have the right to terminate the Term hereof.

13.9. All notices hereunder shall be in writing and shall be given by personal delivery, registered or certified mail, return receipt requested, or by Federal Express, at the addresses shown above, or such other address or addresses as may from time to time be designated by either party by notice. Notices shall be deemed to be given when mailed, except for a notice of change of address which shall be deemed to be given on the date of its receipt.

13.10.(a) You may not assign this agreement or any of your rights hereunder without our express written consent of Distributor, subject to subparagraph 13.10(b) below.

13.10.(b) Monies to be paid to you under this agreement will not be assignable by you without our written consent, which we may withhold in our unrestricted discretion, subject to the next sentence. You may assign royalties to be paid to you under this agreement, provided: (a) No more than one such assignment will be binding on us at anytime, and if we are notified or more than one we will have the right to rely conclusively on priority of notice to us in according priority among them; (b) each such assignment will be subordinate to our continuing right to apply all such royalties due or becoming due in recoupment of all Advances, loans and other offsets which may be recoupable from your royalties, included but not limited to those made under agreements concerned; and (c) no such assignment will be effective until it has been accepted in writing by us. We will not unreasonably withhold acceptance of an assignment which is consistent with this paragraph.

13.11. In entering into this agreement, and in providing your services pursuant hereto, you have and shall have the status of an independent contractor and nothing herein contained shall contemplate or constitute you as our agent or employee.

13.12. This agreement shall not become effective until executed by all proposed parties hereto.

13.13. Any and all riders annexed hereto together with this basic document shall be taken together to constitute the agreement between you and us and the loss thereof cannot be adequately compensated in damages, and Distributor will be entitled to injunctive relief to enforce the provisions of this agreement.

13.14. You have read and fully understand this agreement. You have either consulted with an attorney regarding any questions you may have or have voluntarily elected not to do so.

IN WITNESS WHEREOF, the parties have executed this agreement on the date and year first written above.

_____ RECORDS, INC.

By_____   _____
                                   Artist

My taxpayer identification number (social security number or employer identification number) is _____. Under the penalties of perjury, I certify that this information is true, correct and complete.

GROUP PROVISIONS

20.02. If any member of the Artist ("leaving member") ceases to perform as a member of the group:

20.02.(a.1) You will notify us promptly.

20.02.(a.2) The leaving member will be replaced by a new member, if you and we so agree. The new member will be deemed substituted as a party to this agreement in the place of the leaving member, and you will cause the new member to execute and deliver to us such instruments as we, in our judgment, may require to accomplish that substitution. Thereafter, you will have no further obligation to furnish the services of the leaving member for performances under this agreement, but you (and the leaving member individually) will continue to be bound by the other provisions of this agreement, including, without limitation subparagraphs 20.02(b) and 20.02(c) below. You will not permit any musician to perform in place of the leaving member in making Recordings under this agreement, unless that musician has executed and delivered to us the substitution instruments referred to in the second sentence of this section (2). We will continue to have the right to use the name "_____ ", and any other professional, group, and other assumed or fictitious names used by the Artist at any time, in connection with Recordings of the Artist's performances made at any time; no leaving member will make any use of the name "_____ " or any such other name in any circumstances.

20.02.(a.3) If you and we do not agree on replacement of the leaving member, then, without limiting any other rights we may have, we will have the right to terminate the term of this agreement by notice given to you at any time before the expiration of ninety (90) days after our receipt of your notice. In the event of such termination, all members of the Artist will be deemed leaving members as of the date of your notice to us under section 20.02(a)(1) above, and subparagraph 20.02(c) will apply separately to each of them.

20.02.(b) Each Advance becoming payable under this agreement after the leaving member ceases to perform as a member of the group will be reduced to one-half of the amount prescribed in paragraph. The royalty percentage rates applicable under paragraph 9.01 to Records derived from Master Recordings made under this agreement after the leaving member ceases to perform as a member of the group will be reduced by one-half (1/2).

20.02.(c) You and the Artist grant to us separate options to engage the exclusive services of each leaving member as a recording artist ("Leaving Member Options"). Each Leaving Member Option may be exercised by us by notice to the leaving member at any time before the expiration of ninety (90) days after the date of: (1) our receipt of your notice under section 20.02(a)(1), or (2) our termination notice under section 20.02(a)(3), as the case may be. If we exercise a Leaving Member Option, the leaving member concerned will be deemed to have entered into a new agreement with us containing the same provisions as this agreement, except as follows:

20.02.(c.1) the new agreement will apply only to that leaving member, and all references to "you" and "the Artist" will be deemed to refer to the leaving member.

20.02.(c.2) the term will commence on the date of an exercise of such Leaving Member Option and may be extended by us, at our election exercisable in the manner provided in paragraph 1.02 of this agreement, for the same number of additional periods as the number of option periods, if any, remaining pursuant to paragraph 1.02 at the time of an exercise of the Leaving Member Option (but at least two such additional periods in any event);

20.02.(c.3) the Minimum Recording Commitment for each Contract Period of such term will be   [Albums] [Sides] with an overcall option equivalent to that granted to us in paragraph 3;

20.02.(c.4) the [Advance] [Recording Funds] prescribed in paragraph will be;

20.02.(c.5) the royalty percentage rates in respect of Master Recordings made during that term will be   % (U.S. Album sales),   % (U.S. Single sales),   % (other Album sales), and   % (other Single sales), instead of the royalty percentage rates prescribed in sections 9.01(a)(1), 9.01(a)(2), 9.01(b)(1), and 9.01(b)(2); and 20.02.(c.6) if your royalty account under this agreement is in an unrecouped position at the date of an exercise of the Leaving Member Option, one-half of that unrecouped balance will constitute an Advance recoupable from the royalties payable under the new agreement.

ARTIST'S ASSENT AND GUARANTY.

To induce _____ (the "Company") to enter into the foregoing agreement with _____ (the "Agreement"):

1. [Each member of] the Artist:

1.(a) represents to the Company that he has read the Agreement and has had the legal effect of each of its provisions explained to him by a lawyer chosen by him;

1.(b) assents to the execution of the Agreement and agrees to be bound by all grants, restrictions, and other provisions of it relating to the Artist; and

1.(c) acknowledges that the Company will have no obligation to make any payments to the Artist in connection with the services rendered by the Artist or the fulfillment of the Artist's other obligations under the Agreement, except for the payments specified in paragraph 5.01, subparagraph 13.05(b), and Article 18.

2.(a) [Each member of] the Artist:

2.(a.1) guarantees, absolutely and unconditionally, the full performance by (the "Furnishing Party") of all of the Furnishing Party's obligations under the Agreement; and

2.(a.2)   agrees to indemnify and hold the Company harmless from any loss, damage, liability or expense (including but not limited to attorneys' fees and legal expenses) which arise from any failure by the Furnishing Party to fulfill the Furnishing Party's obligations under the Agreement, or which are incurred by the Company in the enforcement of its rights under this guaranty.

2.(b)   The Artist's liability under this guaranty is direct and immediate, and is not conditioned upon the pursuit by the Company of any remedy it may have against the Furnishing Party. This guaranty shall not be revocable at any time or for any reason, including, without limitation, any modification of the Agreement with or without notice to the Artist. No failure by the Company to exercise any of its rights will operate as a waiver of those rights or any others.

_____

[_____]

RECORDING AGREEMENT
EXPLANATORY NOTES

PREAMBLE:

A preamble identifies the parties who will sign the agreement, for instance, an artist and a record company. If the artist is a group, all of the individual members will be listed, and the contract will apply to each of those individuals separately, and to all of them performing as the group. Sometimes the contract is with a loan-out company, such as a production company, which in turn will furnish the services of the artist to the record company. In that case, the record company will require a separate letter signed by the artist which will be attached to the agreement. In that letter, the artist will confirm that the artist's loan-out company (production company) has the right to furnish the artist's services. This type of document is commonly referred to as an inducement letter.

Basically a record deal is a financing deal where a record company agrees to finance a certain number of recordings for an artist. In return that artist agrees to record exclusively for that record company. The record company in most cases is granting the artist an unsecured loan (it is not guaranteed to be paid back if the artist is unsuccessful). In return, the artist usually grants the record company the right to keep up to 96 percent of the profits, should there be any derived from that artist's recordings. Sometimes if the artist's accounts are in an un-recouped position, broadly meaning the artist's percentage points multiplied by the number of records sold does not equal the amount of money the record company has contributed to the artist and the recording of the album, the record company gets to keep all of the profits derived from that artist's recordings. Unfortunately this is what occurs most of the time.

1. SERVICES/TERM

1.1/1.2/1.3. Most recording agreements are structured for an initial term which begins when the agreement is signed, and will continue for seven to ten months from the delivery of the first album. This enables the record company to evaluate the performance of that album and decide whether they want to finance another album. Record companies maintain the sole right to decide how long to continue the agreement on an album-by-album basis. This means that most record companies will only guarantee to finance one album at a time and will reserve the right to finance additional albums. The ability to reserve the right to finance subsequent albums is referred to as an option. More importantly, this means that under normal circumstances once the artist signs a record contract the artist has no choice as to whether or not she wants to continue to record for that record label until the contract with that label is over. Usually, the record company will insist upon seven or eight options to finance subsequent albums. Occasionally, an artist with some bargaining power can reduce the number of options to between three and five albums. In addition, an artist with bargaining power can insist upon the record company's committing to finance more than one album at a time. The most essential element of a recording agreement is that it binds the recording services of the artist exclusively to the record company. This means that once an artist signs a recording agreement, he or she may not record for anyone else during the term of that agreement. There is an exception for sideman performances which we will go into later. This does not mean that the artist cannot render live performances which are not recorded, or engage in other musical activity which does not involve the recording of records.

1.4. If the recording agreement is with a production company who has signed a distribution agreement with a record company to provide the services of the artist, a paragraph such as this provision should be included for the protection of the production company. It states that if the production company's distribution agreement ends before the production company has received all of the albums it is entitled to from the artist, the production company will be granted six months to one year to obtain a new distribution agreement and reinstate the terms of the original recording agreement it has with that artist. Before an artist agrees to such a provision, the artist should insist that any new distribution agreement entered into by the production company must be with a major record company or a label distributed by a major record company, that in no event should any new agreement change the terms of the artist's original deal with the production company, including the total number of albums the artist is required to record for the production company, and the royalty percentages she is entitled to.

2. RECORDING OBLIGATION.

2.1. Usually, an artist is required to record and deliver one album in each contract period. Occasionally, a record company may prefer that the artist commence with the recording of one or two singles, with the option to finance a full album only if the single(s) is/are successful. Some recording agreements are structured so that the record company can demand two albums in the same contract period (the second album is called an "overcall" album). However, so long as the total number of albums required does not exceed seven or eight, there is no real difference between this structure and the more traditional structure of one album per contract period.

2.2. Most record contracts require an artist to deliver the first album within three to five months of the date the contract was signed. Likewise, most record companies require artists to deliver subsequent albums within three to five months of the start of each new contract period. For some artists, this is not a reasonable amount of time because it can take longer to record an album, especially if the artist is meticulous. However most record companies do not enforce this provision strictly so long as the artist is diligently working on completing an album. If an artist fails to deliver within this time period, the record company has a variety of ways to address the delay. (See 11.3) There are also instances where the delay in the completion of the recording of a album is caused by the record company. The reason for these delays can range from an A&R person looking for the right songs for the artist, to the record company being over-burdened with other recording commitments. In the case where the delay is caused by the record company there is usually no cause for concern. However, both Gary and I have seen situations where delays in completion of the recording have led to the record company terminating the artist's contract. Such cases usually occur when the record company and the artist cannot agree upon the music the artist should record.

2.3. This provision is intended to clarify the fact that the record company expects to receive newly recorded studio masters from the artist.

2.4. This clause is standard legal mumbo jumbo that is self explanatory.

3. RECORDING PROCEDURE.

3.1. Most record companies will insist upon the right to maintain creative and financial control over all recording. Occasionally through negotiation, an artist may obtain certain approvals from the record company, including the right to mutually approve all creative elements with the record company. On rare occasions, an artist may obtain sole creative control. However, as a practical matter, since the record company will be in control of the marketing and promotion of an album, it makes little sense for an artist not to obtain the record company's blessings on the creative elements to be recorded, in order to ensure its support and enthusiasm. Notwithstanding the above, there are times when a record company prefers to have an artist retain all creative control, especially if that artist is also a producer and/or songwriter with a track record of writing and producing hits.

3.2/3.3. All major record companies are affiliated with the unions mentioned in these paragraphs. Accordingly, these provisions are included in order to ensure compliance with the requirements of those unions. Once an artist signs a major recording agreement, he or she will be required to join these unions, and will be contractually obligated to work only with union musicians, or vocalists on his or her albums. In reality, most artists and producers record with whomever they choose, whether they are members of the union or not.

3.4. This is a common provision that gives the record company the right to make a decision at any point in the recording process to not continue to finance that project. However, this provision is not strictly enforced, and the artist should negotiate for a 10 percent over budget cushion before the company can pull the plug for financial reasons.

3.4.(a) This is a protective provision to ensure that an artist is not forced to record or perform with another artist that he or she does not feel it is appropriate to record or perform with.

3.5. This paragraph describes in detail the form in which recordings are required to be delivered to the record company. These requirements will vary slightly depending upon the record company, but will include the primary elements listed in this clause.

3.6. In addition to union requirements, record companies are sensitive to the requirements of the INS (Immigration and Naturalization Service), and will insist upon compliance with its requirements by the artists and producers on a project. Over the past few years record companies have become increasingly insistent about following immigration laws as they apply to employment. Every person who records for a record label must sign an I-9 form, which states citizenship status.

3.7. Under most recording agreements, the artist is responsible for engaging and paying producers, and for that matter, engineers, mixers, and anyone else rendering services on the recordings. Any payments to these individuals comes directly out of the artist's recording budget/fund. This includes royalties which would be deducted from the artist's royalty rate. As a practical matter, most record companies will handle the actual third party payments to producers, background singers, engineers, studios etc., and will deduct the amount of those payments from the overall recording budget/fund. They will also pay the producers their royalties directly. This is accomplished by what is called a letter of direction, in which the artist directs the record company to pay producer's fees and producer's royalties directly. (See The Complete Producer Chapter). In some cases, the producer will be employed and paid by the record company, and the terms of this compensation will be established in advance. For example, your A&R person at the label may also be a staff producer for that label. Artists should negotiate for approval over the amount of compensation to be paid to any staff producers because whatever the amount of pay the producer receives as fees and royalties will be deducted from the artist's recording budget and royalties. The range of staff producer fees is from $1,000 to $5,000, with $1,500 being one of the most common figures in use.

3.8. This paragraph goes into more detail on the INS (Immigration and Naturalization Service) requirements.

3.9. This paragraph requires the artist to obtain written agreements from producers and sidemen in forms which are supplied by the record company. This assures the record company that they have received permission from the individuals who performed on the project to use the performances, ideas, names and likenesses of those individuals. These forms are usually referred to as release forms.

4. RECOUPABLE COSTS

4.1. Most record companies will insist upon administering the recording budgets for new artists, and will pay all recording costs directly. If an artist has a track record, the artist may negotiate for the right to administer his or her own recording costs. This structure is referred to as a "recording fund." Recording artists should not expect to receive session payments through the union for their own performances on their records. However, record companies will make the required pension and welfare payments based on the sessions performed by the artist. This ensures that the artist will qualify for benefits, which include health insurance and participation in the pension plan.

4.2. All recording costs are recoupable from the artist royalties. These costs are broadly defined in most recording agreements and will include any expenses incurred in the recording, including the final mastering process. Mastering is the final audio process. It is always performed after the final mixes have been approved by the record company and is the process in which recordings are prepared for manufacturing. Although it is not that time consuming it can be very expensive. Some limit on mastering charges can be negotiated. In addition, any special packaging, and other promotion expenses such as videos and independent promotion, will also be recoupable. Artists should try to negotiate a limit on the amount of these recoupable costs as follows: 1) Insist upon approval or consultation with regard to album artwork, which may include special packaging and therefore additional packaging costs that are recoupable. 2) Insist that only 50 percent of the video and independent promotion costs be recoupable from the artist royalties. 3) It is most important to be sure that mechanical (publishing) royalties are not used to recoup recording costs. (See publishing chapter.)

4.3. Record companies will insist that the artist be responsible for completing the record within the budget established and approved in advance by the record company. Sometimes an artist can negotiate an additional 10% -15% over budget contingency in the event that the record ends up costing a little more than anticipated. Most record companies will resist this provision. It is also advisable to limit responsibility for excess costs to factors reasonably within the artist's control. As a practical matter, if a company is excited about the progress of an album, the record company will routinely reconsider the original budget and elect to cover the additional recording costs. These additional recording costs will be recoupable from the artist royalties.

4.4.(a) In a situation where the record company is administering or paying the recording costs pursuant to an approved budget, the artist will be entitled to a separate artist advance. One-half of this advance will typically be payable when recording commences and the balance will be paid within 30 days after the delivery of the album. Some record companies will pay a portion of the advance for the first album upon signing the recording agreement. This signing advance will be deducted from the recording budget of the first album. Some record companies will attempt to pay the artist advance in monthly installments in order to ensure that the artist does not squander the money. In very rare circumstances, the artist can insist upon receiving the entire advance either upon signing or upon commencement of recording. It is difficult to pinpoint a specific artist advance as standard. The range varies, depending upon the bargaining power of the artist. It can be as low as $6,000, which is the minimum for exclusive recording agreements entered into in the state of California before 1994, or as much as hundreds of thousands of dollars. A typical range for a new artist is usually somewhere be between $15,000 and $50,000. The amount of these advances should increase over the course of the deal. An often-used contractual device to reward an artist for success is what is known as a sales formula. This formula is intended to take 2/3 of the royalties earned by the artist from the previous albums as the amount of the advance for the next album. Record companies will insist upon a maximum amount which is usually double the amount of the minimum advance. If the recording agreement is negotiated as an overall fund, as a opposed to a budget and advance structure, the payment terms and structure of the formula will be modified. Even if the agreement is set up as a fund, the record company may insist upon administering the recording costs. In this event, a portion of the fund will be payable upon commencement of recording, usually 10 percent to 20 percent of the total fund, with the balance, if any, paid to the artist after the deduction of all recording costs within 30 days after delivery of the album. The basic structure of the formula will be the same, except that there will be no deduction for recording costs since the overall fund will include recording costs, and obviously the minimum and maximum fund amounts will be much larger to include those costs. Again, the range is difficult to pinpoint. The amount of the fund may be as low as $20,000 or as high as $1,000,000 or more. The typical recording fund for a new artist on a major label is between $150,000 and $250,000.

The artist should be careful to ensure that she is not penalized on future records as a result of going over budget on a prior record because, contractually, this may result in the artist's not receiving advances on those recordings. Since this money may represent the only income that the artist may receive during the recording process, the artist must insist upon receiving at least 5 to 10 percent of his or her minimum recording fund upon commencement of the recording of each album.

The last scenario is one wherein the agreement is set up as a recording fund, but the record company allows the artist to administer and pay all recording costs. Under this structure, the total amount of the fund will typically be paid either to the artist or producer in equal payments of 1/2 upon commencement of recording and the balance within 30 days after delivery of the album. In order to ensure proper cash flow, the artist should request 25 percent of the fund upon commencement of mixing, leaving only 25 percent payable after delivery of the album. Under this structure, the artist becomes responsible for paying all recording costs.

Because of union considerations, the artist may need to become a union signatory company for purposes of hiring and paying union musicians and vocalists, or she may elect to run all union contracts through the record company. The benefits and risks of the various structures described above depends largely upon the artist. Most artists would prefer to administer their own recording funds. This enables the artist to maintain control over the process, and make better deals with musicians, singers, rental companies, etc., who would prefer to be paid in cash, rather than having to wait for processing of payments through the record company. However, this process is not without risks and additional costs. The time and paper work involved in administering a recording fund can be extensive, and may require the artist to hire an accountant and/or project coordinator to supervise the writing of checks, processing of invoices, and the completion of other paper work. In addition, record companies tend to be less flexible if a project administered by an artist goes over-budget.

If the artist is a producer, and/or has his or her own home studio where much of the material can be recorded, it is probably worth the risk and additional cost to insist upon the right to administer the funds. For an artist who has no experience in producing records, it is probably advisable to let the record company administer the funds. If the artist develops experience in the area of administering finances, this is always a point to be renegotiated at a later date.

Finally, under a fund structure, the artist assumes the risk that the project can be completed for less than the budget allowed in the recording contract. Otherwise the artist will not be able to retain advances. On the other hand, if the agreement is structured so that the artist is guaranteed a certain advance, this may give the artist the comfort of knowing that a certain cash flow can be counted upon.

4.5. This provision relates to the California law that requires that artists be guaranteed a minimum amount of compensation in order for a company to preserve its rights to that artist's exclusive services. This law is widely misunderstood. It does not mean than an artist who is not guaranteed that minimum amount can break the contract. The record company can still sue an artist for breach of contract in that instance. It does mean that if a record company fails to provide the minimum amount to an artist, that company cannot stop that artist from recording for another company. A word of caution: Before attempting to break a contract based on a company's non-compliance with this provision, you should consult with an experienced entertainment attorney. It also must be noted that this rule is only applicable to contracts that are governed by California law. Many record companies are headquartered in New York and will insist that New York law apply to the interpretation and enforcement of their recording agreements. The down side of this for the artist is that New York has no minimum compensation law. It should also be noted that for contracts entered into after January 1, 1994, the minimum amount of compensation has been increased as follows: $9,000 for the first year, $12,000 for the second year and $15,000 for every year thereafter. For those interested in a more detailed discussion of this unique California law, there are numerous articles in law journals on the subject.

5. RIGHTS

5.1/5.2. The basic concept here is that all recordings belong to the record company. This includes outtakes (recordings delivered to the record company that have never been released), demos and any music recorded during the term of the recording agreement, whether or not the material is used. Occasionally, an artist will be able to negotiate for control of outtakes. As the owner of all recorded material, the record company will maintain broad rights, including the right to use the recordings on albums, to license those recordings for use in films, to couple those recordings on compilation records with recordings of other artists, etc. In some circumstances, an artist may negotiate approval rights over uses of his or her recorded material.

5.3. According to this provision, if a record company fails to release a delivered album within a certain amount of time, the artist has the right to terminate the relationship. This is a vital form of protection to ensure that an artist's recordings do not sit on a record company's shelf while the artist's career remains in limbo. In some cases, the artist may choose to negotiate in advance for the right to buy back the unreleased masters at the end of the contract. As a practical matter, since the option to buy back masters always exists, it is preferable to negotiate buy backs at the end of the contract when the real value of the masters can be determined.

5.4. This paragraph contains examples of approval rights, and marketing restrictions which an artist may negotiate. Other types of approvals and consultation rights include the selection of material to be released as singles, sequencing (the order in which songs will appear on an album), the album cover art work, and in some cases the marketing and promotion plans. As a practical matter, an artist with effective management will be involved in the decisions. However, record company attorneys do not like to guarantee that involvement contractually.

5.(a) NAMES AND LIKENESSES

5.(a.1) In addition to owning all material recorded, the record company will insist upon the exclusive right to use the artist's name and likeness (i.e portraits, pictures, and photographic treatments of the artist) in connection with the exploitation and promotion of the artist's recordings. In many cases, record companies will attempt to obtain even broader rights to an artist's name and likeness which would extend to usage on other forms of merchandise, such as t-shirts, hats, jackets, and concert programs. Since this may be a vital source of income for an artist, it is important to resist granting these rights to the record company. This provision is an example of how merchandising rights may be limited to materials paid for by the record company such as album cover artwork. It also provides that the artist receives 50 percent of any profits derived from merchandising uses of such material.

382 Recording Agreement Explanatory Notes

382   *Recording Agreement Explanatory Notes*

5.(a.3) This is an example of how much control a record company will allow an artist to have over the uses of his or her name or likeness.

7. ROYALTIES

The computation of royalties is a complicated process. The royalty rate given to an artist is supposed to correspond to the retail or wholesale price at which the artist's records are sold. However, it is not as simple as it sounds. Record companies use a series of complicated deductions and adjustments that they factor into that equation. As mentioned above, the basis upon which the royalties are calculated is either on the retail or wholesale price of a particular record. The retail price is the price of a record when it is sold to a consumer at a record store. The wholesale price is the price a record store pays a distributor for a record. Most record companies compute royalties based upon the retail price. A few companies, such as Sony, compute royalties based on the wholesale price of the record. The wholesale price of a record is usually half that of the retail price. Therefore, a deal in which royalties are based upon the wholesale price should contain a royalty rate which is double the royalty rate applicable to a deal based on the retail selling price. In most record deals, the artist's royalty rates include royalties that would be payable to any third parties, such as producers and mixers. Most producers will expect to receive a royalty of between 3 and 4 percent of the retail price. The average retail royalty rate for a new artist will be between 10 and 14 percent. More established artists may get up to 18 percent, or even more in rare circumstances.

It is a good idea to negotiate for increases in the royalty rate over the course of the deal. There are two ways to negotiate increases in royalty rates. There are increases based upon sales and increases based upon the record company's decision to finance additional records. The most common sales-based royalty increases are given at the point when a record reaches sales of 500,000 copies (which is gold in the Unites States), and again at 1,000,000 copies sold (platinum). The most common royalty rate increases based upon a record company's decision to finance more recordings will be given for either every new record or every other new record. The most common of those increases will be one half percent per escalation. In some instances the escalation can be a full one percent.

In order for an artist to receive the full royalty rate as stated in their recording contract, the artist's albums must be sold at full price in record stores in the United States. For all other types of sales, the royalty is computed as a percentage of the full royalty rate. In other words, the artist's royalty rate as stated in the contract will be reduced depending upon the format of the record (single, extended play, EP, or album), the configuration of a sale (i.e compact disc or cassette), the price at which the record was sold, the country in which the record is sold and the kind of sale (record clubs, military sale or mail order). A good singles royalty rate is 10 percent. Occasionally, sales escalations for singles will also be negotiated.

7.1.(b), 7.2, 7.3, 7.4 and 7.5 all deal with reductions in the royalty rate. Regarding foreign sales, most major record companies are affiliated with a Canadian company, and can pay between 75 and 100 percent of the U.S. royalty rate for Canada. An 85 percent rate for Canada is a good rate. The other major territories are Japan, the larger European countries, and sometimes Australia and New Zealand. For these territories, the artist should attempt to negotiate a royalty rate based upon 75 percent of the royalty rate received in the United States. In many cases, the record company will not pay more than 66.6 percent as a royalty rate for the above mentioned countries. For the rest of the world, the most common royalty rate is 50 percent of the royalty rate the artist receives in the United States. Sometimes an artist can negotiate royalty rate increases for sales outside of the United States.

7.2. Record clubs, such as Columbia House, are organizations that offer records at a discount to their members in exchange for a membership fee. Since records through a record club are discounted, the record companies like to reduce the artist's royalty derived from those sales. For these sales a 50 percent royalty rate reduction on the artist's royalty is common. Sometimes an artist can negotiate a separate royalty rate for records sold through record clubs. A good royalty rate for records sold through record clubs is 8.5 percent. Since record companies do not pay royalties for records that are not sold, an artist should negotiate for payment on at least half of all records given away by a record club as a promotional item to encourage new membership. See record royalties chapter.

7.3. This provision deals with a variety of sales for which an artist can expect to receive only 50 percent of the full royalty rate.

7.4. For situations in which an artist's masters are licensed to other companies, the artist will be paid based on 50 percent of the record company's net income derived form those licenses. In this provision, the definition of what is net as opposed to gross income for the record company should be clearly defined. In that definition net income should be defined only as the gross income, minus the record company's out of pocket expenses.

7.5.(a) This paragraph addresses additional types of record sales for which the artist will be paid a reduced royalty. One important concession which is reflected in this paragraph are holdbacks on price reduced sales, such as midline and budget sales. Holdbacks restrict a record company's right to reduce the price of an artist's records until those records have been available at full price for a certain time period. Since most recordings today are sold in the form of CDs and cassettes this is obviously unfair to the artist and producer.

7.5.(b) The royalty rate for compact discs is an issue which is hotly debated. Artists' attorneys have maintained that there should be no reduction in the royalty rates simply because the price of a compact disc is higher than the price of a cassette or vinyl disc. Nevertheless, record companies have successfully towed the line in forcing artists to accept a percentage of their royalty rate for CD sales. Typically this percentage is between 70 and 85 percent. In addition, the price upon which the rate is computed is typically not the full retail price, but rather a constructed wholesale price which ends up being only slightly higher than the equivalent price of a cassette.

7.5.(c) This is an interesting provision that has to do with new technologies, such as DAT. Typically, record companies will insist that royalties paid to an artist for sales of the records contained on new technologies be computed at an even lower rate than they are computed for compact discs. The artist should attempt to negotiate a royalty rate that is identical to the royalty rate at which they are paid for compact discs. In addition, it is a good idea to negotiate a rate for these new technologies that never is less than the royalty payable for cassettes. To accept a lesser rate is also unfair to artist and producers.

7.5.(d)   A multiple record is a project which contains more than one album's worth of material in a single package. The most common of these is a double record set. The royalty for a multiple record should be based on a formula, such as the one used in this contract, which is intended to compensate the artist for the additional price which a record company will charge for a multiple record.

7.6. Because videos are primarily used as promotional items, very few artists achieve a status where their videos can be sold. Therefore, for most new artists, video royalties will not be an important issue. Nevertheless, these provisions give you an idea of how record companies treat these issues. A royalty rate for videos manufactured and distributed by the record company will typically be 50 to 75 percent of the artist's royalty rate for records.

7.7. There are a number of types of records for which record companies do not pay royalties at all. Examples are listed here. These records are commonly referred to as "free goods". An artist should negotiate some type of limit on the number of records that a record company can distribute at no charge, and thus not pay an artist a royalty. Although policies vary from company to company, the most common limits are that no more than 15 to 20 percent of the total number of albums, and not more than 33 percent of the total number of singles distributed can be non-royalty bearing free goods.

7.8. A joint recording occurs when an artist records with another recording artist. In this case, the artist's royalty will be divided by the number of artists on the recording, unless the artist negotiates his or her own terms with the other artists. The most common example is a duet.

7.9. Similarly, if an artist's masters are used on records with recordings by other artists, the artist's royalty rate will be divided by the total number of recordings on the record, or in the case of a video, the total playing time of the video. The most common case of this would be a compilation record, such as "Rock & Roll Hits of the Seventies & Eighties"

8. ACCOUNTINGS

8.1. Record companies keep track of royalties owed to an artist and send the artist statements called "accountings." Most record companies account to the artist twice a year. The actual accounting periods and payment dates vary from company to company. On rare occasions, an artist can negotiate for quarter-annual accountings — payments four times a year — and/or payments within 60 days of each accounting period. A critical issue concerning accountings involves the number of records on which a record company has the right to withhold payment of royalties. These withheld royalties are commonly referred to as "reserves," and are intended to protect the record company in case records which are distributed for sale are later returned to the record company as unsold product. Most record agreements will leave the actual amount of reserves that the record company has the right to withhold to the record company's discretion. It is essential for an artist to negotiate a limit to the amount of royalties a record company can withhold. Reserves should not exceed 25 to 35 percent of the total number of albums shipped, or in the case of singles 50 percent. It is equally important for the artist to negotiate how reserves withheld, but not used for returns, will be paid to the artist. The time period for which the record company can withhold reserves should not exceed two years. Also, any reserves withheld should be paid to the artist in equal payments with each accounting statement the artist receives during the withholding period. For example, if a record company withholds $10,000 in royalties for a period of two years, every time the artist receives a royalty statement during that two year period, they should receive a credit or payment of $2,500 until those reserves have been exhausted.

8.2. This provision deals with how record companies pay foreign royalties.

8.3/8.4. An artist should negotiate for the right to examine and inspect the record company's books if the artist feels that the record company has made mistakes pertaining to the amount of royalties due the artist. These provisions are commonly referred to as audit rights. Record companies restrict the artist's right to conduct audits by limiting the time period within which the artist may object to a royalty statement, and/or sue a record company. Record companies further restrict an artist's audit rights by forcing the artist to follow strict notification and procedural guidelines. Failure to comply with these guidelines will result in the loss of audit rights with respect to the royalty statements in question. The restrictions contained in this contract are typical of the type of limitations most record companies will try to impose on an artist.

9. MUSICAL COMPOSITIONS

9.1.(a) In addition to receiving artist royalties for the sale of records, record companies are required (pursuant to copyright law) to pay the songwriters and publishers of the material contained on that records what is called a "mechanical" royalty. The rate of this royalty is regulated by law, and is referred to as the "statutory rate." The current statutory rate is 6.6 cents per song per record that has a playing time of five minutes or less. The amount of this rate has been increased several times, and is likely to be increased again in the future. Most record companies will require the artist to grant to the record company a rate which is 75 percent of the statutory rate required by law. Artists should negotiate for the rate to be determined no earlier than the date the master containing the composition is delivered to the record company.

Compositions which are subject to this rate are commonly referred to as controlled compositions. In most recording contracts "controlled" compositions are customarily defined as any musical compositions written, owned or controlled by the recording artist, or his or her producer. For the ways these provisions affect a producer, see the complete producers chapter. These provisions will apply to records sold in the United States and Canada. In rare circumstances, an artist with bargaining power can negotiate a rate closer to the real statutory rate. As with record royalties, increases in the 3/4 rate can be based upon sales of albums, or increased over the course of the agreement.

Sometimes, record companies who are affiliated with publishing companies will offer to increase the mechanical royalty rate in exchange for the artist's agreeing to enter into a co-publishing agreement with its affiliate. In fact, in many cases, record companies will insist upon such an arrangement to enter into the recording agreement. An artist should negotiate aggressively not to grant publishing rights as part of a record contract, even if the record company offers an increase in the mechanical rate. The reason this is so important is because publishing royalties derived from the use of songs written by the artist on the artist's own records may be the only royalties that the artist may see. This is because, as discussed earlier, publishing royalties are not affected by recording costs and other expenses that are charged to the artist's account by the record company. If you are unable to avoid granting publishing rights to a record company, you should at least negotiate that they pay you separate advances for these rights. For more information on what these advances should be, refer to the publishing agreement and its explanatory notes. Most record companies won't pay publishing (mechanical royalties) on free goods or songs that are in the "public domain." Public domain songs are songs that are not protected by copyright, usually because they are old songs whose copyright has expired. "The Star Spangled Banner" is a good example of a public domain song.

However, it is possible to negotiate for payment on 50 percent of free goods in some circumstances. It is also possible to get a record company to agree to pay mechanical royalties for arrangements of public domain material which qualify with the performing rights societies ASCAP or BMI as royalty bearing compositions. (For more information on ASCAP and BMI see the chapter on publishing).

Finally, record companies will insist upon reducing publishing royalties for songs contained on records that are not sold at full price in retail record stores. The rate for these sales is usually 3/4 of the 3/4 rate or 1/2 of the full rate. This is a difficult provision to delete from most recording agreements.

9.1.(b) In addition to limiting the rate at which record companies will pay publishing royalties, record companies limit the amount they will pay writers and publishers per record. The most common limit is 10 times 75 percent of the statutory rate per album, or 5 times that amount for EPs, or 2 times that amount for singles, or 3 times that amount for other configurations, such as 12 inch singles. This means that if the number of songs contained on an album exceeds the number of songs that a record company will pay mechanical royalties on, either the artist, writer or publisher will be penalized in the form of reduced royalties or the reduction of other monies that might otherwise be payable to the artist. In some cases, it is possible to negotiate an increase in the maximum number of songs to 11 or 12 for albums sold as compact discs. In circumstances where the artist is not a writer, it is also important for the artist to negotiate an increase in the maximum amount of royalties to 10 to 12 times the full statutory rate. Again, see the chapter on publishing for more details on how this can affect an artist or producer. Most record companies will resist this request, and may only agree to make this allowance for 1 or 2 outside songs per album.

9.1.(c) Unlike record royalties which are paid twice a year, most record companies will agree to pay publishing (mechanical) royalties four times a year. Other than that, the issues regarding payment of publishing royalties are the same as they are for record royalties.

9.2. In addition to paying an artist who is also a songwriter publishing royalties at reduced rates, record companies will insist upon the right to use an artist's songs for free in that artist's videos. Occasionally, record companies will agree to pay a nominal fee for non-promotional uses of an artist's songs contained on that artist's videos if that video is commercially exploited.

9.3. This paragraph deals with the artist's responsibility for obtaining licenses for songs not written by the artist or the artist's producer. In addition to trying to negotiate for the full statutory rate for these songs, it is important that an artist not be obligated to obtain these licenses, but only that the artist agree to use best efforts to obtain the licenses for songs that they did not write.

9.4. If the artist has entered into a co-publishing or songwriter arrangement prior to negotiation of the recording agreement, not only is the artist required to notify the record company, but it is likely that the artist must refer the negotiation of the terms of this paragraph to his or her publisher. The publisher will then have sole control over the terms of licenses that are granted to the record company concerning songs written by the artist.

10. WARRANTIES

10.1(a)/(b)/(c) A "warranty" is the artist's acknowledgment that statements made by or on behalf of the artist in the contract are true. These are basic warranties concerning the artist's exclusive obligations to the record company. Although it is unusual for recording artists to be restricted from producing material for others, more record companies are insisting upon extending the artist's exclusivity to producing services as well. Obviously this is something the artist should resist.

10.1.(d) This provision is an example of what is called a "re-recording" restriction. It basically provides that in addition to not recording for anyone else during the term of the recording agreement, the artist also may not record the songs she recorded for that record company for anyone else during the term of the agreement and for a certain amount of time after the term of the agreement. Usually, the re-recording restriction time period will be for 5 years after the artist first delivers the song to the record company or 2 years after the termination of the contract, whichever is later. Recently, record companies have started insisting upon the right to approve the use of any songs recorded for the record company in advertisements and commercials.

10.1.(e) These are warranties that guarantee the record company that the artist will comply with all union requirements and abide by union rules.

10.1.(f) These are warranties that assure the label that all materials and recordings delivered to the record company by the artist are in fact original.

10.1.(g)/(h) These paragraphs confirm that no one rendering services such as producers, sidemen, and guest artists appearing on any recordings of the artist will make any claims against the record company.

10.2.(a) This clause is referred to as a "sideman" provision and must be included in any exclusive recording agreement. It basically permits the exclusive recording artist to record as a non-featured (background) performer on other artist's recordings. This exclusion is subject to certain restrictions, some of which can be overly protective for the record company. Except for the requirement that the artist give the record company credit (for example "artist appears courtesy of Brooklyn Boy Records") most record companies do not strictly enforce these provisions and will allow most artists to do as many sessions as a sideman as they like. Even if an artist wishes to perform with another artist in a featured capacity (e.g. a duet), depending upon that artist's position with the record company, the artist is likely to be granted that permission.

10.2.(b) If an artist is restricted from acting as a producer, it should only be under limited circumstances such as those described in this subparagraph.

10.3. Another important exclusion from participating in other projects which an artist should attempt to negotiate falls under the broad category of what is commonly called "permitted" recordings. Under this provision, the artist is allowed to render musical performances in audio-visual programs such as movies. However, as with the sideman provisions, this exclusion is subject to restrictions such as those listed here. For example, the artist's performance in that instance cannot be released on a soundtrack album without the prior consent of the label.

10.4/10.5. "Indemnification" is a legal term which means that if a claim is made against a record company that is provoked by something the artist did or did not do, the record company will hold the artist responsible for any loss it suffers as a result of that claim. For example, if a third party sues the record company claiming that the artist stole their song, the record company would look to the artist to cover the cost of defending that claim. Indemnification will include the record company's right to withhold monies from the artist that would otherwise be payable to the artist until the claim has been resolved. The record company's right to withhold sums should be limited as set forth in this paragraph. An artist should also negotiate the right to participate in the defense of any such claim, and to consent to any settlement. Most record companies will only allow an artist the right to consent to settlements over a certain dollar amount (typically $2,500 to $5,000). Artists should also attempt to negotiate a limit on these obligations so that indemnification would only apply to claims that are actually resolved in court against the artist and the label. This protects the artist against a false claim. However, most record companies will not agree to such a request, arguing that it is not their responsibility to bear the financial burden of defending even false claims.

11. FAILURE OF PERFORMANCE

11.1.(a) Since record companies control every aspect of the recording process, the artist needs to negotiate a provision stating that if the record company refuses to allow the artist to complete an album, the artist has the right to terminate the contract and be compensated for the time and energy spent working on the project. Record companies will try to limit the compensation to the session payments the artist received for his or her services prior to the termination of the project. An artist should attempt to negotiate for payment of the full amount of any artist advance promised by the record company for the album in question.

11.2. This provision is called a "force majeure" clause. It is included to protect record companies in the event that an Act of God prevents them from fulfilling their obligations under the agreement with the artist. It allows them to freeze the running of the term of the contract during any such event. An artist should negotiate for a limit on the amount of time that any such suspension can last before the artist would have the right to terminate the agreement. A typical maximum time period during which a contract may be frozen or suspended due to an Act of God is from six months to a year.

11.3. This provision outlines some of the rights that a record company has in the event that an artist fails to fulfill his or her recording obligation. The most severe remedy is the right of the record company to demand that the artist actually repay any advances previously paid to the artist for a record that is not delivered. Some record companies will eliminate this provision entirely. Most will not. However, it must be pointed out that few record companies will invoke this provision, except in an unusual circumstances where an artist willfully refuses to record without reason.

11.4. This provision is intended to cover a situation where an artist becomes physically unable to fulfill his or her obligations to the record company. A period of time for which an artist should be allowed to recover from any such disabilities should be negotiated. A typical recovery period for an artist would be ninety days. As a practical matter, most record companies will allow an artist as much time as is needed to recover from any disabilities without invoking penalties.

12. DEFINITIONS

Gary and I decided not go over every definition, but will limit our comments to the most important provisions that require negotiation.

12.1. As mentioned several times in these notes, it is important to exclude the payment of mechanical royalties (publishing royalties) from the record company's right to recoup advances paid to or on behalf of the artist. It is also important not to allow a record company to use royalties earned under one agreement to recoup advances which may be paid to the same artist under a different agreement with the same record company. For example, if an artist were to perform on a soundtrack album which is distributed by his or her record company, the artist would not want the royalties from the soundtrack album applied against his or her unrecouped advances under his or her recording agreement. This practice is commonly called "cross-collateralization" and is always a difficult point to negotiate with record companies.

12.6. This seemingly innocent provision can have significant economic effects upon an artist. For certain artists, such as Rap and R&B artists, certain record formats such as 12-inch singles can contain a number of different versions of the same song. Under this definition, the artist would only be paid publishing royalties for one version of that song. This is a point that is difficult to negotiate, but is worth the effort. Specifically, the artist should request that the record company pay publishing royalties on at least two or three versions of the same song on a record.

12.15. The definition of net sales is another way in which record companies reduce the artist's record royalty rate. In this definition, net sales is defined as 85 percent of actual sales. Some record companies use a 90 percent definition and only a few actually define net sales as 100 percent of actual sales. It is pointless to go into an explanation of how record companies justify this reduction because this point is neither justifiable nor negotiable.

13. MISCELLANEOUS

Gary and I decided not to address every provision included under the heading of "miscellaneous," but we will address the more important ones.

13.1. This clause is referred to as a standard notice and cure provision. It states that before a record company can be considered to be in breach of an agreement, the artist must formally notify the record company in writing of the breach and give the record company time to correct the problem. The amount of time that is commonly allowed for a record company to remedy any alleged breaches ranges from 30 to 60 days. An artist should attempt to negotiate into the contract with the record company that in the case of the record company's failure to pay that artist on time any monies due, the record company should be allowed no more than 15 days to pay the artist the past due amount.

13.3/13.10. Assignment as used in a recording contract means the record company has the right to transfer the ownership of the artist's contract and or masters to a third party. It is important for an artist to limit the record company's right to assign a contract only to companies which are affiliated with the record company in question or companies with which the record company may merge. Otherwise, the artist could find himself or herself in business with a company that they know little or nothing about. Even if a record company assigns the artist's contract to a third party, it would be wise to negotiate that the record company in question remain obligated to the artist under the original terms of the original contract if the new company does not live up to those terms. If it is important to an artist, most record companies will agree to allow the artist to assign his or her right to receive royalties to a third party, but will limit that right to not more than one assignment, and sometimes only to the artist's loanout companies.

13.4. In this provision, the parties are choosing the jurisdiction of law that will apply to the contract. Because California is most favorable to artists, an artist should choose California as the jurisdiction that will govern the contract. However, most record companies will attempt to use New York as the state whose laws will govern the contract. No matter how strong a case the artist may make for the application of California law, this provision is usually not negotiable.

GROUP PROVISIONS

If the artist is a group, a provision similar to this will be included in the recording agreement. It starts off by requiring prompt notification to the record company of any member who leaves the group. It then provides that the record company and the artist will mutually decide whether to replace the departing member. If the leaving member is replaced, the new member will be required to sign onto the existing recording agreement. If the record company and the artist cannot agree on a replacement member, the record company will have the right to terminate the agreement and consider all of the members of the group to be leaving members. This provision may include a reduction in royalty rates and advances if any members leave the group. However, the artist should be able to get the record company to agree to delete this part of the provision. With respect to any leaving members, the record company will retain the right to sign them to separate agreements. If the record company signs a leaving member to a new agreement, the term of that contract will most likely be inferior to the terms of the original group contract under which the leaving member was signed. What may not be clear to members of a group who sign a recording contract is that by signing any contract that contains this type of provision they are in fact agreeing to accept the inferior terms of any future agreement for their services as a solo artist with that record company. It may be difficult to get the record company to delete this provision, but it should be negotiated aggressively. In no event should a reduction of more than 25 to 33 1/3 percent of the terms contained in the original agreement be permitted. In addition, the term of that new agreement with the leaving member should be limited to the amount of time remaining on the original group agreement. Finally, the leaving member will remain responsible for his or her share of any unrecouped balances under the original group agreement as of the date of departure from the group.

Notwithstanding, as a practical matter, if a record company believes in a leaving member enough to sign him or her to a separate recording agreement, that leaving member will be in a position to re-negotiate a better deal at that time.

ARTIST'S ASCENT AND GUARANTEE (INDUCEMENT LETTER)

In the event the artist is signed to the record company through a loanout company or production company, the record company will require the artist to sign a separate document for the direct benefit of the record company. This document will be called either an ascent and guarantee, or if it is in the form of a letter, it will be called an inducement letter. In this document the artist will acknowledge to the record company that he or she understands the recording agreement even though he or she is not officially signing it personally, that all payments will be made by the loanout/production company to the artist, and not by the record company to the artist, and that the artist assumes responsibility for the agreements, representations, and warranties which are made by the loanout/production company on the artist's behalf in the recording agreement.

The Future
of the
Record Industry

I have always believed that in order to know where you are going you must first know where you have been. It is in this spirit that I write this chapter. I am by no means attempting to document the history of the music business. There have been other writers who have done a fantastic job at that. Instead, I am attempting to abbreviate a series of events as they relate to the future of the recording industry. I will also attempt to give an overview of the role technology has played in this ever-changing industry.

THE BEGINNING OF THE RECORD INDUSTRY

Although the recording industry is relatively young—about seventy years old—it has experienced some dramatic changes. These changes have not only been in the way recordings are made and sold, but also in the final product itself. The first recorded music was played on a machine called a gramophone. You've seen them in movies and in antique shops. They have a large v-shaped cone protruding from the side and a handle that winds a motor which turns a platform where a record is placed. The resulting music was not of particularly high quality, especially if you consider today's standards. But nonetheless it served its purpose of bringing music into the home of the average person. The phonograph was later invented by Thomas Edison, and thus the name phonograph record was coined. Records in those days were made of a substance called lacquer, which is a derivative of crude oil, and it was the main format for most recorded music until about 1982. But we'll talk about that later.

RECORD MEN

The recording industry, in the beginning, just like every other major industry in America, was run solely by males. I shudder to think of how much we have lost to sexism and how much farther along this society would be if it had enlisted the creativity and help of women as equals. But since we didn't, I'll explain the record business as it was started by record men.

Record men were combination producers, promoters, artist managers and road managers. They did just about every job that is now associated with the record industry except perform and play the music. In today's record industry each job is done by a separate department within a larger organization called a record company.

Before the record industry was as we know it today, record men would arrive in town with an artist in tow and a recording made by that artist, in hopes of securing radio airplay. As a result of airplay, the artist would become popular in that city and would, therefore, be booked to play live performances. In those days, live performances were the artist's only way of earning money. There were no record or publishing royalties because records were not sold. They were strictly a promotional item. After the artist would finish performing in one city, she and the record man would leave for the next town. Somewhere along the line, somebody got the idea to sell records to the general public. They realized that if the general public liked what they heard on the radio enough to want to see the performer live, they would also want to have a copy of the artist's recorded performance as a memento. That was the beginning of the record industry.

JAZZ, CLASSICAL, SWING & THINGS

The first recordings were called 78s. The 78 rpm record made 78 complete turns, or revolutions, on the turntable per minute. All recordings in those days were mono — the music came out of one speaker and had no left and right separation like today's recordings.

The music sounded thin and lacked a fullness. Most music in the early days of recorded music fell into the classical category. That remained so until jazz musicians like Benny Goodman, Duke Ellington, Fats Waller and others came along. Big bands presented the music of the day. The musical style was called "big band" because that's exactly what it was — music played by big bands. The sound was big, the style was big and the reception by the general public was big. Actually the type of music was swing. Swing became the most recorded music of the day. As odd as it might sound, jazz became to the thirties, forties and fifties what pop & hip hop music is to the industry today. Swing was the beat. In fact, if you listen carefully, you can hear the influence of Swing in our modern day hip hop style.

After 78 rpm records gained in popularity the gramophone was replaced with an electronic counterpart called the phonograph. This electronic device had better audio quality and was capable of playing at both 78 rpms and 33 rpms. Thirty three revolutions per minute became the industry standard for albums, at about the same time that Les Paul, a brilliant guitarist, invented stereo and the electric guitar. These innovations were the first in a long line of technological advancements that would affect the recording industry profoundly. Between then and now there have been 8-track cartridges, the ill-fated quadraphonic systems (which consisted of four channels instead of two, but never caught on with the consumer), the electric organ, Fender Rhodes piano, and of course the synthesizer.

New styles of music were being conceived all over the world, but none caught on with the youth like American music. In the 1950s Doo Wop was born and was the first music to hit mainstream America that emanated from urban centers. Even pictures of the groups that sang Doo-Wop were images of mostly men singing songs of love, pain, fun, and dance with intricate harmonies on the street corners of America's inner cities. Record companies as we know them today were in full swing. Columbia, RCA, and Capitol concentrated on white artists who sang and played jazz and pop music.

In the early sixties Motown began setting the pace of popular music with groups like the Shirelles, Martha Reeves and the Vandellas, and Smokey Robinson and the Miracles. Motown became the prototype of record labels that relied upon black musicians and singers as their main source of talent and revenue. These predominantly R&B labels included Chess Records, Volt Records and Stax. They found their talent mainly in the south and because of that, their musicians were more familiar with and utilized a heavier Blues influence than the groups from the north. Artist like Jerry Butler, Isaac Hayes, and Etta James were signed to these labels.

By now Motown was burning up the charts with The Temptations, The Supremes, Marvin Gaye and Junior Walker and the All Stars. Motown was, in fact, playing a significant part in American history by providing one of the most influential cultural expressions of its time. No other musical form had penetrated the fabric of American society like the music of Motown.

Up until about 1970, most music was played on traditional instruments—instruments easily recognized by the public. Pianos, organs, guitars, drums, and horns were the main instruments used in popular music. Then musicians and arrangers started creating unique sounds by combining the sounds of the traditional instrument groups and using traditional instruments in non-traditional ways. The Beatles were famous for this kind of experimentation. In fact, they were as famous for creating new recording techniques and this kind of experimentation with sounds as they were for writing and singing great songs.

In 1970, synthesizers found their way into popular music, which made it easier to create unusual sounds, although they did not reach their full recognition until around 1980. Groups like Electric Light Orchestra, Yellow Magic Orchestra, and brilliant musicians such as Chick Corea, Stevie Wonder and Herbie Hancock began changing the direction of popular music by employing the synthesizer as the main instrument used in their recordings. Yellow Magic Orchestra was more pop-dance while Electric Light Orchestra was more rock oriented. Both enjoyed success and a wide acceptance. Chick Corea and Herbie Hancock fused the use of electronic instruments with their own unique blend of Jazz.

One of the earliest records to have worldwide success that made extensive use of the synthesizer was Stevie Wonder's "Fulfillingness' First Finale." Stevie's curiosity and musical talent led him to the forefront of American music. He was seen as an innovator and musical genius. A few years after releasing "Fulfillingness' First Finale," Stevie Wonder recorded and released "Songs in the Key of Life." It became the most important record of its day. Stevie Wonder became an icon. Not only did Americans and Europeans recognize him an incredibly gifted musician, but music lovers all over the world began seeing Stevie Wonder and the music he made as a guide into their social conscience. Stevie's blend of gospel, jazz, funk, rock, along with his messages of peace during wartime, struck a chord with the American public. His extensive use of electronic keyboards played a role in the acceptance of technology into the mainstream of music. By 1980, almost all popular musicians used electronic instruments on their recordings. Even classical music could not escape the clutch that electronic instruments had on the recording industry. "Switched-On Bach" was the most famous of the classical records that utilized synthesizers. By 1983 more records were being made with synthesizers than with real musicians. Drum machines and sequencers had found their way into the average musicians arsenal of electronic gadgetry. A tragic side effect of these innovations was the fact that a lot of musicians were driven out of work as a result of the synthesizers' ability to emulate almost any acoustic instrument. By the way, the synthesizer was invented by Bob Moog.

In the early to mid 1980s, rap infiltrated the music industry and spread like wildfire. Many hardcore R&B musicians, pop musicians and music enthusiasts claimed that rap was not a form of music at all and that it would fizzle out as quickly as it appeared. They were wrong. Like the sounds of Motown, rap music has become the most important cultural voice of today's youth. It has spread to other countries as both entertainment and as a vehicle for social commentary, and is recognized worldwide as the voice of American youth.

THE OLD AND THE NEW

In the early days of the music industry, the technology was crude at best and the sound of the music reflected that. But as the public interest in recorded music grew, I imagine that the desire also grew for recorded music that sounded more like the real thing. Once the march toward modern times started, there was no stopping it. We have seen the 33, 45, and 78 rpm records all go by the wayside in a relatively short period of time. The extended 12 inch single, the eight-track cartridge, and LP have been discarded and replaced by the more desirable digital formats. The four products that fit into this digital category are CD, DAT, Mini Disc, and Digital Compact Cassette (DCC). These relatively new and affordable formats have made the highest quality sound, that was in the past only available to high tech recording studios, now available to consumers as home entertainment products. They also boast a durability that was not achievable in the older analog, non-digital record, cassette and eight-track formats. All four digital formats share the distinct quality of being more compact than their prehistoric relatives. I'm sure anyone who has maintained a large album collection within limited storage space greatly appreciates this.

MTV

Then came videos and MTV. MTV became as important to the music industry as records themselves. It quickly became the most effective way to market and promote a new artist. Unfortunately, when MTV hit, the public became obsessed with the physical qualities of artists much more than they were with the artist's music. This was not the fault of MTV as much as it was that of the viewing public. Never before had physical image played such a large role in the success of so many artists. The public, in general, was excited and entertained by artist with hit songs who could also dance or had an interesting physical appearance or video concept. Unfortunately, this created a problem for artists whose main attraction was their music.

During the 1980s, if an artist was uninteresting to watch and was unsuccessful in teaming up with a video director that could spruce up his image, all was lost. For a while, watching MTV was the favorite pastime of young America. Because of that, MTV also became the platform from which most record companies sought to break new pop stars. During this time record companies also shifted their approach to signing new artists. Instead of signing new artists primarily upon their musical prowess, they looked for artists that could be marketed on MTV. What was once the music business became the marketing business. With the popularity of MTV and its ability to thrust a new artist into the limelight so effectively, radio stations could not help but rely upon MTV as a gauge as to what was hip and what was not. Consequently, if an artist received substantial air time on MTV, the chances were excellent that the same artist would also enjoy extensive airplay on radio. The combined air play of radio and MTV is a sure-fire sign that a song will become a hit. Videos were so popular that they became sale items themselves.

Good music can stand alone. Its inherent qualities do not require videos to increase its value. People have enjoyed music without videos for centuries. Truly good music, when heard by the listener, can sell itself. That fact is becoming increasingly apparent to record companies, because they are releasing fewer videos these days. Word has it that labels feel videos no longer enhance record sales enough to justify their production. They have finally gotten the picture. Videos have finally found their place in the music industry as a tool that can help promote, market and sell records, and as a visual aid that allows the viewer to see into the minds of the recording artist getting a closer look at what the artist might have been feeling when he or she performed that song for the first time.

WHERE WE ARE NOW

And so, as we sit back in our living rooms with blissful smiles upon our faces and sounds clear as mountain springs caress our ears, another monumental wave of change is roaring in and will be upon us quicker than you can say, "I want a record deal." These sweeping new changes will not only affect the way we as consumers purchase recordings, but also the way the creators of music think about and approach all sound recording projects. Engineers, record companies, artists, producers, distributors, radio stations and consumers alike will feel the impact of this new wave. You will see great recording companies brought to their knees as the creators of music are brought closer to the consumer. In the future, the word distribution will take on a whole new meaning.

FIBER OPTICS & CABLE

Fiber optics will play an important role in the future of the entertainment industry. Cable companies will develop fiber optic networks that will make it possible for the consumer to order feature films, video games, clothing, music, virtual activities and just about any product or service that can be purchased via television. The television, telephone and computer combined will become a digital home shopping mall for your entertainment, educational and recreational needs.

The programming of television and radio will also evolve into interactive formats. You will no longer be forced to watch your favorite program at a fixed time. Instead, you will be able to browse through a database of thousands of titles and choose what you want to watch or listen to, when you'd like to watch or listen to it.

A test version of this type of programming is already in use. Cable television has the Sci-Fi channel, CNN News, The Cartoon Channel, and Cinema Classics, all programmed to give the viewer exactly what they want, when they want it. Incidentally, the Congress just passed a law allowing cable companies to go into the phone business and phone companies to go into the cable TV business.

We are about to witness fierce price wars as each company fights for its share of the other's market. Prior to the passage of the legislation mentioned above, telephone companies were not allowed to venture into the cable TV business because of anti-trust laws. Congress was afraid of monopolies that might develop. The same law applied to cable companies. But both cable TV companies and telephone companies have been lobbying Congress to allow them to do business in an open and competitive environment. The millions spent on the installation of fiber optics puts both the telephone companies and cable television companies on the cutting edge of the communication industry. Given the high quality results that fiber optic installations bring, both industries want to compete in the same markets. So don't be surprised if in the not too distant future, your telephone company will bill you for both telephone service and cable television service.

DIGITAL RADIO & INTERACTIVE TELEVISION

Imagine if every radio station played only one kind of music, the kind of music we like. Wouldn't it be grand? Jazz lovers could hear jazz 24-7. All the hip-hoppers of the world could hip and hop to their hearts' content. Classical fans would be in heaven, while rock and rollers could rock and roll more than California itself. Cable and fiber optics have made it possible to have digital music piped right into our homes. It's happening right now. Television radio is what I call it.

Here's how it works. You turn on your television set and turn to the station that plays the music you like, and listen until your ears fall off. Listings of the names of the artists and song titles appear on screen along with a catalog number. This enhancement allows listeners to order whatever they like right from the comfort of the very couch on which they relax. And in a few days that product will show up on their doorstep. That's better than any radio station I know. Besides, radio stations often fail to announce the names of the artists whose music they are playing.

Although television-radio format has brought us one step closer to being able to have music delivered to our homes via our telephone lines, a more advanced form of home music delivery, via telephone equipment combined with television as a visual aid, is already being developed. The television will play the role of showcasing products while telephones will become the delivery method. This new system will allow the viewer to download via their phone lines a digital copy of the latest movies, videos, music, and virtually any on-air programming, for viewing at their leisure.

How will all of this affect the creators of music? Through cable technology, fiber optics, and satellite technology, musicians will be able to conduct recording sessions with players and participants in different parts of the world simultaneously. This will eliminate the constraints of time and travel. If for example, you wanted Eric Clapton to play guitar and he is in London and the rest of the band is in the USA, no problem. You all will be joined together via video and sound transmission systems that allow real time interaction between Mr. Clapton and the rest of the band.

Writing sessions will be conducted with participants thousands of miles apart, eliminating the time and expense of travel, not to mention jet lag, immigration, customs and the rest of the unwelcome surprises that come along with traveling and working in a foreign country. Demos and new recordings will be delivered to record companies, publishers, and managers via fiber optic telephone and cable lines.

This new technology, combined with already existing devices and software, will open up grand new possibilities for the creative individual. Becoming a record company or publisher of the future right from your home studio is a distinct possibility. Gone are the days of big recording studios costing hundreds of dollars per hour. The only exception may be when a large live recording room is necessary. Soon mastering studios will be a thing of the past. Instead you will invite the engineers into your home recording studio to do everything from pre-production to mastering.

CD-ROM – OUR SAVING GRACE?

There is already software and hardware available that allows the user to edit film and video on home computers. I see the music demo of the future becoming a full audio-visual presentation with the sophistication that up until a short time ago was not achievable unless hundreds of thousands of dollars were spent. I'm excited by these new opportunities because they will allow the artist to take full control of her music, visual images and ultimately, her career.

CD-ROM has become the buzzword of the recording industry. Artists such as the former Prince, Peter Gabriel and Elton John have been the first to explore this medium. Musicians and performers must consciously search for new ways to excite the consumer or be left in the dust of their competitors. CD-ROM is a perfect platform because it puts an enormous tool into the hands of creators and visionaries that will revive the luster and romance once associated with the recording industry.

Artists of the past enjoyed a dedication from their audiences that was close to fanaticism when compared to the cynical fans of today. Fans back then wanted to know what the artist ate for breakfast, what the artist's favorite pastime was, who influenced the artist musically. Any information about the artist was received with enthusiasm and excitement. Artists also enjoyed longer careers because a mystique surrounded their image. Most popular musicians today are overexposed and the public interest wanes quickly. There does seem to be a decrease in the number of videos, which is a step in the right direction. Over-exposure of an artist breeds contempt from the public which leads to diminished record sales.

CD-ROM will take over where videos left off. I would like to see the development of CD-ROM in the recording industry stay in the hands of the artist. By doing so, it will allow the music industry CD-ROM market to be developed on its own and not by a handful of directors that are willing to settle for emulating the latest visual hit. If artists are responsible for developing their own CD-ROMs, there will be less music released because artists would need time to develop their CD-ROM package. CD-ROM may be just the shot in the arm the record industry has needed to put the mystique back into its image.

NOT TOO LONG AGO

I remember a time not too long ago when I was growing up, and music played a big part in everyone's daily life. Like now, most of us listen to the radio every day. But somehow it was different then. We had the utmost respect for artists and their work. When I was growing up, we didn't have videos that flashed the same artist repetitively, day in and day out on our television screens. When an artist was scheduled to appear on TV, everyone was there to watch the show. Seeing a recording artist on television in those days was a rare thing. The television became the focus of the entire family. Even my mother, who was devoutly religious, loosened her grip and settled down to watch James Brown, Steve Wonder, Tom Jones, and just about anybody who was a big star. There was a certain mystery and awe surrounding artists in those days. We the fans came to know our favorite singers, bands, musicians and performers through their music, and when we were lucky enough to see them on the tube, we cherished the moments. Those performances became the talk of the neighborhood for weeks on end.

The music industry seems to be getting back to basics. More acoustic and traditional instruments are finding their way into recordings again. More songs are being released that have imaginative lyrics and lush harmonies. More bands are starting to surface and live music is seeing an incredible resurgence. Musicians are becoming more educated about the music industry and more independent record companies are popping up everywhere.

I hope these pages have helped you in some way. It has done a great deal for me to be able to share this information with you. I have a sincere wish that this book will stimulate you into at least considering keeping your creative projects in your hands as much as possible. If not, I hope it will at least help you understand the way things happen in the record business and you will learn a great deal about how to take care of yourself and your projects as they roll off the press. If done properly, rewards will be just what you expect and deserve. All it takes is a little courage and the will to go forward. Good luck and stay well.

Kashif,

Please extend your gift of knowledge by telling your friends and fellow musicians about this book and if they would like to obtain a copy, an order form is provided in the back of this book.

[ORDER FORMS]

Please extend your gift of knowledge by telling your friends and fellow musicians about this book and if they would like to obtain a copy, an order form is provided in the back of this book.

[ORDER FORMS]

PRODUCTS & SERVICES OFFERED BY
BROOKLYN BOY BOOKS

Everything You'd Better Know About The
Record Industry Book $39.95

Features 409 pages of easy to understand information about the inner workings of the record industry. Written by Kashif, a producer of hits for Whitney Houston, Kenny G., George Benson, Dionne Warwick, etc. Its ease of reading and its candid nature has made this book a big hit among newcomers to the industry as well as veterans. Billboard Magazine calls it a must have!!!

Book and Audio Cassettes $79.95

Includes 5 Digitally recorded cassettes for a total of 6.6 hours of audio instruction on how to find success in the record business, and the book for one low price. Great tool for learning on the run.

Book and Compact Discs $89.95

Includes 5 Digitally recorded CDs for a total of 6.6 hours of audio instruction on how to find success in the record business, plus the book for one low price. Complete with indexing for subchapters.

Book and Floppy Discs $59.95

IBM or Macintosh Formats
3 Contracts, their explanatory notes and the book for one low price.

Musicians Phone Book $25.95

Pages and pages of the telephone numbers and addresses of managers, producers, manufacturers, distributors, graphic artists, attorneys, etc. All located in the music capital of the world, Los Angeles.

A&R Directory $65.00

Get the most up to date listing of all the A&R Executives. It includes the phone numbers, addresses and fax numbers.

Publishers Directory $65.00

Get the most up to date listing of all the Creative Directors at the top Publishing Companies. Includes the phone numbers addresses and fax numbers. and assistant's names. A must have for those seeking publishing deals and contracts.

Brooklyn Boy News Letter $25.00
Per Year

A monthly newsletter informing you about the latest changes in the industry. It is also a great way to network with other musicians, singers, managers, producers, lawyers, promoters etc.

> Add $6.00 for Shipping and Handling on all items.
> Add $12.00 for Shipping and Handling on multiple item package deals.

Use the order form or to expedite your order, call (800) 974-7447
Send orders to Brooklyn Boy Books, c/o RIIS P.O. Box 3029, Venice CA 90294-3029

~ ORDER FORM ~

Please send me the tools for my success as indicated below. I have filled out the order form and enclosed a check or money order for the total or I have filled out my credit card information below.

Fill in requested product(s) below	Price per Copy	Number of Copies	TOTAL
SUBTOTAL			
Shipping & Handling Add $ 6.00 per single item ordered. Add $ 12.00 per multiple item package ordered.			
Arizona Residents, add 7% sales tax.			
GRAND TOTAL			

Name: _____ Telephone: (___)

Address: _____

If paying by check, **please make checks payable to Brooklyn Boy Books** and fill in the following:

Drivers License #: _____ Year of Exp: _____ State: _____

If paying by credit card, please fill in the following:

[ ] Visa   [ ] MasterCard   [ ] Discover Card   [ ] American Express

Account #: _____ Exp. Date: _____

Signature: _____ Name on Account: _____

Mail order form to: Brooklyn Boy Books, c/o RIIS P.O. Box 3029, Venice CA 90294-3029 or call (800) 974-7447 to expedite your order.

~ ORDER FORM ~

Please send me the tools for my success as indicated below. I have filled out the order form and enclosed a check or money order for the total or I have filled out my credit card information below.

Fill in requested product(s) below	Price per Copy	Number of Copies	TOTAL
SUBTOTAL			
Shipping & Handling Add $ 6.00 per single item ordered. Add $ 12.00 per multiple item package ordered.			
Arizona Residents, add 7% sales tax.			
GRAND TOTAL			

Name: _____ Telephone: (___)

Address: _____

If paying by check, **please make checks payable to Brooklyn Boy Books** and fill in the following:

Drivers License #: _____ Year of Exp: _____ State: _____

If paying by credit card, please fill in the following:

[ ] Visa   [ ] MasterCard   [ ] Discover Card   [ ] American Express

Account #: _____ Exp. Date: _____

Signature: _____ Name on Account: _____

Mail order form to: Brooklyn Boy Books, c/o RIIS P.O. Box 3029, Venice CA 90294-3029 or call (800) 974-7447 to expedite your order.

Call (310) 827-0923 and ask about:

Kashif University

a

TWO DAY INTENSIVE COURSE ON THE RECORD INDUSTRY

ALSO COMING SOON

"I'LL DO IT MY DAMN SELF"
(A LAYMENS GUIDE TO INDEPENDENTLY
RELEASING YOUR OWN MUSIC)
BY KEVIN HAREWOOD

"HONEST ABE"
computer program
The first computer program ever to calculate
how much your royalty payments should be.

Visit our web site at:
http://www.pacificnet.net/~kashif

or

E-mail Kashif at:
kashif@pacificnet.net

RECEIVE A FREE FLOPPY DISK!

A $65.00 value absolutely FREE!!!
Just fill out and return the questionnarie below and receive a FREE floppy disk containing recording, production, and publishing contracts.

- (fold here and tape before mailing) -

~ QUESTIONNAIRE ~

YES. Please send me the FREE floppy disk filled with contracts negotiated by Kashif. I have filled out the questionnaire below. <u>Please put me on your mailing list.</u>

Indicate what disk format you require (check one).   ☐ Mac Format   ☐ IBM Format

We know your privacy is important to you. We assure you that your information will only be used to bring you more information that will help you toward your career goals. Further, this information will only be used by Brooklyn Boy Books/Records & Educational.

Name:

Address:

Home Telephone: (   )   Work Telephone: (   )

What type of computer do you use?

What programs do you use?

What instument(s) do you play?

What kind of music do you listen to?

Do you own any other music books? If so, which one(s)?

How did you find out about this book?

Mail Questionnaire to: **Brooklyn Boy Books, c/o RIIS, P.O. Box 3029, Venice CA 90294-3029.**

Place postage
here before
mailing.

Brooklyn Boy Books c/o
Recording Industry Information Service
P.O. Box 3029
Venice CA 90294-3029.